In the Words
of the Faculty

~~~~~~

*Perspectives
on Improving Teaching
and Educational Quality
in Community Colleges*

Earl Seidman

~~~~~~~~~~~~~~~~~~~~~~~~~~~~~~~

In the Words of the Faculty

Perspectives
on Improving Teaching
and Educational Quality
in Community Colleges

Jossey-Bass Publishers
San Francisco • London • 1985

IN THE WORDS OF THE FACULTY
Perspectives on Improving Teaching and Educational Quality
in Community Colleges
   by Earl Seidman

Copyright © 1985 by: Jossey-Bass Inc., Publishers
                      433 California Street
                      San Francisco, California 94104

                            &

                      Jossey-Bass Limited
                      28 Banner Street
                      London EC1Y 8QE

Library of Congress Cataloging in Publication Data

Seidman, Earl
   In the words of the faculty.

   (The Jossey-Bass higher education series)
   "Published in cooperation with ERIC Clearinghouse
for Junior Colleges"—T.p. verso.
   Bibliography: p. 283
   Includes index.
   1. Community colleges—United States.   2. Community
colleges—United States—Curricula.   3. College
teachers—United States.   I. Title.   II. Series.
LB2328.S43   1985   378'.125   85-45066
ISBN 0-87589-669-3 (alk. paper)

Manufactured in the United States of America

The paper in this book meets the guidelines for
permanence and durability of the Committee on
Production Guidelines for Book Longevity of the
Council on Library Resources.

JACKET DESIGN BY WILLI BAUM

Published in cooperation with
ERIC Clearinghouse
for Junior Colleges

FIRST EDITION

Code 8543

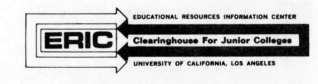

EDUCATIONAL RESOURCES INFORMATION CENTER

Clearinghouse For Junior Colleges

UNIVERSITY OF CALIFORNIA, LOS ANGELES

The Jossey-Bass
Higher Education Series

Consulting Editor
Community and Junior Colleges

Arthur M. Cohen
University of California, Los Angeles

Preface

~~~~~~

Community colleges have become a key component in our system of higher education. And the work of the faculty is central to the success of community college education in this country. Yet despite the contribution community colleges make to the ideal of providing equitable educational opportunity in the United States, the issues of how faculty members in these institutions understand and make meaning of their work, what concerns and pressures they face, and how they understand the inner workings of community college education have received relatively little attention in professional literature. These pages give community college faculty the attention they deserve.

With enrollments down, these are not easy times for community colleges. In order to attract additional students, they have enlarged upon their original mission—providing transfer and career-terminal education—by attempting to serve almost every adult educational need that is not already being served by existing institutions in their communities. This expanded and diffused mission has created dichotomies and dilemmas that faculty must face in their everyday work; at the same time, governing boards and administrators must contend with the demographic and economic realities of potentially shrinking enrollments.

At this critical time in the development of community colleges, *In the Words of the Faculty* provides a way for governing boards, administrators, and faculty leaders to understand how qualitative issues within the walls of their colleges, for which they can and must take responsibility, interact with broader societal, economic, and demographic issues over which they exercise little control. This book offers recommendations for alleviating some of the problems that now confront community college faculty, recommendations that take account of the constraints within which community colleges operate.

The issues this book brings to the foreground include the consequences of a dichotomized curriculum, inequities in collegial relations, interdependent issues in teaching, and the double edge of one of the most time-honored characteristics of community colleges: student-centeredness. What is unique about this volume is that these concerns are voiced, not by outside critics, but by the faculty who work within community colleges. Not only are the issues raised by faculty members, but to a considerable extent they are presented in their own words. In the major interpretative chapters, the important themes are illustrated by extensive excerpts from faculty interviews; six chapters offer profiles of community college faculty at work presented entirely in their own words. These profiles present a wealth of concrete detail and provide reflective and incisive analysis by the faculty themselves. These personal portraits will help readers better understand their own experiences and their own institutions.

Research from two consecutive studies conducted over a three-year period provides the foundation for this book. The first study was sponsored by the Exxon Education Foundation and concentrated on community college faculty in Massachusetts. The second study was sponsored by the National Institute of Education and allowed for research in California and New York, as well as further study in Massachusetts.

That the results of these two studies could be presented to a great extent in the words of the faculty who work in community colleges is a result of the methodology used: in-depth phenomenological interviewing. Basic to this methodology is the assumption that understanding the perspective of the individuals who work within an institution is essential if one is to comprehend how that institution operates. Furthermore, this method assumes that the meaning participants find in their experience affects the way they carry out their work. This study was designed to draw its understandings, its identification of major issues, and its recommendations from the meaning the faculty themselves made of their work. Research is often conducted by people outside schools and colleges and designed to tell those inside how to do their jobs better; this study attempts to combine the outside perspective of the researcher with the inside perspective of the faculty whose description of their own experience and reflection on the meaning of that experience provide valuable insight into the problems within the community college.

Governing board members who are concerned with what directions to take, with what new policies to develop, with what vision is necessary to provide effective leadership for their colleges will find, in the words of these faculty members and in the themes that are highlighted, important insights into the major issues community colleges are facing and directions for action that can be taken. Administrators who are deeply concerned about the future of their colleges and who are plagued by the gap between themselves and their faculty imposed by their increasing size and bureaucratization will find a way to bridge those divisions. Presidents and their chief executive officers, deans, division and department chairpersons, and any administrator concerned with the professional sustenance and renewal of their faculty will gain through this book concrete understandings that can provide the basis for any potential professional development efforts. Administrators concerned with averting conflict before it becomes destructive to the institution or with learning what is really important to their faculties before going to the bargaining tables will find many instructive comments. Finally, administrators who want to seize the initiative rather than react to problems will find a discussion of the issues of concern to their faculties.

Faculty will find a new way to approach the major issues they confront in their everyday work. They will see that they have much in common with colleagues who teach in college settings very different and far removed from their own. Faculty who have become accustomed to taking individual responsibility for their work, who may have concluded that the problems they face are primarily matters of their individual personalities, will see that the structure in which they work contributes significantly to their daily work experience. Teaching is often an isolated and lonely endeavor. To admit that one has problems or is feeling severe stress, or to articulate successes and hopes for the future is not a common experience in faculty lives. Through the accounts of their colleagues in these pages, faculty members may develop a deeper and richer understanding of their own experience in the community college.

In addition to the benefit for faculty who are already in community colleges, those who are now considering or preparing for a career in community colleges will gain valuable insight into the complexities of that work. They will benefit from the experience of those already in the field. This book presents case studies—faculty profiles arranged by subject matter—and an analytical text that weaves together the major issues. A glance at the table of contents will reveal the wide range of issues, from curriculum development to collegial relations, to pedagogy, to the issue of research and writing, as well as the broad coverage of subject areas, both academic and career-oriented, including chapters on minority faculty and counselors.

Overview of the Contents

To highlight the themes that connect the work of individual faculty members in community colleges, to present the concrete detail of their work, and to build on their experience, this book is organized into three parts. In Part One, excerpts from the interviews with a large number of the seventy-six faculty members who were interviewed are interwoven to focus on the major concerns confronting these community college faculty today. Part Two presents the experience of twenty-one of the faculty in profiles composed almost entirely in their own words. The profiles present a rich, concrete, and detailed insiders' view of working in a community college. Part Three synthesizes the earlier findings, focuses on how best to support the efforts of faculty, and makes specific recommendations for administrative and faculty action to improve the quality of education in community colleges.

Part One, "Determining and Understanding Faculty Concerns," describes the context within which community college faculty work, the method used for interviewing the faculty, and the major issues they are now facing in their work.

Chapter One describes the sense of shrinking horizons, diminished power and opportunity, and shifting social imperatives that have come to characterize the current community college setting. The chapter describes the ambiguous position of community colleges in the higher education hierarchy and the developing debate in the critical literature on community colleges, both of which complicate the work of community college faculty in the 1980s.

Chapter Two presents the method of in-depth phenomenological interviewing used in this research. It emphasizes the importance of having faculty members reconstruct their work in detail and reflect on its significance. The chapter describes the interviewing technique that can lead to an "inner voice" being heard that will allow readers, especially those who work within community colleges, to relate to the stories and experiences recounted in the chapters that follow.

Chapter Three discusses the false dichotomy that has arisen between career education and academic curricula. That dichotomy has long had significant implications for minority students; the debate between W. E. B. Du Bois and Booker T. Washington is still being waged in community colleges. The curricular divide also has implications for the status and power of faculty in both career and academic fields. Academic faculty, threatened by the turn to vocationalism, struggle to maintain a significant role in the college. Vocational faculty, buoyed by the wave of students entering their programs, nonetheless sometimes feel that they play a less central role than their academic colleagues. Such vulnerabilities have consequences for both the academic and the career education faculty who want to promote a more well-rounded education for their students.

Chapter Four further explores relations among career and academic faculty and pays special attention to relations between male and female faculty, minority and nonminority faculty, and counselors and their faculty colleagues. This chapter describes the inequities that have developed among community college faculty. These issues divide and enervate the faculty and have a negative effect on the colleges' ability to provide equitable educational opportunities for all their students.

Chapter Five outlines five interlocking issues that community college faculty must face in their teaching, no matter what their field. The verbal performance of community college students, especially in reading and writing, presents increasingly complex problems for teachers across the curriculum. The concern over verbal performance relates to a trend toward less writing and greater reliance on so-called objective, machine-scored tests. The chapter also discusses with considerable caution the promise of microcomputers to offer solutions in this fundamental area. The chapter concludes by discussing the interrelated issues of standards and dropouts, both of which plague the work of community college faculty and demand critical attention.

Chapter Six discusses one of the root causes of the sometimes frenetic days pictured in the faculty profiles presented later in the book. Time to think, plan, respond to student papers, read, and write seems to be almost nonexistent for the faculty while they are on campus. On campus, faculty must keep their doors open to students. The chapter discusses the double edge student-centeredness has acquired for both faculty and students in community colleges. While not promoting a callous disregard for the students' needs, this chapter encourages both faculty and administrators to reconsider the time-honored notion of student-centeredness; faculty need time to carry out the work at the center of their responsibilities.

Part Two presents profiles of twenty-one of the seventy-six faculty who participated in the study. These profiles present the work of community college faculty in their own words. With the exception of Chapter Eleven, the profiles are grouped by the subject matter the faculty teach. Each profile presents a case study of what it is like to teach in the faculty member's subject area in the community college. Chapter Seven presents four profiles highlighting the difficulties English and humanities faculty experience in today's community college. They struggle to teach students, many of whom are uncomfortable with reading or writing and sometimes have little apparent patience with the questions teachers of the humanities know are important to consider. The humanities faculty work against a strong current of vocationalism and a fragmented sense of education. The irony of their work is that they hold the real key to power and opportunity for the students who come to community colleges seeking job preparation. As the faculty in these profiles point out, their students will be consigned to dead-end jobs if they do not learn enough to be comfortable with reading, writing, and critical thinking in their fields.

Chapter Eight presents the complexities of teaching math and science to students who have often had little prior success with these subjects. Attracted to the community college by the promise of training programs leading to jobs, many students take math and science courses in the hope of making up past deficiencies. But the cumulative nature of learning in math and science, the prerequisite of strong math skills for advanced work in science, and the basic difficulty some students have with reading the texts, all combine to present enormous problems for math and science teachers. These complexities and the faculty response to them are presented in the profiles in this chapter.

Chapter Nine reveals the difficulties of teaching the social sciences in community colleges. Social science faculty cover topics directly related to notions of progress. They are committed to asking questions about how society ought to work, questions that can be discomfiting to students whose lives intimately reflect social inequities. Their students seem more concerned with learning skills that will get them jobs rather than with questions that may strike them as idealistic if not irrelevant. The profiles describe the complexities of contending with the anti-intellectualism that can accompany a narrow view of vocational education.

Chapter Ten focuses on the experiences that career education faculty share with the academic faculty. Some of the vocational faculty are the most eloquent concerning the false dichotomy between intellectual and manual labor. Many vocational faculty know that training the hand cannot be separated from educating the mind, and they work as hard as their academic colleagues to have their students see the necessity of overcoming their discomfort with, and sometimes their alienation from, conventional academic skills. The profiles in this chapter also highlight the issues of status, power, and opportunity that face career education faculty, especially women, in the community college.

Chapter Eleven presents the profiles of three minority faculty members who work in predominantly nonminority institutions. They must confront all the problems their nonminority colleagues must face, and in addition they must deal with discrimination in their everyday work. Their profiles include stories of having to work twice as hard to stay even, and of subtle and not-so-subtle hints of racism. The profiles also describe a qualitative impact of minorities in their colleges that far outruns the actuality of their numbers.

Chapter Twelve highlights the hierarchy that exists among professionals in community colleges. Neither administrator nor faculty member, the counselors in these profiles do the work of both, but without the power of the former or the autonomy of the latter. The profiles reveal the difficulty of the job of counselors who are regarded as workhorses by the administration but as idlers by some faculty. The profiles also describe the sensitivity and insight counselors develop as student advocates in their colleges.

Part Three reviews and synthesizes the voices of the faculty heard in the earlier chapters, identifies key issues underlying the work of faculty, and offers recommendations for concerted action on the part of those concerned with the future of community college education. Chapter Thirteen points out that the time spent in the classroom is only a small part of faculty work. Reading, writing, thinking, exploring, gaining more knowledge and experience in one's field, planning, and preparing are all crucial to the work of community college faculty. In the United States, where there is much ambivalence about intellectual work, it is not easy, conventional, or popular to urge that community colleges affirm the intellectual core of faculty work. In fact, the dichotomy between teaching and research that has long existed in community colleges works against such an affirmation. In this chapter, I urge administrators and faculty to affirm the intellectual core of all faculty work and to revamp policies and procedures in their colleges to support that work.

Chapter Fourteen summarizes the major themes developed in the preceding chapters, highlights their interconnections, and presents fourteen recommendations for administrative and faculty action. The recommendations deal with the issues of curriculum development, professional relationships, pedagogy, relationships with students, research and writing, and the intellectual core of faculty work. Based on the experience of committed teachers working within community colleges, these recommendations call for qualitative changes in thinking that require perhaps additional effort and understanding, but not necessarily additional money. Perhaps the most distinguishing characteristic of these recommendations is their promotion of increased respect for those who work within community colleges.

Acknowledgments

I am grateful to the Exxon Education Foundation and the National Institute of Education for their support of the research that provided the foundation for this book. The opinions, findings, conclusions, and recommendations expressed are those of the author and do not necessarily reflect the views of the Exxon Education Foundation or the National Institute of Education.

Many colleagues and associates at the University of Massachusetts at Amherst contributed to this work. Special thanks go to Conrad Wogrin, director of the University of Massachusetts Computer Center, and Charles D. Lyman, associate director. Richard Morrill, of the university library, and Mario Fantini, Richard J. Clark, Ronald Frederickson, Judith Gourley, Verne Thelen, Sharon Gorman, Sheryl Jablonski, Terry Eddy, and Margaret Malone, colleagues and associates at the School of Education, made important and timely contributions that I value. My thanks also to Oswald Tippo, Linda Papirio, and Tevis DuBois. Debbie Britzman, Grace Flisser, Myron Glazer, Christopher Hurn, Byrd Jones, and Rudine Sims read early drafts of chapters and shared their perceptive responses for which I am grateful.

Arthur M. Cohen, as consulting editor, and Florence B. Brawer responded insightfully to the plan for the book and to the manuscript. Clifton F. Conrad served as an outside reviewer and offered important suggestions for revision. They contributed significantly to what strengths there may be in the book, and I deeply appreciate their consideration.

Gene Winter in New York and Tom L. Clark in California, as well as significant others whom I cannot name, facilitated our contact with participants in the study. To them and especially to the community college faculty, staff, and students whom we had the privilege of interviewing, I am grateful.

Special mention must be made of three people who made central contributions to this work. First, Patricia Driscoll, staff consultant at the University of Massachusetts Computer Center. She was consistently thoughtful, insightful, and expert in her work and served as an outstanding professional resource. Patrick J. Sullivan was co-investigator and then associate investigator on the two projects that led to this book. During our many hours of conversations and work together, he deeply influenced the thinking that went into this book; I appreciate his colleagueship. Mary Bray Schatzkamer was our research associate and has continued to contribute significantly to the book through her skilled and sensitive reading and editing. I value the depth of her understanding and look forward to her own writing based on her research on returning women students attending community colleges.

My wife, Linda L. Seidman, to whom this book is dedicated, and our daughter, Rachel, and son, Ethan, gave much to me, each in their own ways, as I wrote this book. To them I extend appreciation and love.

Amherst, Massachusetts   Earl Seidman
September 1985

Contents

The Author

Earl Seidman is a professor in the School of Education of the University of Massachusetts at Amherst. He received his B.A. degree in English (1959) from Oberlin College, his M.A.T. degree in English and education (1960) from Harvard University, and his Ph.D. degree in education (1967) from Stanford University.

Seidman teaches and conducts research in the areas of English and higher education, teacher education, the teaching of writing, and qualitative research methodology. From 1968 to 1975, he was associate dean of the School of Education at the University of Massachusetts. He has also been a member of the English Department at the University of Washington in Seattle and has taught English in high school. He is a member of the National Humanities Faculty.

In the Words
of the Faculty

Perspectives
on Improving Teaching
and Educational Quality
in Community Colleges

∾ Part One ∾

Determining
and Understanding
Faculty Concerns

∾∾∾∾∾∾∾∾∾∾∾∾∾∾

On a day-to-day basis, community college faculty work with students and interact with colleagues, administrators, and support staff to carry out the mission of their college. Through the countless details of their experience, the faculty come to understand the central realities of education in their institutions. Because of the fast pace in their colleges, the increasing bureaucratization of their institutions, and the individualistic nature of faculty work, what they know about education in their college is not often fully expressed and is infrequently shared with either colleagues or administrators. Faculty meetings, departmental gatherings, negotiating sessions at the bargaining table, and grievance hearings do not often provide a forum for determining and learning from what faculty know about their work.

The depth, sophistication, and thoroughness of faculty knowledge is an indisputable but relatively untapped reservoir for those concerned with improving community college education. Part One presents major concerns of the seventy-six faculty members who were interviewed in this study. These faculty members teach in twenty different community colleges in California, Massachusetts, and New York. The community college systems

1

in these states have different histories, different levels of funding, and different methods of governance. Some of the colleges are in urban settings; others are in suburban, small town, and rural locations. Despite these wide variations, individual faculty members told stories and recounted experiences that connected to one another. Those experiences touched on the crucial issues of curriculum, collegial relations, teaching, and working with students. These concerns are explored in detail in the six chapters in Part One.

1

Changing Conditions
in Community Colleges

Introduction to the Study

Community colleges mean the opportunity for higher education to millions of students in the United States. One out of every three undergraduate students in this country is enrolled in a community college. Some commentators estimate that as many as 50 percent of all minority students who attend institutions of higher education do so at community colleges (Astin, 1982, p. 132; Olivas, 1979, p. 25). For over four million minority and nonminority students each year, the notion of what college is and the sense of power and opportunity that a higher education can offer are shaped by experiences in a community college. To a considerable degree, the tension between the ideal and the reality of equitable educational opportunity is expressed in the myriad daily events that take place within them. At the center of working out that tension are community college faculty. Their work has consequences not only for those within community colleges but also for the entire system of higher education in the United States.

At the same time, community colleges have come to a critical and perhaps pivotal point in their development. A serious debate

3

has arisen over their fairness, their effectiveness, and their economic efficiency. (See, for example, Karabel, 1972; Zwerling, 1976; Pincus, 1980; Breneman and Nelson, 1981; Astin, 1982; and a comprehensive summary in Cohen and Brawer, 1982, pp. 342–365.) Perhaps even more significant than the critical debate is the fact that for the first time in twenty-five years, declining enrollments are being reported in community colleges across the country. One response by community college spokespersons is to cite economic and demographic factors, essentially out of the control of the community colleges, as being among the basic contributors to the decline in enrollment (Wolfe, 1985, p. 1). Growth and numbers have been central to the thinking about community colleges in the last few decades. As community colleges enter this critical period in their development, a possible danger is that those concerned—legislators, members of governing boards, administrators, and faculty leaders—will fail to examine the qualitative issues within their control that may be interacting significantly with the demographic and economic factors often cited.

In fact, however, the leveling off of growth offers the opportunity—and the decline in enrollments the imperative—to examine qualitative issues that lie beneath the numbers. These qualitative issues may have as much to do with the current state and future of community colleges as the quantitative facts of the higher education marketplace. The marketplace is subject to periodic fluctuation. The qualitative matters that lie at the heart of teaching and learning are less changeable.

At the center of teaching and learning in the community college are the faculty. The chapters that follow offer insights into the major qualitative issues faculty face in their everyday work. The experiences they reconstruct illuminate the tension for students and faculty alike in community college curricula that are dichotomized between training for jobs and education for life. Their stories reveal that collegial relations, once a source of energy for developing new programs and for considering new approaches to teaching, have become infused with hierarchical divisions and inequities, leading once enthusiastic colleagues to feel frustration or to maintain what they describe as a low profile in the college. In the chapters that follow, community college faculty speak compellingly about problems that plague their teaching in institutions dedicated perhaps above all else to good teaching and accessibility to students. They speak of their concern for the declining verbal power of their students, the difficulties of teaching writing, the substitution of so-called objective, machine-scored tests for written essays, the problem of the student who one day just disappears, and the erosion of standards. Their stories illustrate, in addition, the ambiguous results for both students and faculty of the dedication to a student-centered ethos in the community college.

In profiles presented in their own words, the faculty reconstruct details of their everyday work experience and the meaning they make of it. English, humanities, math, science, and social science faculty speak of the complexities of working in an institution that has become increasingly career-oriented. Career education faculty speak in their profiles of the pressures unique to their subject areas and of the concerns they share with their academic colleagues. For both academic and career education faculty, the profiles tell of a major concern for the sustenance and renewal of the central intellectual core of their work.

This inquiry focuses on the work of faculty and other professionals in the community college who have significant instructional responsibilities. Faculty, of course, do not work in isolation. Members of governing boards, administrators, secretaries, custodians, registrars, admissions officers, bookkeepers, telephone receptionists, cafeteria workers, security guards, computer operators, and the students themselves all interconnect with the work of faculty. While everyone who works in a community college is important to the effectiveness of the college in meeting its goals, the faculty are at the core of any teaching and learning enterprise. How the faculty understand and make meaning of their work affects the way they carry out that work and ultimately the success of the community college. That is the subject of the chapters that follow.

Historical Considerations

The historical, societal, and organizational context in which faculty work shapes and gives meaning to that work. First conceived as a junior college early in the twentieth century, the community college has changed markedly in some respects since its inception. On the one hand, the expansion of the community college into its current role as an institution that serves almost any and every community educational need was not foreseen by the founders. That diffusion of purpose has, in fact, contributed to the complexity of the work of today's community college teacher. On the other hand, major characteristics of today's community college were part of the original concept of the junior college. Advocates of the junior college urged its establishment as a way of providing a buffer between the expanding high school populations seeking higher education and the newly developing, specialized, and professionally oriented university. Their language conveyed the dichotomous assumptions of the time concerning gender, social class, and education. One advocate spoke, for example, of the junior college as "providing particularly for that class of men who are mechanically minded and of women who are domestically minded, the opportunity to improve their abilities" (Eells, 1931, p. 289). Speaking of the popularity of the new junior colleges, Eells wrote, "The junior college has popularized education. Where a local junior college is established, probably the number of people who 'go to college' is at least doubled. It would be unwise and unfortunate if all of these tried to enter a university and prepare for professions which in most cases are already overcrowded, and for which their talents and abilities in most cases do not fit them" (1931, p. 289). One of the major functions of the newly established junior college was to provide "terminal education" for those who were not "fit" for four-year colleges and universities. In the 1980s, those in community colleges must contend both with the ramifications of the dichotomous thinking of the early advocates of the junior college and the diffusion of purpose promoted by more recent community college leaders.

After the Second World War, large numbers of returning veterans sought a college education. They swamped four-year colleges and universities. Junior colleges, and later public community colleges, expanded at a high rate to relieve the pressure on the four-year schools. A significant number of students who attended the junior college persisted in seeing it as a first step toward a four-year degree. Community colleges began to be seen as instruments of the official federal policy of providing expanded educational opportunity (Medsker, 1960, pp. 9-10).

In the 1960s and early 1970s, at the time of the civil rights movement and the "War on Poverty," the notion of expanded educational opportunity was further enlarged to include the idea of more equitable educational opportunity. When the community colleges began to be seen as part of the nation's attempt to provide equitable educational opportunity to all who would seek higher education, the community college was placed, and placed itself, at the crossroads of conflict in our country. The tension was and still is between the United States' liberal ideology, which stresses equal opportunity, individualism, and the possibility of upward social mobility (Hartz, 1955), and the realities of the way social class, race, and gender interact with our economic system. Community college faculty are still buffeted by the crosscurrents of this conflict between ideology and social and economic realities. In the 1960s and early 1970s, however, there was so much enrollment growth and such a sense of unbounded horizons that the tensions arising from the conflict could be submerged, or perhaps relieved, by the corresponding expansion of faculty, facilities, budget, and the development of new programs.

Assassinations, the Vietnam War, Watergate, the oil embargo, inflation, the hostage crisis in Iran, the arms race—all interacted to bring the social ferment of the 1960s and early 1970s to a halt. Some of the outward form of the ferment remained, but little of the substance. As one faculty member in an urban Massachusetts community college said about the sixties, in comparison to the eighties, "It was a different time. It was a time when I guess we felt that we could have an impact on society. . . . That was, I thought, the Kennedy legacy. . . . We could resolve the civil rights issue; we could ease the tensions of the cold war by limiting nuclear weapons; . . . it was possible to put more Americans to work and spread the distribution of wealth around. Martin Luther King was saying . . . that nonviolence could have an impact."

Nostalgia may lead some to romanticizing the sixties, and hindsight may lead others to skepticism, but in fact some faculty were attracted to the community college because, among other reasons, it represented a movement consistent with their sense of social imperative. One social science faculty member in a New York state community college said, "There was a great deal of enthusiasm. The school was just being built. Students were coming who, at least for the most part, never anticipated ever going to college. They were hungry for whatever college implied, even the intellectuality of college. They looked for that; they wanted the vocabulary, the discussions, the politics, the philosophy. . . . It was a constant, reiterated theme . . . from the administration: we are pioneering." But the notion of "pioneering" started to wear thin as the difficulties of doing such work with diminishing resources began to be apparent. The same faculty member went on to say, "It got to the point that when they said 'pioneering,' you started to look to pull arrows out of your body."

The seventies saw the community college growth begin to level off. As enrollments began to stabilize, many colleges sought new students through community-based programs. They reached out to adults in the local community to provide for them almost anything in which they might be interested. Indeed some leaders of the community college movement were inclined to put more emphasis on the outreach to the community through lifelong education programs than on the notion that the community college was a college first and foremost. (For a full discussion of this development, see Cohen and Brawer, 1982, pp. 251–282.) The move to emphasize noncollegiate efforts combined with the increase in the need for remedial courses, the sharp turn of students to vocational programs, the diminishing role of the traditional liberal arts courses, and the decline in the rate of transfer of students to four-year colleges and universities to produce considerable uneasiness among many faculty in community colleges. (See, for example, Slutsky, 1978, and a synopsis of that article in Cohen and Brawer, 1982, p. 67.)

Community college faculty in the 1980s continue to face a diffuse sense of mission, but they no longer have a sense of expanding, almost unlimited horizons. In fact, after decades of growth, there are indications that community colleges are losing enrollments (Meyer, 1984, p. 3). When they talk about the growth period of the sixties and early seventies, current community college veteran faculty remember a sense of possibility, autonomy, and the ability to get things done. Faculty now face increased bureaucratization, centralized coordination, and attempts to control colleges at the state level (Cohen and Brawer, 1982, p. 68). Campus administrators increasingly began to play a middleperson role between state officials and faculty. As economic conditions tightened in the late 1970s, and as competition for students grew among all institutions of higher education, the enlarged bureaucracy turned to dealing with limits rather than possibilities.

The consequences of shrinking resources and concomitant increased bureaucratic decision making have been significant for everyone within community colleges, faculty as well as students and staff. One faculty member said, "When I started, the college was a pretty euphoric thing. It was a small place. It was OK to experiment, to wonder about things. . . . But as it grew it became more systematic. More rigid, more rules, more committees, more administrative structure." The F.T.E. (full-time equivalent) student became the criterion for almost all decisions. One senior humanities professor described some of the consequences: "[The F.T.E.], that's what makes the game; that's what you play by, and if you don't, you are going to have to do something. . . . I know one fellow, I was in the dean's office when he stuck his head in. . . . He had just been told he would have to teach a night class as part of his day load. He had been teaching his art history classes for all these years. He created all this material; it really is an excellent class, but his day classes are just dwindling away; and so he was told that he had to teach a night class as part of his load. He was upset. He had been there a lot longer than I had . . . probably since 1952 or '53."

For some faculty the response to the F.T.E.-driven decision-making process was to search for ways to make their academic programs connect to vocational programs. For example, Martin Brenner, whose profile appears in Chapter Seven, said that his music department was conceptualizing a program to prepare people for the recording industry. In many schools marketplace considerations, long present in most institutions of higher education, began to dominate. Faculty found themselves face to face with the realities of the marketplace and the demands of entrepreneurship in the community college. Most faculty who participated in the study were not purist about their calling and were willing to do what had to be done to meet the "needs" of their college; most administrators were described as being sensitive, thoughtful, and as considerate as possible in a very difficult time of shrinking resources. Nonetheless, threats to faculty's sense of identity and security were implicit in their having to consider "retooling" themselves and becoming, in a sense, academic utility infielders.

In the sixties and early seventies, the sense of breaking new ground in the community college, and the excitement of participating in an educational movement, had as one of its central sources of energy the imperative to provide equitable educational opportunity. In the 1980s that energy is difficult to sustain when it ceases to be part of a broader societal imperative. One English teacher remarked, "I remember in the sixties I would say that I teach in this community college, and people were impressed because you were doing a significant thing. . . . It is no longer fashionable to work with the poor." While it may no longer be "fashionable" to work with the poor, Breneman and Nelson point out that "compared to students in other sectors of higher education, those in community colleges are more likely to be, on average, less wealthy, members of minority groups, older, part-time, working, and less well prepared" (1981, p. 22). These basic characteristics of community college students make it especially hard for them to persist in school (Astin, 1982, p. 183). By implication these characteristics of the student body make the work of community college faculty extremely complicated and difficult, especially when compared to faculty in four-year, residential institutions. In the sixties and early seventies there was broad social support and considerable respect for such efforts. In the eighties the response is much more ambivalent. As Eugene Bowen, whose profile appears in Chapter Eight, put it, "I think a lot of people say that the community college is wonderful and it is a wonderful job that you are doing. . . . But then they say little things with subtle hints, and things come out that give you the deep-seated impression that they think that your job is not really that great."

The Higher Education Hierarchy

As we have seen, community colleges have held an ambiguous position between the high schools and the four-year colleges and universities. The history, financing, and governance of community colleges reflect that ambiguity. But there is no ambiguity concerning their status in the hierarchy of higher education. Despite the difficulty, complexity, and social significance of their multiple missions, despite the confrontation with what others in higher education have been able to evade because of the very existence of community colleges (Jencks and Riesman, 1968, pp. 490–492), despite many instances of true local pride, and finally despite salaries that compete with and sometimes outrun salaries in four-year institutions (in states like California), there is a nagging, pervasive sense, for both faculty and students, that being at a community college means being near the bottom of the higher education totem pole. (London, 1978, p. 55, argues that for vocational faculty with a different reference group this is not necessarily true.)

Working in a hierarchy at any position has consequences for the worker. The profiles that appear in Chapters Seven through Twelve indicate that for many community college faculty, their position near the bottom of the higher education totem pole is a significant part of their consciousness. The response of some community college faculty is to extol the merits of the community college as an environment over the four-year college and university because of the lack of pressure to publish. Others express the sense that while the community college may not be high in the hierarchy, it is better than teaching in a high school. For still other faculty, particularly women, the community college represents a level of achievement they had not even considered possible for themselves. For others, in contrast, there is a sense of not being where they had hoped to be.

No matter what the particular response, however, most community college faculty experience their position in the higher education hierarchy as affecting their sense of themselves. Community college faculty simultaneously face the realities of their students' struggle with the American dream and their own. How they react to their position on the totem pole affects their commitment to their work, as will be evident in the following chapters.

In addition to these individual responses, the position that community colleges hold between high schools and four-year colleges and universities has resulted in a number of structural and operational conditions which significantly affect the work of community college faculty. Perhaps the most obvious of these conditions is that community colleges are two-year schools. The institution and its faculty have less time with their students than either high school or four-year college teachers. Faculty tend to be limited to teaching introductory courses in their fields. In addition, faculty in community colleges are urged to make teaching and accessibility to students their first priority. To support that priority, early junior college leaders established a dichotomy between teaching and research that is maintained in today's community college. A student-centered ethos has become one of the hallmarks of a community college (O'Banion, 1972, p. 23). The chapters that follow reveal that all of these structural and operational facts of life for community college faculty have enormous consequences for their everyday work and their long-run response to their role.

Increasing debate over community colleges' present efficacy and future directions, more and more bureaucratized decision making, a shifting sense of societal imperative, a position low in the higher education hierarchy, and dropping enrollments—these are all elements of the context in which community college faculty work. This shifting context results in a level of complexity of community college faculty work that defies the two-valued orientation of either criticism or advocacy. The complexities of community college education are so intertwined with the complexities of life in the United States, that simply criticizing community colleges for the broader societal inequities reflected in them does community colleges and their faculty a serious injustice. On the other hand, it is important not to dismiss the difficult realities of community college education since these realities in fact mark a critical point in the history of the community college as an institution.

Community college faculty experience the concrete realities of working within a context that has shifted dramatically while retaining characteristics manifest since the inception of the junior college. When given the time and opportunity to reflect on their experience and those realities and to construct their own analyses of the resulting dichotomies and dilemmas, faculty convey the authority of those who work with the issues on a day-to-day basis.

The research in this study approaches what faculty know and understand about their work through the method of in-depth phenomenological interviewing. The following chapters discuss major issues in faculty work and serve to highlight the connections in the experience of diverse individual faculty members working in a wide range of community college settings. For all those interested in the future of community colleges, what the faculty say in this book can lead to a qualitative understanding of critical issues in community college education and can provide a sound basis for addressing those issues.

2

Interviewing the Faculty: Discovering What Faculty Really Experience and Do

The Rationale for the Method

The major premise of this book is that understanding the experience of community college faculty members is central to understanding the complexities of community college education in this country. A basic approach to study the complexities of any organization is to understand the experience of those who comprise the organization and carry out its processes. One way to approach that experience might be through participant observation. But participant observation places the burden of constructing meaning almost totally on the observer. A goal of this study, in contrast, is to have the meaning we make of the work of community college faculty informed as much as possible by the way the faculty themselves understand their work. In-depth phenomenological interviewing provided the best access to that understanding. (See Becker and Geer, 1969, and Trow, 1969, for a discussion of the comparative values of in-depth interviewing and participant observation.) The model of in-depth phenomenological interviewing we used was suggested by the work of Kenneth Dolbeare and David Schuman (Schuman, 1982).

14

It is not the purpose of phenomenological interviewing to get answers to questions, to test hypotheses, or to "evaluate," as the term is normally used. At the root of in-depth, phenomenological interviewing is an interest in understanding the experience of other people and the meaning they make of that experience rather than in being able to predict or control the experience.

The purpose of in-depth phenomenological interviewing, then, is to have participants reconstruct their experience and reflect on the meaning they make of that experience. In trying to know and understand the interviewees' experience, it was thus important to understand that they were neither subjects nor objects of our study; instead they were participants in the research work. The people we interviewed were constantly active in the research; their individual experience, by the very nature of the process, was affirmed as significant.

For our part, we did not seek "answers" to questions because answers do not adequately reflect the complexity of a person's experience. We did not concentrate on their opinions because we wanted to understand the concrete details on which their opinions must have been based. We were not testing hypotheses because our goal was to understand their experience and to develop our own understanding from the meaning they made, rather than to use them to prove or disprove a notion we had. In order to gain access to the meaning the faculty made of their experience, we explicitly asked them to concentrate on reconstructing, and reflecting on, that experience. That the meaning an individual makes of his or her experience is accessible when the individual reflects on the constitutive factors of that experience is convincingly argued by Schutz (1967). His book, *The Phenomenology of the Social World*, provided the primary theoretical underpinning for our approach to in-depth interviewing.

Selection of Participants

In selecting participants we made an early decision to study the work of community college faculty and professional staff who had instructional responsibilities in a wide range of settings. We were not interested in any single community college site. We

selected participants who worked in community colleges in large
urban centers, in small towns, and in suburban settings.

The study was carried out in two phases.[1] The original
study, sponsored by the Exxon Education Foundation and begun in
1979, concentrated on participants who taught in community
colleges in Massachusetts. Massachusetts ranked forty-eighth in the
nation in per capita expenditures for public higher education
(Chambers, 1979). Most of the funding for the state-wide community college system came from state sources (Garms, 1977). As we
expanded and deepened the research through the second phase of
the study, sponsored by the National Institute of Education, a major
goal was to understand whether the stories and experiences collected
in the Massachusetts interviews were particular to Massachusetts
faculty because of the low level of funding and the centralized state
organization of community colleges.

We therefore decided to do the additional interviews in the
NIE cycle of the study in states that have contrasting characteristics.
California was selected because it has a longer history with community colleges than Massachusetts, was third in the nation in per
capita expenditure for higher education (Chambers, 1979), and, at
least before Proposition 13, had a system of governance and funding
more balanced among state and local sources than Massachusetts
(Garms, 1977). New York state also provided a useful contrast to
Massachusetts and California, in addition to being accessible to the
researchers on a regular basis during the academic year. New York
ranked twenty-fifth in per capita appropriations for public higher
education (Chambers, 1979) and provided an even more balanced
formula for funding among state, local, and tuition sources than
either California or Massachusetts (Garms, 1977). In addition, both
California and New York provided access to community colleges
that were much larger than those in Massachusetts.

---

[1] Patrick J. Sullivan, co-investigator of the Exxon study and the associate
investigator of the National Institute of Education study, Mary Bray Schatzkamer,
research associate, and the author were members of the research team that conducted
the interviews and worked with the resulting material. Mary Ellen Kelly also
conducted interviews of students in the first phase of the research.

Thus, the contrasting levels of appropriations for public higher education, the different formulas for funding and governance represented in each state, and the wider range of size of institutions determined the decision to interview participants in California and New York state. Additional participants from Massachusetts in this second, NIE-sponsored phase of our study were also included. A faculty member who had taught in Illinois and one who had taught in Colorado were asked to participate in the study. In addition to interviewing community college faculty and professional staff who had instructional responsibilities, a sample of twenty-four students distributed evenly in Massachusetts, New York, and California were interviewed. While the student interviews contributed to our understanding of faculty work, for the purposes of this book we have focused almost entirely on the faculty interviews.

The goal in selecting individual participants was to build a pool that was fair to the larger community college faculty population. Recent reports indicate that the percentage of women faculty in community colleges is growing. In 1980 it was approximately 40 percent (Wolk, 1980, p. 192; Gilbert, 1980, p. 3). In the final sample of seventy-six faculty, thirty-two were women; 42 percent is a figure consistent with the national population.

The statistical picture of minority and nonminority faculty in community colleges is infused with many problems, as is described by Olivas (1979). Olivas reports that in the early seventies, nonminorities accounted for 95 percent of the faculty in community colleges and minorities for 5 percent. Nothing in what Olivas or other sources present indicates that that figure is rising at any significant rate, and there is even some suggestion of decline. If the 5 percent figure had been adhered to in our study, we would have interviewed a total of only four minority faculty. However, because issues of equitable educational opportunity are central to the mission of community colleges and because the experience of minority community college faculty contributes to an understanding of the issues, we decided to include more minority faculty than would be called for if we had used numerical representation as the only criterion. Of seventy-six faculty and staff participants in our study, therefore, twenty-one were members of minority groups.

Another major consideration in the selection of participants was the division in community colleges between faculty considered "liberal arts" and those classified as "career education" faculty. In *The Culture of a Community College,* London (1978) built a strong case for saying that faculty who teach in liberal arts transfer programs have a different sense of their work than do faculty who teach in vocational programs. The literature is replete with statements about the increasing importance of vocational programs in community colleges. Indeed, in California it is reported that more than three-fourths of the students in community colleges are enrolled in courses to learn specific vocational skills and have no intention of completing a program or transferring to a four-year college (Watkins, 1983).

Yet despite the evidence that a dichotomy between liberal arts and career education exists, there is very little statistical data on the relative number of career and liberal arts faculty. Partially that is a problem of definition; there is an increasing number of faculty who would normally be considered "academic" teaching in "vocational" programs and who thus blur the distinctions, at least on one level. (See Cohen and Brawer, 1982, pp. 200–203, 221, for a more extensive discussion of the blurring of such distinctions.) Grant and Eiden (1980, p. 104) gave some guidance in the matter by reporting on areas in which community college faculty earned their highest degree as of 1972–1973. At that time 20 to 33 percent of community college faculty held their highest degrees in vocational areas. Of the seventy-six faculty and staff participants, nineteen, or 25 percent, were faculty in vocational areas, a figure that is fair to the historical picture but perhaps a little low given the recent upsurge in vocational education in community colleges.

In addition to considerations of gender, nonminority and minority status, and career education and liberal arts program affiliation, issues of age and experience, highest degree held, and whether the faculty were tenured or nontenured were also taken into consideration in selecting participants. Wolk (1980, p. 192) indicated that 15.3 percent of community college faculty held the doctorate, either the Ph.D. or the Ed.D. In our sample of seventy-six faculty and staff participants, twelve, or 15.78 percent held the doctorate. Wolk (1980, p. 192) also reported that the average age of community college faculty members was forty-four and that ten years was the average length of teaching experience. Among the faculty and staff participants in this study, the range of age and experience was consistent with these figures.

In selecting the participants, we took other factors that were less concrete into consideration as well. For example, during an early round of contact visits we met with a group of faculty who had just endured a divisive conflict between faculty and administration, resulting in the forced resignation of the president. It became clear as we talked with this group of faculty that their perceptions of their work experience would be deeply affected by this recent clash. Although we considered for a short time including some faculty from this school in our sample because such political battles are not irrelevant to the work of community college faculty, we decided that we wanted to avoid participants who had an axe to grind, at least to the extent that we could discern this ahead of time. Nor did we want the research to become associated with local political battles.

Similarly, participants who had been recommended to us as "stars" of the faculty were bypassed in the selection process, although certainly some who were chosen for other reasons turned out to be stars in their departments. The study was focused on the everyday experience of faculty who carry out the work of community colleges and not on celebrities on the faculty whose experience might be more affected by their status than by the nature of their work in the college.

Also included in the group of participants were seventeen people who had professional staff positions in community colleges, for the most part staff positions that included instructional responsibilities. Among those staff were counselors and staff of instructional resource centers. Only two people who had administrative positions with no instructional responsibility were interviewed.

Contact and Access

It became clear in the research process that how access was established with participants and how contact was made with them affected the actual interview process. The interviewing relationship begins at the point when contact is first made with a potential participant. In achieving access to potential participants and making contact with them, we established a process that was directed toward achieving as much equity in the interviewing relationship as possible. Contact was made with participants through peers and not through people in positions of authority over the participants. We wanted not only to avoid the impression that the research was supported and sanctioned by the administration of a college and that it was a study of one particular site but also to minimize differences in perceptions of power and authority between the researchers and the community college faculty.

As a general guide to the work, we tried to minimize the role of third parties. As soon as possible we took direct responsibility for the relationship that would develop between us and the participants. A contact visit was made with almost every participant before the actual interview process began. These contact meetings would be held either individually or in small groups. In these meetings we explained who we were, what our study was about, how we intended to use the data we collected, and the amount of time and the nature of the commitment we were seeking from participants. In addition to talking about ourselves and our work, we would ask the participants to tell us about themselves so that we could collect information about them relevant to the goals and criteria established for selection. In the entire process the goal was to be explicit about the work and to try to create a situation in which the potential participant made an active choice about whether to participate in the study. Once that choice was made, dates and times for the interview series were proposed.

After having made contact with a participant, secured the participant's agreement to participate, and set up the time and place for the series of interviews, one final step remained as a bridge between the contact process and the interview process. At the appointment for the first interview, but before it actually started, the participants were asked to read carefully a detailed "Written Consent Form" that we had prepared for the project. While the original impetus for the form came from federal regulations concerning the rights of human subjects in research, the form served more than just a legal function. By making the form as explicit as possible about who we were, the nature of the work, the commitment asked of the participants, the uses to which the data would be put, and the rights of the participants, we further clarified the purpose and nature of the work.

The Interview Process

The research design was structured around a sequence of three in-depth interviews with each participant in the study. Each interview in the series lasted one and one-half hours, and the interviews were normally spaced about three days to a week apart. The first two interviews were usually held in the faculty member's office or another room in his or her college where uninterrupted privacy could be assured. Whenever logistically possible and whenever the participant was willing, the third interview took place in the participant's home.

All the interviews were tape-recorded. Taping was essential to the process of interviewing. It contributed to a sense of responsibility on interviewers' and participants' parts alike. Contrary to conventional wisdom, the tape recorder can work to make the participant more comfortable rather than less comfortable with the interviewing process. The tape recorder allows the interviewer to concentrate on what the participant is saying and on the interviewing process rather than on capturing in writing what is said. Further, it provides a full record of what was said. The presence of the tape recorder proved to be a constant and appropriate reminder of the delicate tension between the private voice sought in the process and the public use of the interview material that was intended.

Each of the three interviews had a distinct purpose and focus. The first interview concentrated on the life of the participants before they began to work in community colleges. The researchers asked the participants to reconstruct experiences with parents, siblings, neighborhood friends, and acquaintances, and to talk about their schooling and early work experiences. The second interview focused on what it was like to work in the community college. In this interview participants were asked to reconstruct in as concrete detail as possible how they spent their time and energy in the community college. We concentrated on the details of their experience rather than on their opinions and attitudes, which would have been abstractions of that experience. The third interview focused on the meaning that the participants made of their work in the community college. Given what they had reconstructed in the first two interviews, they were asked to reflect on how they understood the place of their work in their lives.

Each of the three interviews in the sequence had a specific purpose and focus, but within each interview the interviewing technique was open-ended. There was not a set of preestablished questions to which we were seeking answers or a set of hypotheses that we wanted to test. At times we would ask questions that had developed from previous interviews with the same participant, or with other participants, that seemed to reflect common themes. Examples of questions that were repeated in different interviews are "What is it like to be a woman on this faculty?" "What is it like for you to have a Ph.D. in this community college?" On the whole we limited the number of such thematic questions we asked to avoid creating themes in the minds of participants that would have not been there had we not asked the question. When thematic questions were asked, it was after the participants had spent the time they wanted to spend recreating the details of their experience and when such questions seemed connected to the experience that they had presented.

The methodological goal in the interviewing was to have the participants reconstruct and reflect on the concrete details, the constitutive factors, of their experience. The interviewers' primary task was to frame the interview and to be active listeners. We most often asked questions when we did not understand something that had been said, when we wanted to hear more detail about what a participant was discussing, or when we wanted to guide the interview within the framework established for that particular interview. We would also ask a question when we thought that what we were hearing was a public, outer voice instead of what Steiner (1978) calls the more private, inner voice. Sometimes a question like "How would you talk about your work today if you were talking with your spouse?" would be effective. Even a technique as transparent as that provided a way for participants who perhaps did not even realize that they were talking in a public, outer voice to switch to an inner voice. (For an extensive discussion of methodological, ethical, and epistemological issues in in-depth interviewing, see Seidman, Sullivan, and Schatzkamer, 1983, chap. 14.)

Working with the Material

The interviewing began in December 1979 and was completed in January 1983. The interviews resulted in approximately 12,000 double-spaced pages of verbatim transcript. The research team spent seven months reading the transcripts of all the interviews. At least three readers read each transcript, marking passages that were of interest. After completing the process of reading and marking the transcripts, the team labeled each marked passage according to categories that began to emerge as the transcripts were studied. To do justice to the interviews, we decided that the material could be presented best in two ways: first, as profiles of community college faculty work experience in their own words; and second, as excerpts from the interviews woven together around important themes that connected individual faculty members' experience. As much as possible, focus would be on the words of the faculty.

The profiles in Chapters Seven through Twelve are composed almost totally of the words of the participants. Where we have needed to interject our own words for the sake of clarity, we have bracketed them. In most cases the order of the profile material is consistent with the order of the interviews. In some cases material from a later interview has been placed in the profile in an earlier position. When material has been taken out of its original context, it has been done only if the new context does not change the meaning of the original utterance.

For the purpose of this book, the focus of the profiles was on the faculty's work in the community college. Clearly much material has been omitted. In reviewing the material and deciding what could be left out and what could be brought together, we made a decision to omit the following: (1) repetitious material; (2) ad hominem material; (3) material unconnected to other passages in the interview or to larger social and organizational contexts; (4) material that would make the participant vulnerable if he or she were identified; (5) material that, if taken out of the total context of the interview, was not fair to the participant.

In addition to composing the profiles, the author edited them where necessary to make them readable. In most cases repetitions common to oral speech but awkward in written form were deleted. Syntactical inconsistencies that occur in informal speech were also edited. In addition, steps were taken to disguise the identity of our participants. The names used in the profiles that follow are pseudonyms; other steps were taken when necessary to cloud the identity of the participants. Finally, in all matters of choice in working with the words of the faculty, three basic criteria were followed: (1) Is the material fair to the participant? (2) Does the material preserve the participant's dignity? (3) Is the material selected for the profiles or for quotation an accurate reflection of the interview as a whole?

By using the method of in-depth interviewing to gain the perspective of the faculty who have worked within community colleges, we hoped to bridge the chasm that often occurs between researcher and participant. By presenting the findings as much as possible in the words of the faculty interviewed, the author hopes to indicate a sense of possibilities for action that might connect effectively to the experience and understanding of the administrators and faculty who work within the colleges.

3

The Deepening Conflict
Between Vocational
and Liberal Education

False Dichotomies

"Should general studies people, which is what they call us, be at this place at all?" the first community college teacher interviewed at the outset of our study said. "Or should the college just be vocational? . . . That is an unresolved issue. General studies people holler and yell, 'Of course we are important,' but it is very hard to make that clear to anyone." Near the end of the study, two years later, in a different part of the country, a theater teacher who also served as the head of her small community college's humanities division said, "I serve on the curriculum . . . and long-range planning committee of the college. I feel like I attend an enormous number of meetings. . . . I would say the majority of the time it is irritating for me because I don't really feel we're dealing with the problems. . . . That is, you know, what is the purpose of the school? . . . The business people want to bring in an AOS degree, which is an Associates of Occupational Science degree. I'm not really sure what that means, but it does mean that you take sixty credits and you don't have to have area distributions. . . . We would be doing away with the requirements we set for our students. . . . What kind of job would we be doing of educating our students?"

The previous summer in California, Edward Thompson, whose profile appears in Chapter Ten and who is a teacher of small motor repair, said: "I have very few people complete the two years in my program. The people that come to me are striving for a job . . . maybe the first one they have ever had. Or they have had a series of jobs that never lasted more than three or four months. They are looking for some kind of skill to get them a little more stability in their life. . . . They get a job and they are done with me. . . . Don't get me wrong. I would like to see my students go through the academic stuff. I push for that . . . [but] I get a lot of guys that you give the first test to and they are gone. . . . When my student leaves here, I want him to know how it is really going to be out there, not how it should be. The social scientist can deal with how it should be, but my students have to know how it is."

Seventy-five miles away in another California community college district, a psychology teacher with a Ph.D. in psychology reported, "More and more are going into vocational areas, that's why the number of courses in liberal arts is dropping off. . . .We just don't have the bodies anymore. I think if public feeling toward education continues the way it has been going for the last couple of years and if the present economic conditions continue, we will become a trade school. . . . It would be very sad for us . . . in the liberal arts."

And so it went during the three years of interviewing community college faculty in Massachusetts, New York, and California. In large urban community colleges, in colleges set in well-to-do suburban areas and in small towns, faculty told stories of how their everyday work and their sense of themselves, their students, and their colleagues were influenced by the divisions established between vocational and liberal arts education, between general and specialized education, between training for work and education for living. Intelligent voices from a wide range of perspectives have called these divisions "false dichotomies" (see Whitehead, 1929, p. 74, and Cohen and Brawer, 1977, p. 97). Yet for all that has been written about these false dichotomies, the dichotomies seem to be becoming more pervasive in community colleges and are having a divisive and undermining effect on the faculty and students.

The Impact on Minorities

The division between vocational and liberal arts education is of special import to minority faculty and students in community colleges. In a 1930 speech, W. E. B. Du Bois said that the debate between the advocates of vocational education for Negroes and those who advocated a liberal collegiate education was not yet settled. He said then that it was not that he did not believe in vocational education; it was that he did not believe that what was being called vocational education for Negroes at the time was actually collegiate level education. Du Bois argued that industrial education was least effectively carried out in school settings where by necessity the curriculum and the equipment would always lag behind that of industry (Du Bois, 1973, pp. 61-62). (For an interesting corollary of that argument, see Cohen, 1969, pp. 139-140, where he argues that vocational education should be taken out of the community college and put back into industry and business, with whom community colleges could subsequently form educational partnerships.) Du Bois argued that the Negro college should provide not just the trained man who would do what the world wants done but also the graduate who could help the world know what ought to be done (1973, p. 68). Du Bois went on to say this: "We need, then, first training as human beings in general knowledge and experience; then technical training to do a specific part of the world's work" (1973, pp. 77-78).

Fifty years after that speech, the same debate, the same lack of resolution, the same feeling of struggle was expressed by black and Hispanic community college faculty who taught at a school whose students were predominantly members of minorities. One of the Hispanic faculty members said, "I believe in the liberal arts. I defend them. In one of my courses today, I was speaking to my students and telling them that the only way that they can be free in terms of an education is to have an understanding of the liberal arts. I told them if you do not go through the experience of the liberal arts, you are missing half your life. And a student confronted me, and he said, 'But I want to go to work. I am poor. I am unemployed.' And I understand that very easily. But I said, 'Keep in mind that if we really want to be independent and participate in the whole political process in this country, we are not going to be able to achieve that working in a factory.' "

A black faculty member from the same college said the following: "What is happening now is that community colleges are moving toward vocational education which means that a lot of our students . . . will be tracked into those positions. . . . This has been the problem throughout history, the issue of industrial education or liberal arts education, beginning from Du Bois and Booker T. Washington. It has not been resolved. . . . I'm not putting down the development of skills. I mean the development of skills is the basis of survival. But there is also the personal sense of existence, of who you are as a human being."

A division chairman at the college, a black and a graduate of Harvard, gave the other side of the argument:

> I don't know. You don't need . . . some of the classical liberal arts types of things here. You have to get started somewhere, and the most viable way . . . would be by getting the basic needs of the community met; by dealing with unemployment, dealing with upping the economic levels of families, getting them off public assistance, and enabling them to at least be aware that there are means by which they can get a toe-hold in society.
>
> The community college that even gives a "second best" type of education is not seen in that light by the people in the community. . . . Despite all the rest that it might do to aspirations, at least it will teach people to read and write beyond the sixth grade level. . . .
>
> A glorified trade school type of operation? . . . I don't worry about whether they are going to be hopelessly trapped . . . as much as I worry that they wouldn't survive if they didn't have those jobs. . . . That's simplistic. I should think more about it. But that's basically how I am going about it, and that's basically how people are receiving it for the most part.

Minority students seem to be taking the issue into their own hands and voting with their feet. Olivas (1979) reports that although it is often contended that minority students are channeled into vocational programs in community colleges, his findings do not support the notion that a disproportionate number in comparison to nonminority students are entering vocational programs. According to Olivas a fair share of minority students opt for the liberal arts transfer programs in community colleges. But the sad fact is, according to Astin (1982, p. 99), that a disproportionate number of minority students gain access to higher education through community colleges and that their chances of earning a baccalaureate degree are substantially reduced by doing so. Breneman and Nelson found data consistent with Astin's position (Breneman and Nelson, 1981, p. 209). Critics speak of a negative effect of going to a community college if your aspiration is a four-year degree.

While many minority students opt for liberal arts transfer programs, the ethos, energy, and resources of the community colleges are decidedly moving toward vocationalism. While the interviews provided much evidence of distinguished efforts of individual faculty in both vocational and liberal arts programs to teach their courses in a spirit and with a method consistent with the ideal of a liberal education, their individual efforts are fragmented and isolated, and become tokens in the face of the larger vocationalized ethos of community colleges. If this is the case, then it may be a cruel irony that when minority students choose the path Du Bois might have urged in community colleges, what they get may only dimly resemble what they thought they were choosing.

Status Within the Curriculum Hierarchy

Despite the fact of the increasing swing toward vocationalism in the community colleges, despite the fact that money, and new and replacement faculty positions, are seldom directed these days to liberal arts areas, despite the fact that all outward signs affirm the strength of vocationalism in community colleges, there is considerable discomfort beneath the surface of the divided curriculum. For example, Edward Thompson, who is profiled in Chapter Ten, said, "When they started this school, everybody thought that because of the geographic boundaries this was going to be the vocational-technical school, because we are where there is industry. The word started to spread that there were great vocational classes over there. The president has fought for the last five years to change that image, but it is hard to erase that stigma from within a community. It is starting to work now, as we have students that have left and have gone to four-year institutions and are coming back to the community." It seems that if a community college is good at its vocational efforts, it must face the notion that vocational education is somehow demeaning to a college.

Not only do presidents worry about the vocational image of community colleges, but vocational faculty within the colleges, despite the fact that enrollments, money, and resources have swung in their direction, often do not feel empowered in the colleges. Some faculty face the issue quite directly. Thompson went on to say: "I get along with the rest of the faculty real well. I am one of the faculty leaders because I am in the union. . . . A long time ago when they used to call industrial arts "manual arts," the type of people they put into that were the ones they didn't think could make it academically. Academic people (not all of them) sometimes tend to think that they might be just a little bit above you because you are doing something like this. That does not exist around here. Number one, I would match my brains and wits with any of the academic people. I don't cower away from them, and I am not afraid to get involved with them. . . . If you don't get involved in things around the campus, which is normally done by the academic people, they tend to start looking down on you."

Across the country in a small-town Massachusetts community college, we interviewed a retired police officer who had risen high in the ranks of a major city police department and who now teaches in his college's criminal justice program. In one part of the interview he commented very thoughtfully on the complexities of the issue of grading, which was of constant concern to the college at large. We asked him if he shared his thoughts with his academic colleagues. He replied that he did not and that he keeps his thoughts pretty much to himself because "I don't think people from the humanities division have ever asked me anything about school administration. I don't think they are interested in what my opinions are. I'm not being critical of them. . . . I don't think those involved in traditional education view the occupational programs as being the equivalent to what they are engaged in. . . . You know, higher education even to me as a youngster meant more than an occupational program." In the same vein, another faculty member said that when he sees someone he has not seen for a long time, "I have trouble when someone says what do you do. I say I am at a community college and I teach secretarial skills and I always invariably add accounting too, because I think accounting is a collegiate level course."

The hierarchical notions associated with "academic" and "vocational" curricula are intensified and complicated when women faculty are involved. Linda Donovan, whose profile appears in Chapter Ten, spoke about what it was like to begin her career at the college in the secretarial department. She said, "I felt that, in many instances, some of the faculty might perceive their job as more important than mine because they were teaching courses that they considered more important. . . . The business division meant males. . . . And, of course, in the secretarial department we could have some females who would be very good but who would always be considered slightly different from the rest of the faculty." A position opened up in the predominantly male business department and, with the encouragement of affirmative action policies, she applied for and got it. She said, "I'm not a member of the secretarial faculty anymore. I'm in the business administration faculty, and over the years I think others' perceptions of my role began to change. I felt that I was beginning to emerge as an equal in other people's eyes."

Roberta DeVane, whose profile also appears in Chapter Ten and who is a woman with a master's degree and many years of experience in nursing, said that when she joined the community college faculty, "I had this feeling that, you know, I was just a nurse and therefore I wasn't quite as good as the rest of the people that taught here because they were . . . college professors. They had their master's. I had a master's, but for some reason it took me a while to get used to the idea that I'm just as good as they were. . . . I didn't want to talk in faculty meetings. I just kind of did my job, and I really didn't feel part of the college at all. That's changed over the years."

Hierarchical distinctions are established, then, not only between career and academic faculty but also within the ranks of career faculty. The existence of a totem pole within the institution is not unique to a community college. A similar study of university faculty would elicit similar observations about hierarchy within university faculties. But the totem pole effect is exacerbated in the community college because some eighty years after the establishment of the junior college, community colleges are near the bottom rung on the higher education ladder. The mission that they were asked to carry out by early university leaders was to serve as buffers allowing four-year colleges and universities to "preserve their academic integrity and concentrate on what they like best" (Newman, 1971, p. 60). That role of buffer has led community colleges to undertake some of the toughest tasks in higher education, which the four-year segment of higher education has been glad to hand over to them (Newman, 1971, p. 57).

But instead of gaining the respect of the higher educational establishment and the general public for the difficulty of the task that has been both imposed on community colleges and that they have sought, community colleges are near the bottom of the higher education totem pole. That sense of being near the bottom affects faculty in the academic areas who are teaching subjects with which a great deal of respect and prestige is normally associated. Eugene Bowen, whose profile appears in Chapter Eight, teaches math at a community college in a suburban area in Massachusetts. At the time of his interview he was completing a doctorate in math education at a nearby private university. He told us that friends of his who taught in four-year colleges spoke of his teaching at a community college as teaching "down there." He spoke of the working-class neighborhood in which he and his family lived when he first started teaching in a community college and of the respect that he felt from his neighbors for the fact that he was a college professor. But then he went on to say, "We moved from one neighborhood to another in the same town a year ago. We picked up a whole new set of friends. . . . Where I am now most of the people are either college professors or they are the director of data processing, or editor of this, or the machine supervisor at some big company. Some of the comments they make give me the impression that they think that community college teachers are beneath them." Bowen, a talented and experienced teacher who has learned to face a wide array of students in his math classes with a feeling of confidence that he can teach them, struggles with the idea of leaving teaching completely and moving into administration. He sincerely prefers teaching to administrative work, but working in a context that undermines the value of his work leads him to consider trying somehow to move up the so-called ladder.

Manual and Intellectual Work

Students and resources may be shifting to vocational programs, yet teacher after teacher in the study seemed to be aware that the skills those students needed most were the skills of reading and writing. Edward Thompson, outspoken on the split between practical vocational education programs and theoretical academic programs, said, "I tell all the students that the amount of money they are going to make is going to be directly tied to responsibility that they are willing to take, and that is going to be tied to the amount of education they have. . . . I tell them that somewhere down the line, they are going to have to bring up their reading and writing. It is imperative. You go to work as a mechanic and the next step up is the service writer, and above the service writer is the service manager."

Janet Ingersoll, whose profile appears in Chapter Seven, worked in a writing center. Her job was to provide outreach to vocational programs. She said, "I worked with a lot of vocational students. They often knew that to get anywhere in their profession . . . they had to improve their writing, but they were very scared of going up the hill where the humanities classrooms are and taking English classes. They march out of the vocational buildings and up the hill assuming that they are going to fail yet once again. . . . The welding instructor was more than willing to say to his students, 'If you can write, if you can write up a report, if you can write up a program or a design for a particular welding project, you're going to end up being a supervisor, maybe running your own company. If you can't do that, you are going to be stuck being a welder, and it's going to make a crucial difference.' "

The irony is that English faculty and other teachers in the humanities hold the key to a real sense of power and opportunity for the students who come to the college seeking job preparation. Many faculty members recognize that, but faculties, administrators, and colleges as a whole seem not to know what individual faculty know. English teachers, as the profiles in Chapter Seven indicate, are asked to teach writing in a format that ignores the complexity of teaching writing to students who have had little success with writing in their previous school experience. While it is true that many colleges set up reading and writing centers for students who need intensive remedial work, it is in the freshman and sophomore English classes that the overwhelming number of students who have very little sense of power, confidence, or competence in their writing are taught. The colleges expect the teachers to teach writing as though their students did not have a complex history with writing, a history of tension shaped by issues of social class, race, and gender. Teachers in these classes most often have a teaching load that assumes no such complexity, and no history of failure on the part of their students.

The result is, as Nancy Warren's profile indicates, that teachers of English face a "soul deadening" load of papers to read, grade, and comment upon, and no real way to ever feel successful at the job. As Warren said, some teachers of English do their work with a constant sense of personal failure that "comes always from the feeling that you could do so much more if you had more time, and you would have more time if you had fewer students and less paper grading and more time to work with the students individually." (See Chapters Five and Seven for more about the critical issue of teaching writing in community colleges.)

Writing is crucial to a real sense of opportunity for all students, and students in community colleges tend to have had a complicated and negative history with writing. To contend with those histories, individual English teachers sometimes make almost heroic efforts; yet as Nancy Warren's profile indicates, try as English teachers might—through their union, through lobbying from professional associations, through personal and collective action— community college administrators, pressed by budget considerations, seem unable to implement any change in the situation that would make a real difference.

Another key to real opportunity for many vocational students is mathematics. Alfred Sohn-Rethel has argued that the crucial dividing line between intellectual and manual labor is the field of mathematics (1978, pp. 101–103). To the extent that students can learn math, they can progress in the physical sciences underlying the technologies for which many are training. To the extent that they can understand the underlying foundation of their career area, they will have the opportunity to move from low-level entry and service positions to positions in which the fact that they are working with their minds will be recognized and they will be compensated for it. It is clear that there is a connection between the science and math curricula in community colleges and students' sense of power and opportunity. As Leonard Braddock, whose profile appears in Chapter Ten and who teaches in a materials testing program in New York state, said, "Testing is nothing more than applied physics, and people coming here with no physics background or chemistry background . . . just can't handle it at the level we think it should be taught. . . . You can't talk about anything in physics without a very heavy orientation in mathematics."

Whether a community college student is headed for a job as a service person, a technician, or an engineer is directly related to how much math and science he or she has had and how well he or she reads and writes. But the problem is that without a strong general education program, the necessary foundation in math, science, and reading and writing is not likely to be established. The deepening division between the vocational programs and general education curricula seems to guarantee that students going into the vocational programs will never get that solid foundation. Faculty like Braddock realize that and do their best to include the necessary math and science into their technological courses; Braddock is even writing a text that he hopes will integrate the basic and applied aspects of his field and present the material in a language accessible to his students. That is a significant effort on the part of an individual faculty member. But most often the awareness of individual teachers does not get translated into curricular patterns that would make a difference.

Like their colleagues in English, math, and science, faculty in social sciences and the humanities face difficult situations in community colleges because of the split between vocational and general education. Lawrence Bauer, whose profile appears in Chapter Nine, spoke of the complicated attitudes his students brought to his social science courses: "So they come into the liberal arts courses with a built-in resentment. I see that in my classes. . . . Most people don't see the connection between why they have to take this course and why they are at the community college. That deeply disturbs me . . . to see the apathetic kinds of responses that these students make to these crucial controversial issues we are dealing with in this world. There are some who genuinely do catch ahold, and they get excited. . . . But by and large, you can talk about an issue for fifty minutes and have a whole class sit there and stare at you with a blank expression and not say a word. . . . It's depressing to me, the feeling that these students are going to go out into the world and virtually separate their intellect from their work."

Students who pursue training programs in community colleges are there because they believe they need the community college preparation to enable them to get a job. They have been persuaded by the notion that there are skills they can learn that will make them employable and that the community college offers access to those skills. It is complicated for those students to go to an institution that promotes a short-term approach to training and jobs and at the same time be confronted by a teacher who asks them to step back and think about long-range social issues. Their reasons for coming to the community college, and the promise of skill training the community college seems to offer, make dealing with issues and values seem irrelevant to them.

At the same time that vocational teachers indicate that their students must learn to think broadly and deeply if they are going to go anywhere in their occupations, the role of social science and humanities teachers in the community college has been steadily decreasing. The type of thinking they ask students to do is relegated more and more to the background. Liberal arts teachers, despite the fact that their vocational colleagues often see them as the real college teachers, increasingly live with the sense that their jobs are on the edge of becoming dispensable in the community college.

What some of the career education faculty in the study wanted for their students was very similar to what their colleagues in the liberal arts said was important for students. Because many of the career education faculty had had long experience in their respective occupational fields, they knew that their students would be limited to entry-level positions unless they understood the place of their work in the larger social scheme and unless they had a grounding in those academic subjects that provided the foundation for their occupational areas. Scott Muller, who teaches refrigeration and heat transfer in a New York state community college, had this to say: "I try to get them thinking about who they are and where they are going or where they are possibly not going. . . . The larger context that I brought was that technical education was not enough, skills are not enough. You have to have not only a general education, but you have to have some sense of self that transcends whatever you are doing. . . . I am trying to justify the fact that these kids can do more than society expects them to. They have been tracked, they have been conditioned by their families. I think they are much more capable. . . . I try to make sure that my students don't feel limitations especially because they seem to have been relegated to the lower academic rungs. . . . Vocational programs tend to be their first and last stop in a lot of peoples' minds. So if anything, I try to convince them that this doesn't have to be their last stop, that this learning can be the beginning of continually turning themselves on to it."

In his article on vocational education in community colleges, Fred Pincus urges that community college educators work with working class and minority students to provide them "with a historical and political context from which to understand the dismal choices they face" (Pincus, 1980, p. 356). In fact, Scott Muller teaches in a way that is remarkably consistent with what Pincus urges. But Muller is even more radical in his approach. He recognizes that mechanical skills cannot be isolated from a larger sense of understanding in the true sense of the word "skill." He knows, as other vocational faculty whom we interviewed know, that students who work with mechanical objects—who are, so to speak, "good with their hands"—cannot be so without being good with their heads also.

Many writers on community colleges have commented upon the false dichotomy between career education and liberal arts education, between training and education, and have urged that the language and actions that perpetuate this dichotomy be done away with. (See Cohen, 1969; O'Banion, 1972; Cohen and Brawer, 1982.) Cohen and Brawer found in their survey study (1977, p. 17) that "when the data were tabulated, the difference among people in the various teaching fields proved less discriminating than did nearly all other measures." That finding was completely consistent with our interviews of faculty in the liberal arts who understood the importance of their subjects to the vocational fields, and of career faculty who understood the necessity for more than technical training.

What many of the faculty in the study appreciated was the understanding that a general education is distinguished from narrow training not by subject matter but in terms of outlook, method, and spirit of approach, no matter what the subject matter (Harvard University, 1945, p. 56). But those faculty teach in a setting that constantly strains that understanding to its limits. The community college, in its press for career education, in molding its curriculum toward training for jobs, is not all that different from four-year colleges and universities. Hurn (1983) has argued that the vocationalization of all the segments of higher education has intensified in the last decade. As one participant in the study, Samuel Berger (profiled in Chapter Nine), a veteran of some twenty-five years of teaching in the social sciences in community colleges, said, "I don't object to connecting up vocation with higher education. . . . At the University every other guy is in a vocational program; he can't wait to go into teaching or medicine or law. . . . If somebody wants to go into nursing, a part of their program must be a consideration of the role of medicine in modern life, and an analysis of the industry, problems in medical care, the distribution of medical care, the economics, the history of medicine. In other words, I want to humanize the occupational interests. . . . When you ask me what I think about occupationalism, I don't say 'Down with it. . . .' The struggle is . . . what kind of occupations and what context you put them in."

Community colleges, so deeply enmeshed in their struggle just to survive, do not offer much support for the faculty members in either the career or liberal arts curriculum who ask the question, "Jobs for what, to what end, why?" The teachers in the liberal arts who attempt to perform that function in the community college have a difficult role. They are swimming against the current. What is more, their students find themselves caught in the great divide. Their world becomes fragmented and the questions their liberal arts teachers ask them to think about seem irrelevant to their reasons for coming to the community college in the first place. Sometimes the reaction of students caught in this bifurcated world is anger; often it is apathy. Sometimes the spark catches, and there is a sense in their eyes of deep appreciation for an idea and of recognition that this is what college is supposed to be like. For the career teacher who recognizes the importance of placing career training in the larger context and who tries to bring a sense of the qualitative into his technical training program, the result of this effort is sometimes to isolate him or her from his nearest colleagues. As Scott Muller put it, "I feel sometimes professionally lonely. I feel that I may have a sense of quality that either I am too naive to give up right now or that no one else shares."

On both sides of the divide, then, there are faculty in the community college who have a broad vision of what the education of their students should be like. Their individual efforts, however, seem to be swamped by a movement that is all too willing to buy into the notion of "postsecondary education." That phrase, as Berger said, is an "awful phrase. It isn't even a commitment to a college. It only says there will be something after high school, not beyond but after high school. At least 'a community college' has the word 'college' in it. The more we draw distinctions within the realm of higher education, or certain parts of it, and [first] say that we have 'a community college' and now [that] we have 'postsecondary education,' the more I think we make it meaningless. I think it [the phrase 'postsecondary education'] is pernicious, although it is quite popular."

The eager participation in a concept called "postsecondary education" on the part of leaders of community colleges indeed seems to undermine the efforts of committed and talented faculty to bridge the great divide in the curriculum of community colleges. Individual efforts of faculty in both the liberal arts and career education are clearly not enough to overcome the historical, structural, and social reasons for the curriculum's developing as it has. Calls for reform of the curriculum must include reorganization of its relationship to the social and economic structure of our society. The division in the curriculum in the community college is in fact a reflection of larger divisions ingrained in our society. Many community college faculty pour their considerable energy into bridging those divides, but in so doing they may be pursuing a familiar but ultimately enervating course of action: namely taking individual responsibility for the consequences of social and structural forces far beyond their control. Individual faculty must have the concerted support of governing boards, administrators, their colleagues and all those concerned with community college education to bridge the false dichotomies that have developed in their curricula.

∽◈∽ 4 ∽◈∽

Diminished
Faculty Relations
and Collegial Support

∽◈∽◈∽◈∽◈∽◈∽◈∽◈∽

Increasing Bureaucracy

Collegial relations play a major role in shaping faculty members' sense of their work and how they carry it out. A counselor in a Massachusetts community college used a telling metaphor to describe her sense of collegial relations. She described herself in the college as being at "the bottom of the totem pole." Ironically, that totem pole image could be used to describe many large modern organizations, but it seemed particularly apt as community college faculty spoke about their work. As institutions, community colleges are near the bottom of the higher education totem pole. Within community colleges themselves, at the top of the totem pole are the governing boards, then the administrators, most of them white males (Olivas, 1979, p. 90). Next come the faculty, and within the faculty, there are different places in the hierarchy for members of academic or career-oriented departments (see Chapter Three). At the bottom of the professional section of the totem pole are the counselors and other nonfaculty professional staff. Beneath the professionals are the "nonprofessional" support staff. Position on the totem pole is seriously affected by whether faculty members are white male or female or members of a minority (see Chapter Eleven). (In community colleges that serve predominantly minority populations or in which there are a larger than usual number of minority members on the faculty, being a white male or female complicates place on the totem pole.)

No matter what one's position is on the totem pole, the fact of its existence has a decided effect on faculty experience. Cohen and Brawer keyed in on this issue when they wrote the following: "The major transformation in the community college as a workplace came when it increased in size and scope. Size led to distance between staff members; rules begat rules; layers of bureaucracy insulated people between levels. Decision making shifted from the person to the collectivity, decisions made by committees diffusing responsibility for the results. The staff became isolates—faculty members in their academic-freedom protected classrooms, administrators behind their rulebook-adorned desks (1982, p. 68)." The increasing size and resulting bureaucratization of the community college expanded and deepened the sense of hierarchy in the colleges. Eugene Bowen, whose profile appears in Chapter Eight, described the effect on faculty this way:

> In the community college . . . there is less and less faculty involvement in the total daily operation of the college. When I first came here, there were about the same number of full-time faculty as we have now, maybe five more. We had two counselors for the whole school, two librarians, maybe four deans, one president, eight secretaries, and that was it. The faculty did everything. We counseled the students, we did this, we did that, and we were just involved in the whole mesh of things. . . .
>
> Now there is a structure. We have nine full-time counselors . . . every dean has an assistant dean. Some of the deans have two assistant deans and an associate dean. All the directors have an assistant director—director of financial aid, associate director of financial aid, director of student affairs. . . . So what started to be a college of one hundred and five

teachers, and eighteen staff, and a president and four deans is now a president and fifteen deans over one hundred staff members of the college. So the staff has actually reached the point where, exclusive of the secretaries, the staff for the college is as large as the teaching faculty, and it [the college] has compartmentalized and pigeonholed job descriptions a lot more and has made it harder to function as a team.

Some faculty and professional staff spoke of their colleges' organization in terms that had an almost military flavor. One Massachusetts community college librarian said, "The president tries to maintain an open-door policy. But yet you walk onto the job and first thing John [his supervisor] told me was we have a hierarchy. You report to me, I report to the dean of faculty, the dean of faculty reports to the president. And the faculty have their own chain too. They have to go through their department chair, then to the division chairman, and then to the dean of faculty."

One response to the increasing sense of hierarchy in the community college is a reluctance on the part of many faculty to be active outside their work with students. Again and again the faculty, especially those with some years of experience, talked of keeping a "low profile" in the college. Some linked the "low profile" to the awareness that it didn't pay to "make waves." Others felt that, while they had devoted themselves to college committees, colleagues who had avoided all involvement were often the ones to get promoted. But most of all, the sense of noninvolvement seemed to stem from a feeling of fruitlessness, of being tired of fighting for faculty power and losing the fight. As Richard Young, whose profile appears in Chapter Nine, said,

I like to control things. I like to control what I do, and certainly don't want anybody controlling me. There was that phrase that Lorraine Hansberry used in *Raisin in the Sun*—an "exhausted insurgent." That's me. I'm an exhausted insurgent and I've had it. How did I get that way? Age. . . . When the institution was younger and new, [there were] a lot of things we

figured we would get done, and some of them worked
out and some didn't. The institution is a lot bigger
now; it's much harder to get things done. How could
you sustain that level of intensity if, in fact, you find
that it is not being productive, or that it seems so difficult to do and doesn't seem likely to be successful?
. . .

I had a feeling that we needed faculty governance here, that the decisions were all made by the
administration. . . . [I thought we needed] control by
the people who are doing the work on the firing line.
Presumably they have a better idea of what is going
on. I guess it wasn't that important.

Another response to the powerlessness that can confront
community college faculty in the face of such hierarchical arrange-
ments is for them to seek power and opportunity by themselves
becoming administrators. A number of faculty in the study saw
moving up to administration as their only opportunity. But at the
same time they realized that they did not like the actual work of
administration when compared to the work of teaching. Eugene
Bowen (see Chapter Eight), who is chairman of his division, is torn
between returning to being a full-time teacher or moving up in the
administrative hierarchy. He expressed his ambivalence in this way:

I am not too happy with myself. Maybe that is
just because I can't live with the high amounts of
frustration that administration involves and the problems that can't be resolved. . . . There are very few
things that I now experience in teaching where I ever
feel a real failure or an internal problem that I can't
resolve. If a kid is absent for two months in the
hospital, I know how to set up makeup tests for him.
I know how to tutor him; I know how to get him back
to where he needs to be mathematically. So I live with
a lot of successes in teaching and that is encouraging.
A lot of times in administration there is a no-
win situation. You are forced to do something that is

> wrong or not fair or inequitable or not in the best
> interest of the student, but it has to be done because
> some administrator or some legislator has said that it
> had to be done that way. I find it hard to live with.

Despite his unhappiness with the world of administration, he went
on to say, "I intend to finish my doctorate [in math education] and
to keep my eyes and ears open for other opportunities. I perceive
that for me the next step of moving upward to administration
would be, if I ever did, assistant dean of faculty at some other
community college somewhere."

It is not an uncommon phenomenon in community colleges—and in public schools with which the colleges share some
structural similarity—to find talented teachers forced to consider
moving to administration because of a sense of very limited power
and opportunity within their teaching positions. The move from
teaching to administration often means a serious loss to the faculty
and students and an ambiguous gain for the individual faculty
member. Being an administrator in a hierarchically organized
system carries with it its own frustrations, which are difficult to
anticipate from the position of faculty. For those who stay in faculty
positions, there is a sense of diminishing power in a setting in
which bureaucracy is increasing and in which faculty authority was
never strong.

Faculty Women

As faculty power diminishes, there is an increasing sense of
faculty isolation and, in Cohen and Brawer's terms, "reclusiveness"
(Cohen and Brawer, 1977, p. 101). One of the costs of faculty
isolation and reclusiveness is that common experiences tend to get
submerged and individual experience tends to be seen as the product
of individual personality, uninfluenced by social and organizational structures in the college. The isolation takes a special toll on
the women and minority members of community college faculty.

The percentage of women has grown significantly among
fulltime faculties, and women now comprise approximately 40
percent of community college faculties (Wolk, 1980). Their growth

in numbers, however, has not seemed to have led to a corresponding growth in power within the colleges. While there are clearly exceptions to the rule, on the whole in most of the colleges at which the faculty in this study taught, men held the chief administrative positions. As Julia Alvarez, whose profile appears in Chapter Twelve, said, "I always felt that I could achieve anything that I wanted to based on my personal qualifications and not related to the fact that I was a woman. But as I look around, I have to face the realities of the system. For instance, as I look at the structure of the college, the president is male, and until recently all the four deans were male. If you look at other colleges, they have women in the position of dean of students, which has always been at the bottom of the totem pole. The next rung would be the directors, and all the directors are men. I will be excluded from positions at a high level because whoever is doing the hiring is picturing a man in that role, or may have a man already picked out."

When women aspire to administrative positions, they sometimes face considerable antipathy. Lucille Pritt, who was a division head in a small college in New York state, explained that she had been nominated for the position through an electoral process by her colleagues in her division. She was in school after the election, and one of her colleagues came up to her and told her that she had really won by a "landslide" over a male colleague, named Bill. A few days later she was called into the Dean's office, and he said,

> "Well, your division has voted you in. You have five first-place votes and three second-place votes." And he said, "But on paper Bill looks so much better than you do." And I said, "You know it's not my decision." He said, "Well, I'm going to recommend you to the president." That was exactly the tone of it: I'm going to recommend you, but I really think Bill had better paper credentials than you. What was I going to say? "Oh yes, Bill does. Forget about me."
>
> So he recommended me to the president. I wanted to know the president's decision because the next Monday was registration and it was already Wednesday, and the division chair has responsibilities

at registration to open sections, close sections, give special waivers. So I waited and waited. The president was supposed to call me and interview me, and the call never came. Finally on Friday, I called our division secretary; I couldn't stand the waiting anymore, and she said, "Oh, yes, the president would like to see you."

So I went down to his office, and he said, "So you want to be a division chair. Why? Why do you want this? . . ." I get the feeling like he is trying to be paternal, and he is, you know, saying, "Aren't you cute"; maybe not quite "Aren't you cute," but a pat on the shoulder will solve everything . . . Eventually he said, "Congratulations," and then I became division chair.

With such little enthusiasm on the part of the college administration, Pritt's experience when she became division head was not surprising. "The administration is male dominated and it is a very chauvinistic administration," she explained. "As division chair, I go to deans' meetings and am the only woman there. And they will make sexist jokes; they don't even realize that they are doing it, because it is so common to them. I don't laugh. I feel, you know, I'm not going to lecture them about how sexist they are, because that's not the way to handle it, but I don't play their games. Like if I were going to be one of the boys I would laugh."

Pritt's experience in New York state was echoed across the country in California. Cheryl Collins, whose profile appears in Chapter Twelve, is a black woman who heads a counseling department. She recounted what it was like for her to attend the regularly scheduled meetings of the division chairpersons with the college president: "There is a division-chair meeting with the president every other week. The president sits at one end of the table, and the dean of instruction sits at the other end of the table, and the rest of us sit and listen. It is a very structured meeting. . . . I'm the only female full-division chair. There is another woman who goes to the meetings because she is a dean. . . . I still find myself being on guard for things in the meetings. I think that the language changes when

I come in. I think that it is a combination of not only being female but I think there is an issue of being young, being black."

When a woman is one of few female administrators in the college there may be even more pressure on her to play by the rules. A female biology teacher in a New York state community college heavily oriented toward technology told of her experience as a science teacher in one of the two departments on campus chaired by a woman in an otherwise male-dominated school. She said, "The stresses are due to a very strict, regimental, unchanging, rigid format that is part of our department and one other department on campus also run by a woman. . . . I think they are always looking over their shoulder. They're always doing everything by the book. . . . I think it's kind of sad because I don't think either of those two women can exercise any freedom. . . . The departments that are run by the men on this campus aren't as rigid."

No matter how much she may know and adhere to the policies of the college, a woman ostensibly in a position of administrative power may not necessarily be treated as such by the men in the hierarchy above her. As one department chairperson in a small Massachusetts community college indicated, "I am really not regarded as a person with power. . . . Even though I was acting chairman last year . . . the dean of the faculty and the president of the college, neither one of those men came to me about any of the three people who were up for promotion. . . . I think that is so indicative of the attitude toward women, where they will put a woman in power or in a position of power, but then they won't regard her in that way. So here, they have the outer trappings. They fulfilled the affirmative action guidelines, and yet in reality they don't really regard women in that way; they don't treat them in that way."

Women faculty who are not involved in administration told double-edged stories about community college teaching for women. The community college offered flexibility to them in terms of scheduling their courses and no demand for research and publication. These conditions allowed them to carry out their often triple jobs of being teachers, wives, and mothers. A psychology teacher with a Ph.D. in clinical psychology discussed the ways in which not having the pressure to publish affected her life: "Working in a

community college made it possible for me to have children, and
having children made it possible for me not to think beyond what
I was doing. And I'm very grateful for the fact that this job in some
ways was nondemanding. . . . It's only now when I begin to have
some free time, when I can come out from under, that I begin to
question what I am going to do, that I could perhaps do with some
more challenge than I have."

Meredith Rand, who teaches political science in a California
community college, explained how she had integrated being a
single parent and a community college teacher. Yet despite the
flexibility in scheduling afforded by the community college, there
were still times when working conflicted with her parenting and led
her to feel guilty. Those times became especially intense when her
guilt was reinforced by insensitive male colleagues and administrators. She said, "I don't know any working mother that doesn't feel
guilty. . . . It's just an operating condition. . . . Sometimes I felt
guilty that I was neglecting my child. . . . Sometimes I felt that I was
neglecting my work. . . . If he were sick, I would go to school and
feel guilty about him, and I would race home and feel guilty that
I hadn't finished my work." She told of what happened a few years
earlier when her son was home sick with the chicken pox. She
stayed home with him the first day. The second day his fever was
practically gone and since she was on the hiring committee that was
interviewing faculty candidates that day, she decided she would go
to school so as not to "mess up" the work of the committee:

> So I left him home and I went to school. . . . I
> taught my first three courses and the hiring committee
> was going to meet at noon. . . . I was anxious that I
> had left him alone, you know, and I called him a
> couple of times, and I had it all set up so that he could
> eat; but still he was so little and was sick and I didn't
> feel good about that.
>
> I was just going to my third class when the
> hiring committee chairman stopped me to say that the
> interviews had all been rescheduled for three-thirty
> that afternoon, instead of right after my class at noon.
> And I said, "Oh, I can't do that. I left my child home.

I can't stay until three-thirty; that means I would be
here till six." And he said to me, "You left your child
home and he's sick. You left your child home all by
himself? What kind of mother are you?"
        I was just devastated. I have never forgiven that
man for that. At some level I am still angry with him
for saying that because of course that was exactly what
I was saying to myself.

She went to a friend's office in tears and he said he would take her
next class and that if she were feeling that way, she should go home.
She said, "I went to the chairman of the committee's office. I said,
'You're right. I should go home. I better go home.' He said, 'Fine,
just be sure that you are back by three-thirty.' " As it turned out, the
candidate did not show up and there was no committee meeting at
three-thirty. But the conflict between her teaching and parenting
responsibilities and her anger at her male colleague was indelibly
etched in her consciousness.
        Linda Donovan, whose profile appears in Chapter Ten,
teaches secretarial and business subjects in a New York state
community college. In order to work at all, she had to overcome
earlier feelings of guilt and family resistance. She was confident in
what she wanted to do and had to deal with male colleagues and
even sometimes female colleagues who seemed to fight her every
step of the way. She moved out of the secretarial department, which
was low on the totem pole, to the more prestigious and male-
dominated business department. But while the move improved her
sense of how she was perceived by her faculty colleagues, she faced
further complexities. She found, for example, that her salary was
way below that of her male colleagues, as a result of how her salary
had been determined when she originally moved from part-time to
full-time status. She said: "I trusted the person with whom I was
dealing on salary issues. There were no printed statistics. So he said
to me that I would be making $1,400 a year more if I accepted the
salary figure than if I were being paid on a part-time basis. And I
said, 'Well, it seems to me that you feel that they are offering me
a good settlement,' and he said, 'Yeah, I think it's pretty good.'
What he neglected to add was 'for someone in your position who

is really using this as a second income.' And I, of course, being as naive as I was, felt once I get there and they discover how wonderful I am, there will be some way of upgrading and equalizing. I am finding that, in fact, it gets worse every year."

In addition to matters of rank and pay, Donovan had to become sensitive to many other issues. She said, for example:

> When I first started working at the college I had lunch all the time in restaurants in the area with many of the male faculty members and it was fun. . . . I enjoyed them as individuals and as professional people. But I was constantly getting comments from some of the other female faculty and some of the other male faculty as well: "Well, how come you're having lunch with Mr. X? What's going on?" But if I were getting those comments, they [the male faculty I had lunch with] were getting them as well, and not only were they getting them from other faculty, they were getting them from their wives. . . . If I would meet their wives, they would say, "Oh, you're the one they mentioned." If I would mention to my husband that I went to lunch with so-and-so, he wasn't all that enthusiastic about it either. So I felt that I was continually having to justify sharing the time with people I enjoyed being with merely because they were of the opposite sex. I don't go to lunch with them very often anymore.

But perhaps the most costly and most difficult aspect of Donovan's work as a woman is the amount of energy she had to expend catering to male egos and submerging her own. She spoke of how she had to act on committees in the college:

> The committees are male-dominated. . . . I've been on a number of committees where problems have been thrown out and . . . I . . . offer a solution. . . . Somehow it gets buried. . . . They would brush it over and just kind of incorporate it, and the suggestion that

was ultimately used was mine. But nobody said, "Hey, that was really a good idea." Men in most instances don't like to admit that women may have ideas that are as good as, if not better than, their own. You know they sometimes feel that in order to maintain their own self-image, they have to keep women at a slightly reduced level. This is a very real thing. Initially it made me . . . angry. I don't like it at all. I don't like to have to subconsciously apologize for the fact that I'm a woman. I like being a woman.

I had a problem in my department that was crucial. . . . In order for me not to alienate the . . . men with whom I had to deal to get the decision that I wanted, I had to make them feel that the outcome was their idea. Once they decided it was their idea, they would love it and present it to me for adoption. They really did feel it was their idea, and they were just patting themselves on the back.

Women make up a considerable percentage of the faculty of community colleges, and it would be unfair to say that there have not been some significant gains in making their workplace more equitable. Yet despite those gains, especially in numbers, women faculty face serious issues of sexism in their everyday experience, and this has an impact on their work and the workings of their colleges. Besides the costs of the direct slights and injuries that they incur in their daily work, there is an opportunity cost that is borne by the college. All the mental energy and effort that is spent dealing with sexism in the workplace is effort and energy lost from the major goals of the college. High-caliber talent enervated and shunted aside is a steep price for any institution to absorb and one that community college leaders should be particularly reluctant to pay.

Minority Faculty

Minority faculty in community colleges do not have the advantage of numbers that women faculty have. Except in some major urban colleges where the student body is predominantly nonwhite, the numbers of black, Hispanic, Asian, and other minority groups are small among community college faculty. (See Olivas, 1979, for a statistical analysis and in-depth discussion of the status of minority students and faculty in community colleges.) While a high percentage of minority students in higher education is enrolled in community colleges (some estimate almost 50 percent of blacks and Hispanics enrolled as undergraduates in the United States are enrolled in community colleges [Olivas, 1979]), the percentage of minority faculty remains quite small. As Cohen and Brawer point out, the affirmative action imperative in community colleges came at a time when the employment of full-time faculty was dropping (1977, p. 5). In addition, in the late seventies, the hiring of minorities became pitted against the hiring of women. The bald truth of the matter is that "despite all the rhetoric about affirmative action, attitudes among community college staff members show a strong bias against giving preferential treatment to members of minority groups" (Cohen and Brawer, 1977, p. 5). The result is that "in proportion to minority enrollment in two-year colleges, minority faculty are even more poorly represented in two-year colleges than in upper-level institutions" (Olivas, 1979, p. 50).

One of the participants in the study, William White, a director of affirmative action and counselor in a Massachusetts community college, said that his college had elaborate procedures in place for following affirmative action guidelines. As director he had to review and sign his name to every appointment, professional and nonprofessional, that was made in the college. However, he commented that despite his position, "One of the interesting things about affirmative action is you can follow all the rules and you can still find ways of discriminating. . . . I don't think a lot of people realize that." Though a greater percentage of minority students attends community colleges than attends any other institution of higher education, the resistance to affirmative action programs at the community college level is as strong and complicated as it is at four-year colleges and universities.

But what is it like for those minority faculty who are hired in community colleges? To some extent, their situation is a function of their relative numbers in the institution (see Chapter Eleven). When, as in most of the community colleges in the country, minority faculty are a few among the many, their experience is different along important dimensions than when, as in some urban community colleges, they are in a more balanced numerical position. (See Kanter, 1977, for a full discussion of the effect of relative numbers on the experience of women, and by implication on minorities, in corporations.)

Josephine Saunders, whose profile appears in Chapter Eleven, was hired in the secretarial department as the first and, for a period of time the only, full-time, black faculty member in a New York college faculty of approximately 120. She spoke of her experience in this way:

I came here in '76 and was the first full-time black instructor that they had had here. There was a lot of adjusting to me when I first came here, and to a certain extent, that is still going on. My first couple of years here were difficult. I guess that's the only word that I can describe it with. The first year that I was here I had to let students and faculty know that I had proper credentials, and that there was nowhere on my diploma that said I was only to teach black folk.

I was the first black person that they had had any real contact with, so they didn't really know how to deal with that. There were instances of my having to justify everything that I did. One instructor could walk into his classroom and say, "This is it," and it would be accepted. I had to walk into the classroom and say, "This is it," and I would have to justify why I said it. . . .

The first year I ignored a lot of stuff because that was, I thought, just part of getting used to the job and the people. You are tested and students test you, and colleagues test; but six and a half years later, it's no longer a test, or it is a test of a different sort.

Saunders found herself getting caught in a destructive circle out of which she and her colleagues seemed unable to break. She said: "There are just certain things that people are not willing to accept about me, being black and the way that I am. One of the comments that was made to me was, 'You never come to see any of us in our offices,' and I say, 'Why must I come to you? . . . that's a concept some whites have. This whole busing thing, you know—black students must be bused over there, but whites can't be bused. It's a one-way kind of thing. So I come in, and I do my work, and I leave, with a minimum amount of interaction." She spoke about how her contributions to the work of her department were received: "I don't perceive myself as being powerful in this division. No, I don't. When I came here, I was told they would be glad to have my input as far as the skills center was concerned because they knew that I had had experience with one from the ground up. So I offered my input at meetings and the suggestions were politely put aside, and then two months later someone came up with the same suggestion and it would pass. That happened a couple of times, and that was again, I thought, because I was new. But it continued to happen. I got to the point where I started to document stuff just for my own sanity."

When Saunders first arrived at the school she saw herself as the "new girl on the block" and didn't think twice about the fact that all the courses she taught required heavy correcting and that her schedule of classes was spread throughout the entire day. But now, she says:

> Given the number of years I've been here, I probably should have, I don't know how to put it, I should have more say, for example, in scheduling. I'm not talking about times. I'm talking about my not being given all the correcting courses, for example. . . . It's difficult for me right now because I don't feel that I'm using the education that I do have and I know I'm not using all the skills I know I've got. And in a sense I guess I'm feeling stuck right now. . . .
>
> I'm angry because I have to fight and I thought that that kind of fighting was behind me, and it's not.

This is 1982 and I did a lot of that kind of fighting in
'64, so how many years is that? You know, when I look
at it, not much has changed. There has been the
illusion that there's been change. I'm angry that I have
to still fight the same kind of fight. Fighting for job,
fighting against what is obviously ignorance and
prejudice—that was the same kind of fight I was
fighting in 1964.

It might be reassuring to understand Josephine Saunders's
experience as a projection of her personality or even as the idiosyncratic reflection of a small-town New York community college. But
in fact the themes she articulated were repeated by male and female
black faculty in other community colleges in settings quite different
from that of Saunders's college. For example, Robert Thatcher,
whose profile appears in Chapter Eleven, is a tenured black teacher
of physics in a well-to-do community college located in a cosmo-
politan, suburban California community college district. Despite
teaching in a college some 3,000 miles away, despite being male,
despite being tenured, and despite his teaching in an area higher on
the totem pole than secretarial studies, Thatcher talked about his
experience in his college in terms that are remarkably similar to
Saunders:

It seems like employers ask a little more of
blacks. Maybe not "ask" but demand a little more. A
little more pressure is put on blacks. I think a little
more pressure is even put on me here at this college.
Invariably, the first week of school, students tend to
ask a hell of a lot of questions, questions that are not
even relevant to the topic, and I think that it is a
situation of feeling you out, seeing whether or not you
know the material. I don't sense that same type of
attitude when they go into a white instructor's class.
I think that it is assumed that he or she knows. But
I think sometimes with a black instructor, it's "Prove
to me that you do know and then I will listen." If I

> differ with the book, it's difficult for them to accept
> the fact that I'm saying the author is wrong, period.

On black faculty being differentially subjected to criticism, he said, "I've seen some white instructors that I know weren't prepared, and there's no overt pressure by the students to do anything about it. I've also seen a black instructor that was ill-prepared, and he got a lot of direct pressure. I'm not apologizing for either instructor. I think you should be prepared, but let's treat both people the same way." He was willing to give the benefit of doubt whenever possible. He said, "One of the problems that you have to watch when those 'subtle' things occur [is] you've got to ask yourself, 'Are those things because of me as a person, or because of me as a black person?' "

Despite his willingness not to see all slights in terms of racism, Thatcher was not willing to ignore racial slights when they occurred. For example, he described his response to the different names his students and colleagues would call him:

> There was one instructor who had a hell of a time calling me by my name. He called me every kind of name. When I'd see him, I'd just call him another name and he got the message.
>
> I had a student that called me "coach." Hell, I'm not a coach, I told him. "I'm an instructor. You can call me by my first name, you can call me Robert, you can call me Dr. Thatcher, but I'm not a coach." Whites will sometimes call blacks "coaches." They have a bunch of strange names they sometimes address blacks with. When you sense that type of thing happening, you just say, "Look, I want you to get off and get on here," and I think when you make that clear, people tend to respect you. The basic thing that I try to do, whether it is on a social level or a working level, is to tell people to deal with me as a person, not any of these stereotype trips. Deal with me as a person.

Like Saunders in New York, however, as much as he demands respect as a person, Thatcher is still subject to the not-so-hidden

slights and injuries of racism. In much the same terms as Saunders
he describes the expectations that whites seem to have that he reach
out to them:

> Coming here I knew that experienced instruc-
> tors like new instructors to sit down and talk with
> them, come in and visit their classes. Again, you
> know, you hate to draw any conclusions, but I find
> myself initiating more, exchanging tests, talking to
> people about classroom situations. I had several in-
> structors that came in, but it was about how to handle
> a black student, rather than handling a student in
> general. It had to be something related to a black
> problem, you know, if they were to come in.
>
> So I think I've really bent over backwards. I do
> the initiating most of the time. So here again might
> be one of those subtle things. As an example, two
> other instructors, or three of us, have eight o'clock
> classes together. I would always come and wait or
> make sure that they were ready to go and we'd all walk
> together. But they didn't do the same thing for me.
> You see, you're always reaching out, but there's no
> one reaching back for you.

Much is asked of minority faculty when they are a few among
many. For example, minority faculty are often perceived as the
"representative" of their ethnic group. One senior black faculty
member in a Massachusetts community college said, "If I am the
only black, and in many situations I have been, then I become what
many people conceive of as the representative of the black people,
which is of course not necessarily true. All black people are not like
me and I am not like all black people. . . . It is an enormous
pressure; there is no need of anybody pretending to you that it isn't
an extra pressure, an extra professional burden, or an extra personal
responsibility."

At the heart of the matter is a question of acceptance as
individuals. He continued: "I don't think there is any question
about it. One of the things that bothers a lot of black professionals

is . . . being cast into this position, because they just want to be a person who holds a job, does his job, and gets paid for what he does just like everybody else. . . . When you say 'accepted,' those of us who are minorities use the term when we are not expected to be any different than anybody else, and we are not expected to accept any less than anybody else, and we are not expected to do any more than anybody else to justify being there."

At the same time that professionals who are members of minorities want to be accepted as individuals by their students and their colleagues, those whom we interviewed were deeply committed to contributing to racial understanding. Some would accomplish this in ways other than overt dramatic action. Daniel Ramirez, whose profile appears in Chapter Eleven, is an American of Mexican descent who teaches history at a California community college. He said, "I perform a positive service just by being here. People come up to me and say, 'You're Italian, aren't you?' or 'You're Portugese.' They assume I'm not Mexican 'because you are not at all like a low-rider,' and after a while I think it occurs to many people that the majority of Mexican people are not 'low-riders'; that indeed if I'm not typically Mexican, I'm not that atypical either. I think people like me play a positive role at this level simply by being here."

Counselors

Just being there, however, is not enough for a group of professionals who may be at or near the bottom of the totem pole in community colleges. Counselors, striving for faculty status, experience many of the tensions expressed by women faculty and members of minority groups and also some that uniquely characterize their position in the hierarchy in community colleges. Garrison reported in 1967 that junior college faculty "express more than a little dissatisfaction with the guidance given to students, both in the high schools and in their own institutions" (1967, p. 65). (See Cohen and Brawer [1982, pp. 169–190] for a comprehensive analysis of the issues that have long plagued counseling programs in community colleges.)

This study approached the issues from the perspective of the counselor at work in the college. Built into the structure of their jobs are factors that could hardly be more enervating. Neither faculty nor administrators, counselors often do the work of both. They teach, do program development, sit on committees, and respond to both internal and external college problems. Because they do not have the autonomy of faculty, they are expected to be around all the time; and because they are around, they can be called upon by the administration to get done what needs to be done. At the same time, they are perceived by faculty as not working very hard. As Julia Alvarez (see Chapter Twelve), a counselor in a Massachusetts community college, said, "Counselors are considered the workhorses. They are really the lowest-level professionals that the college has, the ones that can be given all the extra work and the blame for things that go wrong. Counselors in the past have always been associated with administration. We are held in high esteem by the administration because we solve problems. We answer questions. We make administration's job a lot easier. The problems come with faculty. . . . They have no idea of . . . the diversity of our jobs. A lot of them feel that we just sit in our offices all day and wait for students to walk in and that is all we do. When they see us on all these committees, they feel we are on these committees because we don't have anything better to do."

Alvarez went on to express feelings similar to those which minority faculty members described: "I don't like being at the bottom of any totem pole. I don't necessarily have to be on the top anymore, but I don't feel comfortable being at the bottom. . . . Feels like you are always struggling to prove yourself." That sense of "struggling to prove" results in a heightened sensitivity and awareness to how colleagues are perceiving you. Alvarez said, "For instance, I don't feel comfortable standing in the outer part of my office because people walk by and get the impression that I am not doing anything. If they walk in Friday afternoon and there are three or four of us sitting around a table, they will drop a comment about the counselors sitting around a table talking to each other. So we are constantly having to be careful of our image. If I am going to talk to some other counselor, I usually go into one of their offices. We are very easy targets because we are involved in so many areas of the college. We are here for such a large number of hours, we are so visible, so accountable."

Alvarez's interview could be seen as idiosyncratic, a result more of her personality than of the structure of her work. But Cheryl Collins (see Chapter Twelve), a director of a counseling program in California who has a master's degree in clinical psychology and who earns, unlike Alvarez in Massachusetts, a salary equal to if not better than those of her faculty colleagues, had this to say: "I have to admit that counselors don't have—I don't know about on other campuses—but counselors don't have a really strong reputation. . . . I think that many teachers think we don't do anything. . . . I don't think we are seen in the same way, having the same status as a teacher. . . . Things change so rapidly in counseling that it is very difficult to keep up on those changes and sometimes we make mistakes. . . . We pay a very heavy price for those mistakes in terms of status. And teasing. . . . [It] come[s] through in a joking manner. But when there is that much joking around, you can't help but feel that there is stuff behind it. It's like, 'You guys don't do anything over here all day. Every time I come through here you are just sitting. . . .' Well, it's just very wearing. Counselors feel that they are not valued in the system for what they do." Collins spoke of the negotiation of a new faculty contract: "Recently the campus voted for us to have extra hours. Nobody else's load got increased and our load got increased. The whole faculty approved that. We couldn't get them to see that if they get our load, that they're next; at least the potential is there. But we were vulnerable. And that to me was an indication that they didn't see us as faculty members. It was saying, 'You're not the same as us.' The counselors were really upset about that. People retreated and went into their offices and said, 'Here is my schedule, I am not doing anything else but this.' "

Richard Soletti, a counselor in Massachusetts, thought that as far as he was concerned he had "the best job in the college." He said, "It combines all the parts of what is good about working in a college." A little later in the interview, however, he said, "I am the secretary to the union. That has taken a lot of my time. I really enjoy that part because there is a real battle to be fought, and the battle is the recognition of professional staff, counselors, librarians. These people are not recognized as part of the faculty, not part of the bargaining unit, and we are not administrators. We are kind of in this limbo. And my battle is not only against the other members of the union, but among ourselves—sometimes we don't even consider ourselves faculty."

Soletti liked his job of counselor because he had the opportunity to grow in his experience working with different levels and segments of the community college. But he recognized the tensions in working with members of the college outside the counseling staff and especially with the faculty. He talked about meetings of counselors with faculty departments in the following terms: "I have known counselors who have had horror shows in division meetings. People have turned on them and attacked them. The counselors come back bruised. Like academic advising: I have got to stand up there and talk to thirty-five math teachers. They are brutal. I think those division meetings are a good example of the kind of thing that could happen if you're embarrassed and they put you on the spot and they give you a hard time."

Counselors are cast in an ambiguous position among the professionals in community colleges, and they are subject to being scapegoated for all that can go wrong in the day-to-day operations of a college. Counselors have also been perceived by some commentators as participating in the process of "cooling out" students who came to community colleges with high aspirations only to have to face the fact of not meeting them. (See Clark, 1960 and 1980, for both the original discussion of "cooling out" and a reassessment by the author some twenty years later.) The counselors in this study were aware of the complexities involved in the "cooling out" phenomenon though they may not use that term. Julia Alvarez said, for example:

> There is a certain area that I didn't mention
> that exists, and it bothers me and haunts me contin-
> ually because of my background and because of what
> I know about justice and injustice. I feel that the
> society is very influential on its members; the Amer-
> ican society is very influential toward conformity.
> And I find that in spite of myself, I have been
> influenced to conform. . . . On the other hand, there
> are these feelings that bother me a lot, such as [that]
> the community college tends to perpetuate the system

in which there is injustice. The community college doesn't really question the basic premises of the way the society is set up. It is not a revolutionary force in the community at all, and it doesn't do that much to change the way things basically are. . . . It is an issue that bothers me, but it bothered me more at the beginning than it does now. . . .

Here I find myself saying things that in the past would never come out of my mouth, feeling certain ways, feeling very comfortable with my position, feeling very much an individual, a lot of individual-istic feelings. . . . It bothers me that I have lost . . . the critical attitude toward my surroundings; and I feel it comes from almost feeling that you can't do much to change the system.

What conclusions can administrators and faculty in com-munity colleges draw from these stories of women, minority faculty, and counselors? It is clear that the totem pole effect is very strong in community colleges. The place faculty can take in the hierarchy affects their relations with each other and how they see themselves and finally how they carry out their work. The intensifying of hierarchy in community colleges and the concurrent diminishing of faculty power lead to a sense of isolation that allows common experiences among faculty to be submerged. This situation contrib-utes to a sense of divisiveness rather than shared goals.

It is also clear that the stories of sexism and racism that were told by women and minority faculty members are not unique to community colleges nor is the ambiguous status and scapegoating of counselors. Those same stories are easily reproduceable among faculty in four-year colleges and universities. But what has to concern community college educators is that concurrent with problems of sexism and racism, their institutions have placed on them (and they have eagerly seized) the mantle of equitable oppor-tunity in higher education for all, regardless of gender or race. The egalitarian ideal has been at the heart of the community college movement in the last twenty-five years. Radical critics might call that sense of mission a sham; more conservative commentators might well point out its complexities and argue that, at the least, community colleges should tone down their rhetoric on the subject. But no matter what the perspective, the notion of equitable opportunity is part of how the public views community colleges and how many within them view themselves. That mission is undermined by the increasing sense of powerlessness among the faculty and particularly among women, minority faculty, and counselors.

The hope that many outside and within the community college system have had is that community colleges would be able to educate students so that they might move out of the places to which their race, social class, and gender have tended to consign them. That is a complex task, beset by many antithetical forces outside the community college. If within the community colleges, administrators and faculty are unable to cope with the complexities of sexist and racist assumptions and hierarchical structures as they affect faculty in general—and women, minority faculty, and counselors in particular—then those same assumptions and structures will most likely be imposed on their students. The inequities in the experiences of women, minority faculty, and counselors must give pause to anyone who reflects on the ability of community colleges to provide equitable educational opportunity for a wide range of students.

Facing the Obstacles
to Improved Teaching

~~~~~~~~~~~~~~~~~~~~~~~~~~~~~~~~~~~

What are the central issues that affect the way community college faculty carry out their teaching, the core of their work? What are some of the costs of the pressures they face? What might administrative and faculty leaders learn from listening to faculty talk in depth about their work with their students?

Faculty in community colleges face students who, on the whole, are more likely to be poor, members of minority groups, and less well-prepared than students in other segments of higher education (Breneman and Nelson, 1981, p. 22). Many commentators have noted that the community colleges have taken on and have had imposed upon them a "salvaging" role in higher education. The conceptual complexity of that role is considerable. (See Cohen and Brawer, 1982, pp. 223–250.) The demands it places on faculty seem almost impossible. Moore, decrying a social welfare approach to teaching, recognized that working with a student who has suffered previous educational and social deprivation "demands teaching skill of a high order" (Moore, 1970, p. 64).

Basic Language Skills

The skills and sensitivities required of community college faculty increasingly have to do with knowing how to teach students for whom middle-class standard English may not be the primary oral language, who are uncomfortable with written language, and who are perceived as lacking basic skills in reading and writing. Perhaps most seriously, they have long ago either lost or never had a sense of the pleasure and power that can come from reading and writing. Faculty must keep clear in their minds the difference between the performance of their students and their underlying competence (Chomsky, 1972). Faculty must understand the nature of language performance: namely, that speaking, reading, and writing reflect a complex interaction among linguistic, psychological, and social forces. And that is an exceedingly tall order.

Many faculty in different curricular areas recognize the issue. In problem areas such as math, for example, some faculty believe that the basic issue is reading. One computer teacher in New York state said, "I think it's more a reading and comprehension type of thing. I get students that are reading at eighth and seventh and fifth grade levels. . . . Obviously math will be hard for them because they can't read about it." Jesus Lopez, whose profile appears in Chapter Eight, said that he has students in his chemistry class who are high school graduates, but "You simply have to tell them, you know, that their problem is not that they can't understand chemistry; their problem is not that they can't do math. Their problem is that they can't read. . . . If you can't read a chemistry text, you're not going to learn the subject matter." A vocational teacher in New York explained his students' reading ability as centrally related to their motivation to persist in reading. He said, "I think a simpler book might have been more to their advantage than to try to work with this one. Maybe this is the wrong impression; I just get the notion that among the sorts of individuals we get at the community college, there are the kind of individuals who, if they can read it, and maybe struggle with it a little bit, will say, 'OK, we will give it a shot,' but if they try to read it and it seems on the surface to be overwhelming to them, I think they just give up." Some faculty, deeply concerned by the weaknesses they found in their students' skills with written language, recognized that this discomfort with language had serious implications for their students' conceptions of themselves. As Scott Muller said, "Lousy English skills . . . become a reflection. It is like having a mirror constantly build your mind up. . . . Most of their families have told them . . . that they're not going to be lawyers and doctors . . . they're going to be part of the working class."

The degree of comfort with their reading and writing skills that students bring to the community college has serious implications for them and their teachers. Students' success in any of the curricula in the college and their sense of opportunity for themselves is closely related to reading and writing performance. Faculty's feelings of success in their work, their sense of responsibility to their fields and to the notions they carry within themselves about college-level education interact with their students' relationship to written language. (For additional insight on the impact of this issue on faculty, see Cohen and Brawer, 1982, pp. 235–236.)

What is involved for both faculty and students who must face this issue is an approach to teaching and learning that is a reconstruction of the student's entire educational experience. That type of reconstructive effort was described by Elizabeth McKay, who teaches reading and writing in an urban community college in California. She spoke of a turning point that occurred in her career when she began to work with a student named James Wharton:

> James was a basketball player, and his coach had recommended that he really ought to learn to read. But James couldn't read. And so I sat down with him and figured out how to reconstruct his whole first three years of education. How do you teach an adult the names of the letters of the alphabet, the shapes so that he could write? How do you teach him to put the letters together?
>
> All I remember was what seems now like hours of sitting at the desk with him. But in fact he did learn to read and he went on to graduate from college. He was a real street person. I mean he had the gift of gab. It is really very hard to explain it exactly, but he was much too smart not to learn to read. And in a way that was a turning point for me because I realized that . . . there was something crazy in the fact that he hadn't learned to read. Then I began to see the Jameses

multiply. And we got a little grant. . . . People like
James began to appear out of the woodwork. I mean,
we would have seventy-five and one hundred people
sign up for a class and at that point I began to realize
that there was a question under the questions: Why
are all of these students, and why these students and
not other students, failing to get the rudimentary
skills that twelve years of education should be giving
them?

For students like these, many community colleges have hired
special teachers and set up extraordinary programs. But for many
students who have greater language proficiency than the James
Whartons of our system—those who in fact can read but not
without a struggle and those who can write but are not comfortable
enough with writing to begin to sense the power implicit in being
able to say clearly what is in their minds—there are few out-of-the-
ordinary programs. These students tend to be treated in community
colleges as requiring no additional resources in order to gain a
power with language that they have not been able to gain in their
previous twelve years of education. That assumption places an
enormous burden on teachers of English in community colleges.

A major part of Nancy Warren's (see Chapter Seven) job is
to teach writing to students who are functionally literate but who
have had little success with their writing in the past and have
seldom found pleasure in reading. Understanding that sufficient
practice is a key to learning to write effectively, her department has
adopted a policy that students in writing classes will write at least
three thousand words a semester.

Three thousand words a semester means six five-hundred
word papers a semester for approximately one hundred students.
That means six hundred essays a semester to read and respond to.
In a fifteen-week semester, she must read and comment on approximately forty themes a week. Even if she spent only thirty minutes
on each theme she would have twenty solid hours a week of
marking papers. That kind of concentrated, solitary work cannot be
done in her office at school because of the ethos of accessibility,

which would make it difficult to shut her office door for four hours
a day and say that she is busy reading papers. She does that twenty
hours a week of marking papers at home after school. Allowing one
night off for rest, Warren must spend more than three hours a night
six nights a week marking papers, to say nothing of the time she
must have to prepare for class. And she must look forward to doing
that the rest of her teaching career in a community college.

Her own words capture best the intensity of the problem
facing community college teachers of writing: "The paper grading
problem is my biggest problem with the job. I mean a soul-
deadening, truly soul-deadening load of grading papers. . . . I never
have been able to get over a certain amount of anxiety while doing
it. I could easily sit for two hours and grade a multiple-choice test
that required no thinking or no attention. I don't know whether it
is the feeling of having to mark it in a way to justify your grade,
or whether it is having to be careful to say things that encourage
rather than discourage students, or uncertainty as to whether with
a particular student you should not pay attention to something like
spelling. It requires all your attention."

Nancy Warren and her colleagues have not been passive in
the face of the problem as they perceive it: "We've had endless
meetings and discussions about it. . . . We've sent memos to the
president . . . and talked to the dean, and we've talked and pushed
and complained and had the union representative give them position papers for contract negotiations. So far we've simply never
succeeded in anything. We are always told that there is not enough
money to hire more teachers and that is that." Nancy Warren is not
a political activist; she is a serious, well-educated, committed
teacher. The conclusion to which her thinking leads her is one she
is not comfortable arguing:

> So we don't know what to do. We have cer-
> tainly taken initiatives, but we have been unsuccess-
> ful. In any oppressive institutional system, if you can
> keep the workers from having the time and energy to
> protest and also make them uneasy about their jobs,
> you've got them. And [if you] add to that [the fact] that

they are replaceable easily, you have completely impotent employees. I don't mean to imply that there is
some kind of plot or conspiracy. I don't think there is
anybody sitting around somewhere deciding that a
teacher shall be oppressed. I think it is simply the way
things have fallen out in the course of budget cuts and
lack of concern and interest generally.

While commentators have long seen the community colleges
as acting as "shock absorbers" in the United States system of higher
education (Eells, 1931, p. 48) and as a "safety valve" for releasing
pressures on four-year colleges and universities (Jencks and Riesman, 1968, p. 492), they have seldom commented on what it is like
for the faculty who absorb the shock and take the pressure. Nancy
Warren describes the toll: "In our department there are fifteen or
sixteen for the most part fanatically dedicated, very experienced,
competent people who are slowly being ground down by a system
and arrangement that they feel is impossible. Indeed, if I were really
being dramatic about it, I would point out that our former
chairman who also taught English committed suicide, and we lost
one member to alcoholism; and other people have other problems."
For Warren the consequence of being a shock absorber is that she
feels a constant and pervasive sense of never doing her work as well
as she thinks she should. She understands the oppressiveness of the
system in which she works and yet she still manages to take
individual responsibility. Finally, she is left not quite knowing
what she will be doing in the future and thankful for the vacations
that give her some respite.

Administrators and faculty who read these passages may feel
that perhaps Warren is being too dramatic. Such personal woes
cannot be attributed solely to working conditions in the community
college. Indeed, it is tempting to leave out these "dramatic"
examples from the body of what Warren said in her interview, lest
the skepticism that they can generate be allowed to weaken the case.
Yet somehow community college leaders must face the issue that
there is something wrong in the way the enormous task of teaching
writing is understood in community colleges. The problem rever-
berates throughout the entire college.

Objective Testing

Writing and learning to write have import beyond the skill itself. Thinking is inextricably interwoven with writing (Vygotsky, 1962). When writing is taught and practiced and learned, so is thinking. If the task of teaching writing and offering opportunities to practice writing is limited to English classes in community colleges, the task of writing and thinking becomes isolated and undermined.

For a combination of reasons, however, other departments in community colleges are almost completely eliminating writing from their courses. Whereas in earlier years essay exams and research papers might have been found in courses across the curriculum, many faculty outside of departments of English are dropping all requirements that their students write papers. An epidemic of so-called objective testing, often machine-scored, has swept through community college education across all curricula, resisted by individual faculty as best they can. Warren described the problem: "There certainly is a sense of regret and sorrow that other departments in which the members used to always assign papers have stopped doing so. Their course load has gone up to five courses in sociology, history, government, and psychology. They have said, 'All right, tests can now be graded on a machine.' And they regret it. They feel it is wrong. Yet they feel there is no alternative, and we would agree, knowing what is involved. It doesn't really help the students."

Warren's words are understated. The increasing reliance on objective testing, and the elimination of papers and essay tests, undermines the work of students in community colleges. Evaluation in schools has always served the dual purposes of instruction and sorting. The elimination of writing from the curriculum eliminates one of the major tools of evaluation, a tool that simultaneously teaches students to think about their subjects. The reliance on objective testing separates the instructional function of assessment from the judgmental function, and turns testing into the most mechanistic process possible. At best, objective tests force students to try to figure out what was in the mind of the tester, whereas writing demands that they figure out what is in their own minds. Cohen and Brawer (1977, p. 41) cite a 1968 study which indicates that most history teachers give quick-score tests not because they are best for students, but because they are easier to grade.

Some faculty resist the temptation to move to machine-scored, objective tests and what they represent. Samuel Berger (see Chapter Nine) reflected about his long career as a community college teacher in this way: "I always had essay exams. I came to the conclusion in my own teaching and in my own work that the multiple-choice exam was a terrible obstacle to the improvement of a course. In fact you couldn't change a course because you had to think of the common core. I got to react quite a bit against the multiple-choice exam. I have never used it in my own courses. The stuff that I want to get at, I don't think I can get at it that way." Berger then went on to describe how he used his essay exams for instructional as well as evaluative purposes: "I give them five questions to write on. They have to write on two of the five. I classify them by the best answers. Then I have each student, maybe two or three who wrote the best answer, read them to the others. I am proud that they did a good job and it is so clear to the other students who wrote less satisfactory answers. Very often a black and white student would write the best answer or a black student would write the best answer. I thought that it was very important that the white kids in class should hear that and be able to judge it for themselves. Here is a really top question written with balance and detail [and] with some idea of a thesis. You can't do anything like that with a multiple-choice exam." Lawrence Bauer (see Chapter Nine), who teaches in New York state, said this about the issue: "I see my colleagues resorting to testing systems that really disturb me. They are giving all multiple-choice tests, and they are taking them out of test manuals that are provided by the publisher of the textbook. They run it through a computer and grade it; the students never see where they missed a question, or whether they got a right answer. They don't know anything except a score. I will not give an objective test. I give essay questions, and I write answers to them, and I tell students where they didn't give a complete answer or where they didn't develop it."

Minority faculty teaching in community colleges where the student body is predominantly minority were among the most vociferous in rejecting the idea of objective tests as an adequate approach to teaching and evaluation. Michael Nieto teaches social science in such a college. He spoke of his position and the initial reaction of his students:

> I give them only one type of test—that is, an essay test. I don't believe in the so-called objective test—first of all, because they are not objective, and second, because they cause a lot of confusion. So I explain to my students on the first day why I will not give them true/false and fill-in-the-blank tests. And I get a lot of complaint, because they are trained or schooled into playing around with letters and numbers. I tell them that they have to develop their own ideas in order to be successful and the only way that they're going to do that is by somebody forcing them to read and then write. So I usually give them about five or six questions, essay questions, and they choose three. They have to write on the basis of the reading and the discussion in class. I have seen a lot of progress in the students' doing those tests, even among those who complained at the beginning.

One psychology teacher in a community college in California explained why she thought objective testing was spreading: "There have been increasing numbers of students with minimal skills, incredibly limited communication skills. . . . Many of us try to hold the line, gave essay exams at the beginning. Now, because of the painful factor in reading essay exams of students that can't write, can't express themselves, we've capitulated and started giving objective exams."

The pain involved in reading essay exams of students who do not write well may be the painfulness of realizing the difficulty of the situation both for the students and for the teachers themselves. It is exasperating for teachers to be faced with students for whom a great deal of reconstructive work must be done. It is painful for students to be asked to think through issues and to connect their thoughts with what they have read and heard in class, when they

have had very little success with that process in the past and have
found few opportunities to achieve success in that type of learning.

Nevertheless, community college leaders must confront the
fact that if students who can't write well write less and less, the
problem is exacerbated. By switching to objective tests and giving
students less and less opportunity to practice writing, faculty are
lowering the expectations they have for students. In saying that
their students cannot be expected to learn to express their thinking
in writing, they are consigning students, no matter what curricula
they are pursuing, to future work with little autonomy and less
sense of opportunity. The basic skill needed as a prerequisite for
developing autonomy and a sense of opportunity in work is in fact
the ability to read and write well. Almost without exception,
vocational faculty members in the study stated explicitly that if their
students could not read or write well, no matter what skills faculty
could teach them in welding, graphics, or accounting, their students would be consigned to dead-end positions in their eventual
work areas.

The issue of objective tests is deeply connected to issues of
dignity in relation to community college students. Objective testing
contributes to the feeling of passivity and impotence on the part of
students by asserting first, that there is a body of knowledge held
by the experts and represented by the teacher and the text, and
second, that this body of knowledge is separate from the student and
must be learned correctly as defined by the teacher and text.

Scott Muller, whose profile appears in Chapter Ten, talks
about the attitude his students bring to preparing for tests: "They
moan a little bit. It's almost an involuntary response when they get
the assignment. The mature student looks forward to crunching out
the grade, that sense of progress; he doesn't moan so much. The one
that moans . . . is the one that feels that this is uncontrollable. He
has got to study again. I can verbalize to them that there are other
reasons for giving this test, other than to victimize them. They
should look at it as a learning experience . . . [as] a way to validate
their abilities. In the back of my head, I know how they feel. . . .
They feel victimized. They are constantly struggling with the
question: 'Is this worth it?' "

The process of writing papers and answering essay questions
assumes that there is an active relationship between the student and

the body of knowledge. The student's ability to work with the body of knowledge, to make connections, to see comparisons, and to interpret and interact with the subject matter in an active manner is an important concern. Objective tests reinforce the weaknesses of students. Their increasing use in community colleges is a serious issue for faculty and administrators to consider.

Standards

Faculty also have to face the issues of standards and grades, whether they test with machine-scored tests or essay examinations. In 1960 Medsker reported that 76 percent of faculty in community colleges disagreed with the notion that the junior college is diluting the standards of American higher education (1960, p. 189). Garrison, in his study published in 1967, was able to report: "When asked about standards-for-college work, most instructors asserted that these were not compromised unduly in the long run. 'We've got an open-door college, to be sure,' they would say in effect, 'but after a reasonable time, if these students don't come up to standard, this place becomes a revolving door for them. The main thing is, they've had the chance'" (1967, p. 18).

In the 1980s many faculty did not characterize the situation in the same way. Faculty member after faculty member talked about "lowered standards," "adjusted standards," "different standards," and the "unique mission" of the community college. While some tried to hold the line on standards, doing so caused all sorts of pressures for them and their students.

For example, many faculty who teach in academic courses that are transferable pride themselves on a standard of expectation that would make their course equivalent to the same one taught in a four-year college. But they often face challenges from their students, and in fact from their administrators, in maintaining those levels of expectations. Jesus Lopez (see Chapter Eight), who teaches chemistry in a California community college, expressed his frustrations with students who for a range of reasons would complain about the amount of work in his chemistry course. He said, "I explain to them . . . that this is a course that . . . transfers to a four-year institution. . . . My course is no more rigorous than I feel it would be at a four-year school. I think that's my responsibility to you." Lopez went on to say, "They don't always agree with that rationale. They feel that it's a community college; one ought to perhaps compromise the rigor of your course because it is a community college. I guess I get frustrated and offended by that because I'm expected not to have so rigorous a course or not be as demanding. Some students have come in and said to me, 'You know, if I wanted to do this much work, I would have gone to the university.'"

In defending what he thinks must be the level of expectation for his course, Lopez makes himself vulnerable to losing students. He said that after such a discussion, either a student "will walk away pretty much satisfied that he's not being overworked; or . . . they'll come back and tell me they're not going to take 'your course.' They say, 'I thought I wanted to get into the field, but if I have to go through these courses to get to it, it's not worth my time and effort at this point in my life.'" Faculty who try to uphold a conception of collegiate standards based on their own collegiate education and their knowledge of the field find themselves vulnerable to rejection and resulting self-doubt about what they are doing.

Trying to maintain collegiate standards makes faculty not only susceptible to rejection by students but also, if that rejection becomes widespread, susceptible to a feeling of considerable, albeit ambiguous, pressure from the administration. Some community college administrations send faculty double messages: "Numbers are important," and "Maintain your standards." For example, a psychology instructor and counselor in California said, "When I first started teaching I was covering the whole textbook; I don't do that anymore. They just cannot read a whole book in a semester for whatever reasons. Either you require that and flunk three quarters of the class, or you come to terms with reality: . . . that the administration isn't so thrilled at high dropout rates. So people who hold the line start to worry at a certain point, you know, is this going to be held against them. Second of all, you have to ask if you are serving your students' best interests. . . . There are a lot of questions. . . . You can rationalize on either side of the line. . . . I've capitulated. I see it as a capitulation."

Across the country in New York state, a psychology instructor raised and expanded the same issue. Talking about how she grades students, she said, "There are several hard places. One of them is, Do you grade them so harshly that they give up, which you don't want them to do. But you don't want to be too lenient because then they won't try. So you have to hit the middle ground. Then, of course, you have to be more or less in tune with what everybody else is doing because students are not stupid; they are going to figure that out too. So they are going to start saying, 'Well, so and so does much easier tests or grades easier.' So you don't need that hassle and you could possibly get out of step with the rest of the department. Because again, they want to pass this number of bodies through the institution."

A black faculty member in a hotel and restaurant management program in another college in New York connected the issue of standards to dignity: "I think that there should be more demands placed upon students . . . I think dignity goes along with that." He spoke of his concern that one department in his college was talking about a certificate program for the illiterate, a certificate program where students would be taught how to cook. Students would be tested orally. The college in effect would recognize their inability to write and would accommodate that. In response to that notion, he said the following:

> I can't support that at all. If they do not have the skill to read and write, for whatever reason, I think we should have a program to bring them up to that level or send them back into the system to get that skill, but I don't think we should lower our standards to accommodate that type of student. First of all we would be giving them a false impression that yes, they have a certificate, now they can go out and get a job. They're going to remain in that lower level job. We're not giving them the skills to move up.
>
> My students . . . have to write a term paper. They've never written a term paper before and probably will never write one again, but I challenge them to think. If we lower our standards and say well, I

know you can't write a recipe, but tell me how you
would do it, I don't think we would be doing the
student much of a service.

Computerized Instruction

The literature on community colleges often stresses "innovation." Most recently "innovation" has been connected to computerized, programmed instruction. But the consequence of such
innovation is to remove the student from the basic relationship
between teacher, student, and subject matter, which many community college faculty indicate is the key to teaching and learning.
Understanding that teaching is a relationship, Elizabeth McKay,
who teaches in an urban community college in California, had
limited interest in computerized instruction. When asked to discuss
her experience with computerized and programmed instruction,
McKay responded:

> I guess you could say I don't put much stock in
> it. . . . It works all right for some people in some
> situations, but I wouldn't rely on it. . . . I had a guy,
> an absolutely crazy guy, a couple of years ago, that if
> you touched him he would stand up and fight. I mean,
> you know, "You bumped me, don't bump me." Now
> for him [I plan] programmed instruction. Structure
> this man right down to the last hour. . . . I got
> through the semester with him and it was a miracle he
> didn't kill anybody and I didn't kill him. But you
> know those are real extreme situations. I used pro-
> grammed instruction in a very, very limited kind of
> way. There is something about working with stu-
> dents: I am much more interested in the possibility
> that change comes through relationships than it
> comes through a program of instruction or whatever.
> I mean I don't think those things are opposed to
> change or improved learning, it's just that I somehow
> see the ground as being much more in the exchanges
> than in the material or the book or something out
> there.

Janet Ingersoll, whose profile appears in Chapter Seven and who taught English part-time for five years in another California community college, spoke of the move toward computerized instruction in the following terms:

> The administration has become very interested in machines and all that machines can do and how much cheaper they are in fact than faculty members. They have spent a good deal of time and money flying around the country studying schools that have converted to machine teaching in hopes of being able to convince themselves that it is in fact both cost-effective and student-learning effective. Introductory courses can be put into a machine and students can do self-paced learning and earn unit credit for that.
>
> I have very strong feelings about that. I don't think it works. I don't think it works because I have watched my students try to use machines and because I have tried to use them as well, and there is just not the interaction there is in the classroom. And particularly for students such as the ones who often end up at community colleges, who really need someone to sit down with them and say, "This is what you haven't learned, and we are going to try and figure out why you haven't learned it, and I am here to answer any questions you have. . . ." The trend seems to be absolutely away from that.
>
> They just spent a great deal of money installing new machines and carpeting in their reading center, in hopes that they could get rid of their paraprofessionals they have eventually and make it all machine-controlled. I don't think that's the way to go. And I don't think that is the way to go with writing courses, and there seems to be some push for that to happen with writing. I have some tapes of sentence structure lessons and things like that, which are cute and charming, most of them, and pretty ineffective.

From what I can tell, what it creates is an
administrative stance that seems to say, "We don't
appreciate very much what you can do in the classroom; you know, we understand you are doing what
a good machine can do. But beyond that, we are not
sure that you are doing anything much better." It's
often an attempt on the administration's part, I think,
to be cost-efficient; at least that's been my experience.
They think that if they can plug a certain number of
students into a computer and teach whatever course it
may be, Psych 1 or Typing Skills or whatever, then
that's one less faculty member they have to pay salary
to and health benefits.

Faculty and administrators in community colleges must take
stock of the pressures to innovate by programming and automating
their courses. There is much pressure on administrators to be
innovative, to some extent because quality is difficult to comprehend and assess, whereas some new pieces of equipment stand out
and can be pointed to with pride, whatever their qualitative impact
on teaching and learning.

Faculty are caught in a difficult position. They must work
with students for whom a reconstructive approach to their basic
skills is required. Such an approach requires more time and space,
yet they are faced with teaching loads that assume no such responsibility. It is no wonder that some faculty might themselves be
passive in the face of the computerized, automated instruction
bandwagon. But while perhaps not always heard above the din,
there are voices among the faculty saying unambiguously that
teaching and learning mean primarily a relationship among
teacher, student, and subject matter, and that computers cannot
provide the relationship necessary for the type of learning most
important to students who are learning to think critically.

The Dropout

The issues outlined in this chapter finally lead to the critical
matter of dropouts. We have seen that in community colleges there

is pressure to teach as many students from varied backgrounds as inexpensively as possible. There is also a lack of time and space and perhaps more importantly, no clear mandate to provide the type of reconstructive education across the curriculum that is necessary for many community college students. There is a de-emphasis on writing and reading and an overreliance on objective tests. These tests are often developed and supplied by the publisher of the textbooks rather than designed by the teacher with his or her own goals for the course in mind. In addition, the tests are often machine-scored and results simply posted, so that any instructional function of the testing program is seriously weakened. Finally, students are sometimes urged to connect to microcomputers rather than teachers. While these institutional characteristics do not describe all teachers and all courses and while many individual faculty work against the current, these factors are prevalent enough that it is impossible not to see them as connected to the high-dropout rate of students in community colleges.

While the public at large might be surprised at the indications that perhaps as few as 10 percent of community college students receive an associate degree within two to five years of entering a community college (Breneman and Nelson, 1981, p. 60), the faculty who teach in community colleges know that fact only too well and must confront the problems of dropouts daily. In the face of the high-attrition rate, some commentators have begun to question whether program completion is a reasonable standard by which to judge the success of community college curricula. Breneman and Nelson (1981, p. 55) ask, "Does dropping out represent success or failure? It could reflect success if the student learned as much as he intended and left because he found a job for which he was being trained or failure if he concluded that instruction would not help him in the labor market. . . . Are transfer rates, completion rates, and placement rates appropriate measures of success? Questions like these do not have clear-cut right or wrong answers, depending instead on particular circumstances and on one's educational philosophy."

While such statements have a certain logic, they do not reflect what many faculty in community colleges think; nor does that logic speak effectively to the impact such a phenomenon has on their experience as community college teachers. Teacher after teacher in the study identified the issue of students dropping out of their classes as a problem. Only one faculty member had no problem with the fact that as soon as his students could get a job, they would grab it and drop out of his course and program, no matter what stage they were at. Many of the teachers told us that when they first started teaching, they took students dropping their courses as a reflection on their own effectiveness. For example, a head of a humanities division in a California community college said,

> There were times when it really bothered me that students just all of a sudden disappeared. You work for six weeks of a semester; you are bringing them along; you are exerting a lot of, you know, cheerleading energy and a lot of your professional energy as well; you are conjuring up all kinds of things to help this guy, and he is making some progress; it's slow, it's painful, but he is doing it. And then all of a sudden, bang, you know, for two days he's not in class.
>
> I call a number that he has given me and he doesn't live there anymore. . . . Sometimes I find out what happened; most of the time I don't. That is a recurring frustration in teaching at this kind of institution. The suspicion is gnawing that I didn't do enough for him. We know from studies that have been done that there are a hundred and one reasons that had nothing to do with institutional or instructional control that account for the attrition rate. But it is hard to convert that into any kind of positive statement. . . . I don't think you can turn that around and say it's OK, so you lost 30 percent. We have classes where you lose 30, 40, 50 percent. That's painful. In a number of ways, self-doubt is aroused. You haven't made it with this student. . . . That's a tough one; that's a tough one.

Clearly, the student-centered ethos of the community college, which we will discuss in greater detail in Chapter Six, encourages

faculty to make themselves accessible to students and to be personally interested in the wide range of problems they face. That
interaction heightens the sense of personal investment the community college faculty members may make in their students and inten-
sifies their sense of self-doubt when students drop out.

The high attrition rate not only produces faculty self-doubt
but also frustrates faculty and demoralizes the students. For example, Janet Ingersoll spoke of how frustrating it was to her to spend
long hours marking students' papers in the first few weeks of a
course only to have a significant number of those students drop the
course. She also pointed to the impact of dropouts on classroom
dynamics: "In your evening courses you start out with thirty and
end up with seventeen. And it is hard on the students as well because
our numbers shrink as the weeks go by, and it is demoralizing to
them too. So you are constantly dealing with a classroom whose
dynamics are changing just among the students, and you have to
be the buffer for that and fill in and it is hard. It is very hard."

Part of the frustration gets directed at administrators who
build into their calculations of class size a predicted high dropout
rate. A teacher like Nancy Warren, in effect, has a sense of failure
as a result of the structure in which she is working. She explained
it this way: "The sense of failure comes always from the feeling that
you could do so much more if you had more time, and you would
have time if you had fewer students and less paper grading and more
time to work with students individually." And yet invariably her
classes are scheduled to be large because the administration knows
that a significant number will drop out. By scheduling large classes
they may in fact be creating a self-fulfilling prophecy, since faculty
will have less time to give the type of instructional attention that
they think is necessary.

Faculty in the community college may adjust to the issue of
dropouts by finally adopting the understanding that students drop
for a wide range of reasons, many of which are beyond their control.
But no matter how the issue is rationalized, it remains an issue. For
any teacher who has been thoughtful about planning her course
and who has educational objectives, the notion that completion by
students is not a standard of success is untenable. Despite the
recognition of a wide range of reasons for dropping out, individual

teachers absorb the shock of the high-attrition rates. And no matter how inured they may become to the situation, teachers are affected by the loss of a student, for the very reason that teaching is a relationship. Attrition in the classroom is a serious injury to the relationship that is most important to a teacher.

There is a great deal of thoughtfulness about teaching in community colleges. Much of this thoughtfulness comes from faculty who would reject the notion that teaching in a community college is somehow basically different in purpose and method than teaching in four-year institutions. While teachers recognize that many of their students start off with skills below the college level, given the time and the space to do so, they could bring these students up to collegiate standards. Samuel Berger, whose profile appears in Chapter Nine, put it this way:

> A junior college occupies just about the lowest rank of prestige in the academic world. But I really don't know a difference between a good community college teacher versus a good university teacher. I remember I was told that there is a distinctive aspect to community college teaching, that you are interested in the individual student and you sort of nurse that student, sort of like little children. I had a colleague for instance when he would teach Soc. 102, he would give them a virtual outline of the book. I never did that. He believed that there was a distinctive kind of thing in a junior college, that somehow you have to baby students along. I don't believe that. I find it hard to distinguish or single out any specific respect in which a community college teacher should be a differ-ent kind of teacher or a different kind of human being than a university teacher. . . . I have been told that there are such differences, but I just don't know them.

At the core, Berger argued, "It is not true that kids who were very poor, white or black, that they are somehow not intellectual, not interested in things intellectual. They are usually not given anything to think of intellectually. They are interested in fundamental questions as much as anybody else. There is no intellectual reason to cheapen or lower your level of interest. The problem is how do you meet them at the certain point where they are."

But the complication that administration and faculty leaders alike must consider is that although community colleges have historically separated teaching from research so as to give their faculty more time to attend to good teaching, that time has been consumed by increasing class loads and by an ethos of accessibility to students. The community college is in the position of having to build public and political support through the claim that it can do a more difficult job less expensively than four-year institutions. The pressures created by this claim, in turn, severely impact the working conditions of community college faculty. To complicate the issue even further, much of the concern about teaching is characteristic of the faculty who decry the separation of research and teaching. These faculty stay active in their field, they write (and some publish), and they feel deeply the tension between their understanding of their field and the preparation their students have for responding to that understanding. They affirm the intellectual essence of their work as teachers, in the face of an institutional structure and outlook that tends to deny that essence. These teachers' stance toward their work offers a source of possible initiatives for faculty and administrators to consider as they face the critical issues of teaching and learning in community colleges.

6

Balancing
Commitment to Students
with Other
Professional Responsibilities

The notion of student-centeredness permeates the community college. Its energy derives in part from a stereotypic image of authoritarian university professors interested only in their subject matter and research and caring little for the welfare of their students. In contrast, the community college projects an image of teachers interested in the whole student, teachers who are compassionate toward students' problems and accessible for help with a wide variety of concerns. As O'Banion has written, "The community-junior college emphasis on teaching has a natural corollary—a pressing concern with the classroom learner. Student-centeredness is the hallmark of good classroom teaching. But the community-junior college has earned a reputation for student-centeredness that extends beyond a concern for the student as a classroom learner. The community-junior college seeks the full development of human potential" (1972, p. 23).

The idea of student-centeredness as it operates in community colleges can create considerable stress for many community college faculty. The model can blur teachers' sense of their role, contribute to a sometimes frenetic and almost consuming day-to-day work

86

pattern, and induce a sense of personal responsibility for matters that are basically beyond their control. In addition to contributing to a sense of guilt on the part of faculty who may feel they never have enough time to do their work well, the student-centered model has ambiguous consequences for community college students.

Teacher Among Other Roles

The student-centered model can lead to a confusion of the teacher-student relationship. One psychology instructor in a Massachusetts community college talked about how many students came to speak to him as though he were a therapist. He spoke of the incredible problems the students have and the desperate search for someone to help. He said, "Because I have taught a course in psychology, people were assuming I was a person to go to talk to. So many of the students would come with horrendous problems. I started talking with them and just felt completely frustrated." Because a young computer programming instructor in a New York college thought it important to understand the personal problems his students faced, he sought them out to talk. He said, "I get to know the students personally. Every once in a while, I will go out where they usually go, to the local establishment, and I'll talk to them there. . . . I'll just go and talk to the students and find out, you know, their problems. It's a lot easier to teach and understand some of these people if you know where they have come from and what kinds of problems they have."

A California dental hygiene teacher said, "I don't get into their personal lives. I don't care what they do for social activities; . . . that's their business." "But," she went on, "I'm just here if they need me. . . . It's called the great mother. . . . Well, I don't know if I'm the great mother, but I just see them, you know, as taking beginning steps." A biology teacher in New York repeated the maternal theme. She said, "I don't know, not all students need bolstering, but a lot of them do. . . . They look so grown up, but they're really lacking in a lot of grown-up skills. Maybe I always look on them as children . . . I don't know."

Another faculty member described how she saw herself in the classroom: "I'm a cheerleader. That's what I do here: 'Come on gang, you can do it, I know you can'. . . . Sometimes I don't have that kind of energy." The drain on energy was implicit in how another faculty member described coming back to her office after a class. She said, "I am wiped out because of the teaching and you go back to your office where there are all kinds of people waiting, 'cause they need help, or tutoring, or they need a place to sit down and tell you the story of their life, or they tell you how they are screwed up or whatever."

Therapist, friend, mother, cheerleader, helper—these are all roles with which community college faculty grapple as they try to carry out their basic task as teacher. For some, the additional roles do not seem to provide conflict. A theater teacher in New York state seemed comfortable as she said, "I think it is important to be a teacher who is concerned and who spends time with her students. I think that a lot of students who come here need help in building confidence and courage." A dental hygiene teacher in Massachusetts said, "I am in a profession where I am helping people and I've discovered that I am the type of person who enjoys helping. . . ." But many faculty in the study were struggling with the ambiguities that result from the additional roles. A young graphics teacher in a California community college confronted the consequences of befriending his students. He said, "I think you can get to be too good friends with some students and then you muddy up the teacher-student relationship. You'll get a little too casual with them. . . . I had a couple of students . . . they got so close to me that they figured that they were such good friends, I just mean friends in the classroom, that they didn't have to work as hard. . . . That created bad situations, so I've learned to keep a little distance."

Other faculty said that they tried to discriminate between what was appropriate for them to be concerned with and what was not. In response to a question on how he reacted to students' personal problems, a California electronics instructor said, "Well, that depends on what kind of personal problem. If a student has a reading disability or a physical disability . . . that's something to be concerned about. But I would prefer that he not tell me about his problems with his mother, father, wife, daughter, whomever. I would rather keep those subjects from my classroom. I don't intend to be rude to the student, to keep him from telling me, but that isn't really the image I want to convey. I don't want to be a father to him. . . . I would by far prefer to be seen as a very competent professional. I'm not sure that I'm a good father. I am a good teacher."

Yet in critical situations, the student-centered ethos makes it difficult for teachers to decide what problems are appropriate for them to try to respond to and what problems, on the other hand, should be referred elsewhere, for professional help. In New York state a faculty member talked to us about a student who came to him because she was contemplating suicide: "It was a tense situation for me, because you know the student poured herself out to me. I don't know what kind of advice to give someone who is considering suicide. I drew my faculty office-mate in and he and I talked to her for a couple of hours, trying to counsel her [about] her relationship with her children, her mother, her father, that kind of thing. It was an extreme case."

Some faculty indicated that they had begun to change in their view of how much it was appropriate to reach out to their students. Nancy Warren, whose profile appears in Chapter Seven, said, "I do a lot of advising. I tried to cut down on it some because I think I did too much of it initially. I was not so much counseling but just simply being there and listening to people who came in. And I realized after a point that probably it was simply using up my time and I wasn't helping people who could come in and sit for an hour. Some students, you realize, have very serious problems and need somebody who can give them help. I can listen and I can certainly make some practical suggestions: if somebody who comes in has a problem with a roommate or rent or something, I can talk about those things. But if somebody's really on the edge of collapse, then I try to suggest that they get some professional help."

Faculty are encouraged not only to relate to students on many levels, but to "individualize" their instruction to meet the needs of their students. At times the willingness to individualize means going to great lengths to structure a situation so that students who are having difficulty and who fall behind because of personal reasons can somehow make up their work. Jesus Lopez, whose profile appears in Chapter Eight, said that he was willing to spend Saturday mornings at the college with a student who had been sick. But sometimes his willingness to go that extra step for students made him personally vulnerable when the effort didn't succeed. He spoke of a student in his organic chemistry class whose life "fell apart" and with whom he worked very hard to enable her to keep up with her work. He said, "It never really quite worked out. It was one of those things where the longer it took us to get going, the further behind she got. No matter how much time we had been working together, no matter how much time I was willing to devote to her, she wasn't going to catch up. She didn't complete it. That affected me in a personal way. When you get a little more involved with a student . . . you tend to personalize their triumphs and defeats more."

In addition to encouraging faculty to feel personally responsible for students' success and failure even when circumstances are far beyond faculty control, the pressure to individualize attention can create a deep confusion about what is appropriate to expect of students. Nancy Warren described the dilemma she felt in these terms: "Half the time I say, 'Damn it, look, here it is, this is what the degree from the college means: that you have achieved certain specific things, and you achieve them or you don't, and I give you a grade and that indicates it and that is that.' . . . And the other half [of] the time I think 'Here is this person who can't do this, and it is absurd for him to spend all his time trying to learn to do it. He can do a whole lot of other things. Help him to do those things. The hell with standards and grades and the significance of the degree.' "

In addition to leading to confusion about what is appropriate for faculty to expect of students, sometimes students themselves seem to lose sight of what responsibility they must take for their work. Judith Wesley, who teaches sociology and anthropology in a New York state community college, talked about how students would attempt to use the student-centered ethos to their ends and about the tension that this created for her. She said, "When their not learning shows up on their first test with me, then I get all kinds of personal stories: 'But you know my car broke down.' Or 'I've been having lots of problems lately; things are going badly for me at home.' Or 'I just lost my job.' I used to feel a lot of pressure to soften that 62 that they had just gotten. I was uncomfortable. . . . I kept getting myself backed into corners where I was making decisions about one student and not behaving in the same way with another student, or interpreting attitudes and allowing those perceived attitudes to influence my evaluation of their work. I was just increasingly uncomfortable with that and needed to be clear that everybody was getting the same kind of treatment regardless of how I felt about them."

Wesley did work out a way of clarifying her expectations of her students, and what they could expect of her, that allowed her to concentrate her attention on her teaching and on what students were learning without becoming impervious to their lives. She spoke of a woman in her class who was having difficulty:

> A student came in to see me yesterday. She is an older student who is in my night class. She's thirty-nine years old, got six kids at home, an alcoholic husband, and she got a 58 on the test. She also works. She gets up at five in the morning to do laundry for those kids, keep everybody in clean clothes, pack lunches, and get them off to school. She studied all week long for the test and got a 58.
>
> She said to me, "I paid one hundred and fifteen dollars to take this course, I don't have that kind of money, I can't afford to flunk out. I am determined to get a degree, I want something different out of life. I never was a good student. I quit high school, I got pregnant before I left high school. In those days they kicked you out. I spent twenty years raising kids. I want something different out of life, and I am going to do it."

While Wesley said that she spent a long time listening to this student talk about her life situation, and knew that it was "horrendous," her basic approach was based on her understanding that the student "didn't know the material." Wesley said,

> We spent a long time talking about the way her life is right now and what other kinds of tasks she has and can we find a way to make her studying, the time

that she does have to put into it, more effective.
Obviously, it's not paying off for her.

I said, "I think it's not paying off because you
don't know it. You think you know it, but you don't
know it. If you did you would do better."

We got out her textbook and looked at what she
was doing; and all kinds of mechanical work, mem-
orizing definitions, was what she had been doing in
preparation for the test. She said, "My daughter said
that wasn't going to pay off; I can see it didn't. My
daughter said, 'That's not the right way,' but I didn't
know what else to do; that's how they taught us in
Catholic school: memorize definitions."

Wesley went on to describe her basic response to the student:
"My suggestion was to study with your textbook closed. Read a
section at a time and formulate a question about that, and close
your textbook on your thumb and then say, OK, what did I just
read? She listened very intently and she said, 'I never would have
thought of trying that.' I said to her, 'You know, explain to your
daughter what classical conditioning is. Tell her, and if you can
teach her, then you know it. I learn more than anyone else because
I have to stand up in front of all those people and explain it; so I
read the chapters in a very different kind of way. If you imagine
yourself in that kind of situation, if you had to do that, it would
be very different.' "

After discussing basic study strategies, Wesley went on to
describe how her student could get more out of the class sessions.
She said to her, "When I ask a question in class, answer it. Put your
hand up. You never do that. And she said, 'Well, I'm embarrassed.'
I said, 'You paid your money, get your money's worth. That's what
I'm there for.' "

Wesley described the end of the conversation: "She laughed
and said she would try it. I don't know how well she will do with
that, but we will see on the second test and I'll talk to her before
that second test and see how she is doing."

Wesley was careful not to cross that very narrow line that
exists between what a teacher can try to respond to in a student's

life and what is beyond any reasonable responsibility she can take. She listened to all the problems her student faced, but she concentrated her attention and thoughtfulness on the only aspect of the student's experience with which she could legitimately connect in her role as teacher: how she was studying and how she was experiencing the class. She had worked out after some years of experience the difference between being a teacher and being a "helper." She knew that trying to help students face concerns over which the teacher has no real control can be satisfying in the short run, but debilitating for both the student and the teacher in the long run. She concentrated her energies on those teaching and learning areas in which she had something to contribute, could be effective, and would contribute to the student's independence. She had come to know from experience what Moore (1970, pp. 63–64) had come to see as a major issue facing community college faculty: "Too many teachers consider the task of teaching the high-risk student in the junior college to be academic social work; and making special remedial curricula available to this student is often thought to be academic welfare. Yet this student must be taught—and well." For some in the community college, the line between "helping" students and "teaching" them seems blurred.

The Pressures of Accessibility

The student-centered ethos of community colleges not only pressures the faculty to combine a number of sometimes conflicting roles but also creates an atmosphere in the workday that at times seems almost frenetic. Garrison (1967) found that the inability of faculty to find sufficient time to do their work was a major issue. Some twenty years later, the lack of time to oneself is still a source of major stress on community college faculty.

A very subtle pressure can build in a community college. Making oneself accessible to students is a norm of the job, and success can begin to be partially perceived as a function of how busy faculty appear to be with students. In such an atmosphere, shutting their office doors to grade papers, to read, or to think about the next class may give faculty the solitude they need to get their work done; but if seeking such time to work leads to the perception that a faculty member is not as accessible as he or she should be, considerable discomfort can result. Even though having a line of students outside the office door may drain a faculty member's energy and may inhibit a faculty member from getting all the other work of a teacher done, it is also a sign that the faculty member is really doing the job the community college expects.

In a school in California the notion of accessibility was so pervasive that when a new campus was built, the faculty offices were constructed so that the walls facing the hallways were of glass. Jesus Lopez, whose profile appears in Chapter Eight, described his day in the following terms:

> After class . . . I'll usually come up to my office to do some work. The physical setup of the school, with the study areas being in the center and offices around the periphery [and] the glass sliding doors, precludes anyone from hiding. Normally what happens is I'll go to my office and do some work, but the students will see that I'm in my office and will come in, and I will spend usually the great portion of my time talking with students, handling questions, whether they are in my course or someone else's course. We sort of have a "teacher's fair game" policy around here, so even if they are not in my class, they will wander in and ask me a question. . . . I squeeze in the basic work that I can in terms of grading papers, recording scores, and that sort of task in between students. To keep my sanity, I occasionally flee to the cafeteria for a cup of coffee and stay there til a student finds me and we come back to my office. They're pretty persistent once they realize that you are willing to spend whatever time they want with them. I try to make that a commitment. I tell them, as far as I'm concerned, when I'm at school my job is to interact with them.

The issue of accessibility may be even more exacerbated for a faculty member who is a member of a minority in a community college which has a primarily white faculty and yet a significant number of minority students. Minority faculty members in such situations have to be accessible to all students, but they have a special responsibility to minority students. Lopez said, "We try to serve as role models and [offer] encouragement. . . . We also advise in terms of political issues . . . making sure they're aware of the various programs that the school offers, be it a scholarship, financial aid, job opportunities. I don't know, I guess maybe it's a big brother, big sister role that we play."

In addition to informal advising that a minority faculty member will do with minority students from his or her ethnic background, minority faculty will often be asked to become advisors to the minority students' alliances, clubs, and caucuses that are formed on college campuses. Here the minority faculty play a difficult role of interpreting and sometimes defending the institution to the students and sometimes contending with the institution on behalf of the minority students. Faculty acting as advisors to minority groups find themselves spending time with them on fund raising, planning dances, meeting with students and faculty to encourage minority enrollment in academic areas that seem underrepresented by minority students, and helping students deal with problems they may be facing in the community at large. Lopez summarized his efforts as an advisor to Hispanic students by saying, "I found that it can be very time consuming and can be a major factor in your life if you allow it to be. What usually happens is that we'll burn out after two or three years of being very actively involved with the students, and then we'll take sort of a backseat for a while. . . . Someone else would then take on that primary role."

In those schools with few minority faculty, there is considerable pressure for them to represent minority student interests. It becomes very complicated for them to feel like an individual. Cheryl Collins, whose profile appears in Chapter Twelve, is a black woman counselor in a California community college. She spoke about what it was like to be in such a position.

When I go into a meeting—whatever issue is being discussed—I have to filter it through [the question], "What does this mean for black students?"

Whenever I go into a meeting, I feel that I carry that
responsibility because in most meetings I am the only
minority person, and maybe the only woman. It is like
trying to filter through not only what it means to the
campus at large, but trying to represent also women
and minority students, because when I go back to
another meeting that is with women or other black
faculty, then they see me as their representative. It is
like I just can't go and sit at the meeting. . . . If
somebody doesn't speak up about how does this affect
women or is this fair to minority students, I feel like
I have to represent that. It does feel like pressure
because sometimes I'll go into those meetings and I'll
try to think through [the question], "Am I seeing
everything?" There may not be somebody else there to
bounce that off, and sometimes I'll make a mistake
and I'll go back and say "I didn't think of that." . . .
Sometimes I just want to be there and be me and listen
to what is going on and sit back and not be smart, you
know, and just exist like some of the rest of the people
around the table.

While carrying on special responsibility to minority students, minority faculty in predominantly white institutions must be
accessible to all students. Hidden injuries can occur in the process,
as a black counselor in a small city in upstate New York described:
"I would be in a situation with somebody on a one-on-one basis and
we would talk about some problems and he can feel that he really
has been helped and he will leave and say 'Gee, thank you, you
really helped me out a lot.' Yet I can be on campus and pass the
same individual . . . and just realize that when he walked by he
didn't see me, and know that it is not so much that he didn't see
me as [that] he didn't see me because he would not look at black
people and give them eye contact, because for the most part there
is no need for him to do that."

Private senses of satisfaction also develop as minority faculty
see their teaching and relating to all students as the way they can
contribute to combating racism. As Robert Thatcher, whose profile

appears in Chapter Eleven, said, "When we talk about tearing down racism and discrimination, you can do it in a peaceful way. I've always felt that you could change attitudes by actually being out and involved in something where people are not accustomed to seeing you there. . . . In the process of teaching physics, I have a lot of students who talk to me. They've never had a chance to just sit down with a black person and say, 'How do you feel?' "

The issues of accessibility for minority and nonminority faculty are complicated by some basic structural issues. As Nancy Warren said, "One of the problems for the students at the community college is the lack of community there. Students drive in and drive out, and this contributes to the high-attrition rate. Unless students have friends when they come or join an organization that gives them a kind of center when they are on campus, or find that their classes are kind of cohesive in a social sense, the college can seem very cold, despite the relative smallness, despite the possibility of being friendly with one's instructors." The fact that many students have to work and immediately leave campus for jobs that are often unrelated to their field of study, and the fact that very few community colleges have residential facilities negatively influences the ability of students to persist in school (Astin, 1982, pp. 109, 183). It is extremely difficult for concerned, interested, and accessible faculty to compensate for those basic facts of community college student life as it is now constituted.

The Double Edge of Student-Centeredness

In addition to the pressures student-centeredness imposes on faculty, it has a double edge for the student. It can create a false sense of security and dependence that offers little to the students when they leave the community college. One such student, who transferred from her community college to a large nearby state university, spoke of her experience in making the switch to the university in these terms:

> I just kind of felt like if I did well there [at her
> community college] that I could do it, that I could go
> four years. And that's what gave me the confidence to

go on. It was like a very nurturing sort of situation.
. . .[But] see when I went to the university, I didn't get
that personal touch. I got, "OK, fill this form out,
stand in line. . . ." Nobody was helping me. I was lost
all the time. And then going and talking to somebody,
and he's, like, very brief. . . . It wasn't like he cared one
way or the other. So he'd say, "OK, this is your major
then you take these courses."

[I wanted to ask] "Well, how hard are they? Do
you think I'm capable of doing them? Am I going to
be needing a big transition period? What's going to be
happening?" And no one told you anything.

[At the end of my first semester] you know, I
was on academic probation. I had gotten a D in
chemistry, C in math, and, you know, I did the work
in my public health course, but I dropped my statistics
course a little late. And I had to think of all kinds of
excuses to get out of it. It was like I'm right back
where I started from. It was like a real comedown. . . .
All the fears that I had had came flooding back in and
there I was again. And I wondered, "Was that just a
little flowery school where I went to, where they
babied me and they taught me the way I needed to be
taught? And then it's like here is the cold, cruel world.
And nobody is going to baby you?"

She contemplated switching majors:

I was really at a point where I was confused and
had no counseling—because . . . I was looking for
someone to make the decision for me, and no one
could, basically. I had to do it myself. The only reason
I stayed was because I wanted it so badly. At that point
I would have stayed at any cost . . . I wasn't turning
back. I was determined at that point to keep going. . . .
You've got to remember that a lot of sensitive,
maybe quiet, and shy people go to community colleges. At least that's what I have noticed. You know,

> they had their things that they liked to do, and maybe
> they were verbal in small settings. . . . To turn these
> people loose without having toughened them up a
> little is really kind of unfair.

This student's experience suggests that sense of dependence rather than independence may be an ironic and unintended consequence of the way community college faculty are encouraged to reach out to students.

The dominant note in our study was one of faculty reaching out to connect to their students; however, there were discordant notes of students too angry to allow themselves to be reached and faculty sensing some complexity in the situation of "helping" their students. Judith Wesley told us of the long-legged boys who sprawl in their seats at the back of the room as if to say: "Go ahead, I dare you to teach me something." To her their body posture said: "I'm going to try to get as far away from what's going on in the classroom as possible."

Wesley recounted an experience of having to confront one such student who was intent on cheating on an examination one day. She stopped the cheating and then after class she had what she described as a frank discussion about why he was in the course, what he hoped to get out of it, what he was interested in. On the positive side, she said this of her discussion:

> We really had a good talk. It was the first time
> he had ever looked at me or said anything to me. It was
> clear that he had put me in some sort of category
> which said "teacher" on it, somebody that you need to
> stay away from. He was here because he really didn't
> know what he was going to do. He couldn't find a job.
> He had had a part-time job and had been laid off. He
> had no particular interest or passion for being here.
> And I said to him, "Well, what would happen if you
> dropped out?" Well, he didn't think anything bad
> would happen. He was kind of interested in a science
> course he was taking. . . .

I think he stayed in school for the one science
course he was taking and I haven't seen him since that
time. But after that talk, every time I passed him in the
hall, he made eye contact with me and smiled. It was
like some sort of honest transaction that I had had
with him.

Later, Wesley reflected on her interaction with that student
from a different perspective. She said: "I encouraged this boy to
leave school. I gave him a lot of support for leaving. I helped him.
I asked him to explore what would happen, the consequences of
staying or going. I opened up a possibility he hadn't considered. I
call it "helping" when I really am arranging a situation so that I
feel a lot more comfortable with it. It was useful for me to get the
boy out of the class. His behavior—something had to change. . . ."

Wesley was able to deal with the hostility shown by passivity
and cheating by "helping" the student to leave her classroom. Other
teachers tell of facing more overt hostility. Cynthia Jamison, whose
profile appears in Chapter Seven, described how a student threatened to burn down her house if she didn't give him a good grade.
She had to gather all her nerve to counter his threat with a firm,
no-nonsense counterthreat of her own, which made clear to him
that she would not—in her own words—put up with "that sort of
garbage." She just put a "cork" in his mouth and he never said it
again.

In his study, *The Culture of a Community College,* London (1978) presented additional evidence of hostility and incivility
in the community college classroom. Such behavior may indicate
that the normally unspoken boundaries between the public and
private lives of teachers and students can become stretched beyond
their limits in the community college. The ethos that encourages
faculty to reach across those boundaries may make them vulnerable
to the occasional student who reaches back with hostility.

To sum up, then, the notion of "student-centeredness" that
is a hallmark of community college faculty (Cohen and Brawer,
1977, pp 46-51) is complex, double-edged, and worthy of reexam-
ination. As Garrison pointed out in 1967: "The student-centered
attitude of the two-year colleges has broad implications for the

effectiveness of faculty. The attitude may or may not be laudable; . . . but there is no doubt that it is time consuming, and thus, not so eventually, expensive. Not the least part of the expense is the reduction of time and opportunity for teachers to keep themselves refreshed and up-to-date in their own disciplines" (1967, p. 78).

The passage of time and accumulating evidence make Garrison's comment seem especially discerning and foresighted. It is clear that the cost for faculty of the student-centered model has become very high, the consequences for students ambiguous, and the underlying conception a tangled mixture of social work and teaching. The issue is not that faculty should suddenly become calloused and impervious to the context of their students' lives. But there is a question about priorities, about how faculty time is best spent, and about the assumptions underlying teaching and learning in the community college. After years of practice such priorities and assumptions, which may have evolved at a much earlier period in an institution's history, can be forgotten, confused, and misappropriated.

At this point, it would be more than timely for community college faculty and administrators to reexamine the dominant model for relating to students—the model of student-centeredness—and begin to sort out its consequences for themselves and for students, as well as its interconnection with other fundamental aspects of community college education. As Garrison suggests, student-centeredness is deeply related to the dichotomy between teaching and research and to the intellectual character of teachers' work in the community college. To these subjects, and more, the faculty whose profiles are presented in the following chapters speak in their own words.

Profiles of Community College Faculty

In Part Two, community college faculty talk about their work in profiles presented in their own words. With the exception of Chapter Eleven, the profiles are grouped according to the subject taught. Some of the faculty whose profiles appear in the following chapters have been referred to in earlier chapters. Others appear for the first time.

In these profiles, the faculty reconstruct the details of their experience and the many pressures, contradictions, and hopes that affect their work. By presenting their experience in their own words, these profiles offer the reader an insider's perspective on significant issues affecting the quality of education at the community college. Each profile presents a clear picture of the complexities of teaching that subject area. Taken as a whole, the profiles provide insight into the interconnections among the work of faculty in diverse areas, the difficulties they all face, and themes that connect their experiences. Those who are in the community college will be able to relate their own experience to that of the faculty presented in the profiles. Readers who are planning to enter the community college can better prepare themselves for the realities they will face by reading what the faculty have to say about their work.

One theme that emerges from these profiles is the professionalism of the faculty: they are all very thoughtful about their teaching and about the relationship between their teaching and the goals of their community college. As they recount their experiences and reflect on the meaning of these experiences for themselves and their students, their words communicate the considerable dignity with which they carry out their work.

7

English and Humanities Faculty: Struggling to Improve Students' Writing and Critical Thinking

The 1970s saw a narrowing of the collegiate curriculum offered in community colleges. According to Cohen and Brawer, "Except for political science, history, and literature, many two-year associate-degree-granting institutions abandoned the humanities entirely" (Cohen and Brawer, 1982, p. 287). Moreover, the loss of commitment to the humanities during the 1970s was not a phenomenon unique to the community college. Throughout four-year colleges and universities, there was a flight of students and money away from the humanities as the economic situation tightened and liberal arts college graduates began to have difficulty getting jobs. But the community college, with the support of federal policy, took the lead in substituting a notion of career education for the liberal education that had the humanities at its core. As Cohen and Brawer put it, "The more successful the colleges became in their mission of providing trained workers for the community, the more precarious became the idea of liberal education within them" (Cohen and Brawer, 1982, p. 296).

The irony of this situation is that most of the career education faculty we interviewed insisted that if their students were to have any prospect of moving up in their hoped-for jobs, the skills that the career education faculty offered them were not enough. Both career education faculty and academic faculty argued that if their students were to have a sense of power and opportunity, they needed the skills of reading, writing, and thinking offered especially in the English and humanities classrooms.

While that argument was clearly made by faculty in this study, in fact community college humanities and English teachers face at best ambiguous support for their efforts. In the profiles that follow, four such teachers describe in their own words the complexities of their everyday work. The faculty in English describe the dilemmas they face in teaching writing to many students who have been basically uncomfortable with writing and reading throughout their entire school career. The humanities faculty discuss their attempts to share the central questions, issues, and values of their disciplines in a college context that increasingly seems to separate education from training. In many respects the English and humanities faculty whose profiles are presented in this chapter are swimming against the tide in their work.

Profile: Nancy Warren

Nancy Warren, in her forties, teaches English
in a Massachusetts community college.

I ordinarily have a mid-day or late-day schedule. Which means I leave home at nine or ten, get to the college for a 10:10 or a 11:15 class, usually. I have a class, perhaps followed by an office hour, another class, another office hour, or I hustle around between classes running off dittos that I want to use or getting something brought up from the audio-visual department. I do last minute recording of grades in between classes if I have a free hour, or that is to say an office hour. Only ten minutes gobbling down some lunch, as I am always stuck for eating time during this mid-day schedule. The pace usually seems not exactly hectic but quick and pressured, getting from class to class, and often several people wanting to see you before or after class. Rush into the mail room and go through the mailbox, chat with people who are grabbing coffee quickly between classes. There is not very much socializing because people all seem to be terribly busy. It is always pretty tense. If I have a lit class, I usually will be running over mentally the outline I have in my notes. Sometimes I am preparing a dialogue I intend to have with a student. Planning ahead.

The paper-grading problem is my biggest problem with the job. I mean a soul-deadening, truly soul-deadening load of grading papers. I have not yet found a way to cope with it to make it go faster or to make it less dreary. It is not that the papers are necessarily bad, just the quantity. It is not that I intrinsically hate grading papers but just so many of them, and they are always there, and I am always putting them off. So I am always thinking of them and worrying about it. No matter how good a day is or how bad, if one has got to come home to that, it is on your mind all day. I've got to go home and I've got to settle down and I've got to sit and grade papers for four hours. And I always feel that when I do that, that I somehow have to turn myself off and become a kind of machine and just do it. Why do I hate doing it? Because it takes so long and because I remember years ago, when I was a TA at the university, some guy on the faculty very self-righteously said, "If you don't love grading papers as part of your job, you ought not to be an English teacher." One can be very interested in the student; it is just after you do fifty or a hundred of them, after I do ten, I am tired of doing it. No matter how good the papers are, how inspired, if I spend a whole evening, I am mentally zapped.

I have never been able to get over a certain amount of anxiety while doing it. I could easily sit down for two hours and grade a multiple-choice test that required no thinking or no attention. I don't know whether it is the feeling of having to grade it in a way to justify your grade, or whether it is having to be careful to say things that encourage rather than discourage students, or uncertainty as to whether with a particular student you should not pay attention to spelling. It requires all your attention but doesn't give you any creative stimulation back beyond the pleasure of seeing that a student has understood an assignment, has learned from it and has written something good. I spend a great deal of time dreading doing it, too, which of course just makes it seem like a bigger job than it is.

I've tried all different kinds of things, but at least in writing courses I think if a student is going to write, he deserves to be read. I think some response is necessary; it is an essential part of the job, since three-fourths of the job is composition teaching. Sometimes I resolve not to correct papers in any detail, and I still find that here this student has done something really good and I want to say that it is good, or there is one flaw in an otherwise good paper and I want to point that out. I would find it hard to make a sudden shift. There is also the problem of the students who from time to time, certainly not very often, but sometimes the student who comes in to you and says, "Oh my God, I was writing papers in high school and nobody ever told me what was wrong, and I have now read this and I see what I am doing and now I can correct it." And of course when that happens you are so elated that you feel you have got to give every kid a chance to have that experience. I certainly really go into despair thinking I could have, in fact, at this point exactly twenty-five years of grading papers. One thinks of waitressing or— I don't know.

In our department there are fifteen or sixteen for the most part fanatically dedicated, very experienced, competent people who are slowly being ground down by a system and arrangement that they feel is impossible. Indeed, if I were really being dramatic about it, I would point out that our former chairman, who also taught English, committed suicide, and we lost one member to alcoholism; and other people have had problems. I guess I keep telling myself that any job has a certain amount of drudgery and it's the only part of the job I dislike. (I'm not enthralled with committee meetings.) The good part compensates and I remind myself that I have a summer vacation in which I do not grade papers and get rested up and I always start out each semester with enthusiasm and energy, and then there is this kind of running down as all these papers accumulate and you have done more and more of them. The twenty-five year prospect is very disturbing.

We've done everything we've been able to think of and we've had endless meetings and discussions about it. I think that it is perceived as the greatest problem in our situation by all of us. We've sent memos to the president, and we've had meetings with the president and talked to the dean, and we've talked and pushed and complained and had the union representative give them position papers for the contract negotiations. So far we've simply never succeeded in anything. We are always told there is not enough money to hire more teachers and that is that. Furthermore, if there were more money, there are teachers we need more in other areas. So we don't know what to do. We have certainly taken initiatives, but we have been unsuccessful. In any oppressive institutional system, if you can keep the workers from having time or energy to protest and also make them uneasy about their jobs, you've got them. And [if you] add to that [the fact] that they are replaceable easily, you have completely impotent employees. I don't mean to imply that there is some kind of plot or conspiracy. I don't think there is anybody sitting around somewhere deciding that a teacher shall be oppressed. I think it is simply the way things have fallen out in the course of budget cuts and lack of concern and interest generally.

I think there certainly is a sense of regret and sorrow that other departments in which the members used to always assign papers have stopped doing so. Their course load has gone up to five courses, in sociology, history, and government, and psychology. They have said, "All right, tests can now be graded on a machine." And they regret it. They feel it is wrong. Yet they feel that there is no alternative, and we would agree, knowing what is involved. It doesn't really help the students.

The other departments have different kinds of problems. If you have a general meeting, people are bringing up their problems. Theirs sound equally real to them: problems with staffing, labs, the economics department teaching seventeen courses and only one full-time economics teacher so they are all part-time people, which is not good. There are problems all over—we feel our paper grading thing is the worst but that is because it is ours.

I don't want to portray myself as seeing myself the victim of an oppressive system. I think it is much more complicated than that. Partly a victim of certain hang-ups of my own and partly stuck by one fact of the structure that I feel impotent to do anything about, and it is indeed very oppressive. I don't see myself as a faceless cog in a big machine or something. In fact it seems to me that jobs like this are one of the few places where one still has a certain amount of personal freedom in terms of deciding your schedule and you have summers to do as you wish. I happen to use most of them in connection with work and teaching, but that is a choice and I am certainly not made to do it.

Teaching literature is a very small part of what I do, so one has to have other kinds of justifications and motivations for much of the freshman comp work. On the one hand, there is the need to keep the language usable and train people to use language carefully and thoughtfully. . . . On the other hand, I have the strong feeling about the need for people to express their own feelings and experiences, and these two very basic concerns often seem to me to be in conflict, at least in terms of the kinds of assignments one gives and the way one responds to them. On the one hand, you want people to learn to manage a clear kind of public discourse and learn to read very critically and judgmentally; and on the other hand, you want to free people to get in touch with their own inner experience. I always feel a real conflict between wanting to encourage autobiographical writing and wanting not to come down on it hard in terms of mechanics because of the fear of inhibiting inexperienced writers, and the opposite: wanting to insist on clarity and logic and wanting it to be as objective and detached as possible. It ties up with the paper-grading business because the papers aimed at the public realm tend to be far worse and far harder to grade and less interesting than those in which kids talk about their own experiences.

I do a lot of advising. I tried to cut down on it some because I think I did much too much of it initially. I was not so much counseling but just simply being there and listening to people who came in. And I realized after a point that probably it was simply using up my time and I wasn't helping people who would come in and sit for an hour. Some students, you realize, have very serious problems and need somebody who can give them help. I can listen and I can certainly make some practical suggestions; if somebody who comes in has a problem with a roommate or rent or something, I can talk about those things. But if somebody's really on the edge of collapse, then I try to suggest they get some professional help. I do a lot of just sitting and listening and talking about things that are not related to school. A lot of the students find it is necessary.

In order to work well they need to make that personal connection with the teacher.

I think that in teaching in a community college a big problem is understanding the differences in the situations of the students that I am teaching and my own situation as a student, and simply figuring out how to reconcile the need for academic standards with the very complicated commitments of the students outside of the college. Students are working twenty or thirty hours a week. Since the education I received was terribly important to me, I have the natural desire to perpetuate it. I am always having to come to terms with the difference between what my students want and where they are and where I was.

Many of our students come here because it is small and they feel they have a chance to get to know the faculty. One of the problems for the students at the community college is the lack of community there. Students drive in and drive out, and this contributes to the high attrition rate. Unless students have friends when they come or join an organization that gives them a kind of center when they are on the campus, or find that their classes are kind of cohesive in a social sense, the college can seem very cold, despite the relative smallness, despite the possibility of being friendly with one's instructors. I always urge my advisees to join a club if they have any interest, but that is difficult for them too because of the working. We have an arrangement whereby classes stop at two every Wednesday, and that is to have our clubs meet but many of the students work in the afternoons.

We have a very wide range of students, certainly students who are better than I ever was as a student, better minds, and I guess I have lost the disdain for very average students that I probably had as a grad student. It becomes intellectually interesting to try to understand where the student who is not very good or not very interested is, and to try to work out ways of reaching that student. There are students who can't do certain kinds of things that I want them to do and that creates a lot of dilemmas. Half the time I say, "Damn it, look, here it is, this is what the degree from the college means: that you have achieved certain specific things, and you achieve them or you don't, and I give you a grade and that indicates it and that is that." I set the level, you meet it or you don't meet it, or you meet it to a certain degree. And the other half [of] the time I think, "Here is this person who can't do this, and it is absurd for him to spend all of his time trying to learn to do it. He can do a whole lot of other things. Help him to do those things. The hell with the standards and grades and the significance of the degree. It is the individual student whose personal growth or fulfillment or whatever is the only thing that is important." So I am constantly torn between the two positions. That conflict is one of the sources of stress and strain in the job, one of the challenges too, I guess.

It becomes a very specific kind of problem in two areas. I think one is the problem of reading level of students that I have mentioned before, which is a very serious dilemma—especially when you are overtrained to teach literature and the students are undertrained to read it. The other area where the dilemma is acute is in trying to understand and clarify in your own mind what is important in English courses for students who are in the vocational programs. This has become a growing problem that I think that we've not dealt with very well, thought enough about. The college has changed from essentially a two-year transfer liberal arts college to essentially a vocational training college. What exactly are we trying to do in composition courses and in literature courses? What are our goals? And again one has always got students in those classes, the students who are going to graduate and manage a McDonald's, and also students who are going to graduate and go to an Ivy League school in the same class, so the problem is really acute. I don't know. I don't know. You can't help but have this feeling of, oh boy, here is this kid going to an Ivy League school and I can really teach him the stuff that I know; he is right there ready to learn it, and you feel qualified to do what you are trying to do. [With] the student who is going to manage McDonald's or be a hospital technician, or whatever, it is much harder for me to know what I know or what skills I have that are important for this student. I do feel that there are certain outlooks, attitudes, perspectives that are important for anybody, but how to get them across is a real dilemma.

I think there are always real superteachers who can teach practically anything to anybody. But I am not one of them. It comes back to the problem of what do you teach and how. I think between these dilemmas and the problem of time and correcting I have always the sense of failing, never doing as much or as well as I can imagine doing, coupled with the sense of succeeding very well at times with particular students and particular courses.

I think that sense of failure is due to the structure. . . . The sense of failure comes always from the feeling that you could do so much more if you had more time, and you would have time if you had fewer students and less paper grading and more time to work with students individually, and that certainly is directly connected with the structure. On the other hand, the problem of very diverse abilities among students in one class would remain even if one had only thirty students, and the conflict of how to set standards and a uniform program and to what extent to provide individual programs would still exist, and most of us have had that situation— through some fluke, [a] low student load or a small class. And that, I think, is a problem that is independent of the structure, unless you want to go back and talk about the whole structure of education in the grade schools and the high schools and the whole thing.

I always think of my Ph.D. dissertation as related to my teaching in the community college because I had been working on a textbook that became the dissertation. So I don't think of it as if I had done it on Spenser or something. I sense now that I am further and further away from the things that I studied in college and graduate school. I think less and less about them and teach them less and less. For many years I taught a British Lit course and I haven't done that for several years now. First I taught the whole course for a few years, and then I taught the first half because we had to take turns, and then I stopped teaching it entirely. Last year I taught the first half of an American Lit course and used a new book and it gave me a chance to read a lot of stuff that I hadn't read before, particularly seventeenth and eighteenth century things that were not imaginative literature but more historical documents, and that was wonderful. I really enjoyed that and had a good class and felt again that I was doing what I had been trained for, and this was very nice. I find I have lost whatever interest that I once had in scholarly journals. Once in a while I will pull out an article relevant to something, some particular book that I was teaching. I guess the challenge of trying to figure out, in terms of literature at least, what

to teach and how remains, and I enjoy that. I am always reading
new things.

Now what I will do in the future I am not sure. I am not
really very interested in revising my book endlessly. Even in between
editions this past fall I did something totally different that I had
never done before in a freshman course, didn't use my own book or
anything. It makes me kind of sad sometimes not to use a lot of the
things that I know; it seems kind of unfortunate. When I get really
frustrated with papers, I start thinking of going into the computer
programming curriculum at the college and taking a two-year
degree in that and getting a job at IBM and working an eight-hour
day.

In the best of all possible worlds, if one could get some stuff
published and then occasionally have a semester off to work on that,
and to teach a creative writing course somewhere, that would be
fun. The only thing that really makes me want to get out and
change is the paper-grading problem.

Profile: Janet Ingersoll

*Janet Ingersoll, a doctoral candidate in her
thirties, taught part-time and full-time for five years at
a California suburban community college.*

I ended up teaching at the community college for five years
altogether. Only one full-time year—the rest of it was part-time
teaching, which amounted almost to a full-time load. The part-time
teachers could teach nine units and a full-time load would be
twelve. So teaching nine hours is just one class short of a full-time
load for considerably less pay. As a part-timer, you are paid on an
hourly basis and you are paid only for the time you are standing
in front of the classroom. The pay for full-timers is quite reasonable; in fact, on the whole it's more than most people get paid who
are teaching at the university. But the pay for part-timers is much
worse. The part-timers weren't even asked to turn in requests of
what they would like to teach. You were simply given what was left.
And then there was even somewhat of a hierarchy there. Those of
us who were around the longest were asked first. You know, here

are the fifteen courses that are left, which ones do you want, and then the people who were hired last were the ones who got what was left, and they took it if they wanted it, and otherwise they didn't.

The first few years I was teaching both at the nearby state college and at the community college, so I would drive back and forth between the two and usually teach five writing classes altogether. It was seventeen hours in the car driving a week. And I had two briefcases—one for the community college and one for the state college. I had to make sure that I grabbed the right one when I ran out the door in the morning.

There is this hierarchy in terms of the teaching load in higher education. The respect that is shown to teachers in a higher education setting increases as you get to a school that offers more degrees. The community college instructors are afforded the least amount of respect in the sense that they are only teaching at a two-year college; the state college teachers are afforded a little bit more respect because they are at four-year colleges. And the university faculty is afforded the most distinction because they offer Ph.D. degrees; it's a research institution, and the students who are there and the faculty who are there are very serious. I think for some community college teachers, when you are thrown on the bottom of that pile and you see yourself on the bottom, and in addition to that you are teaching students who, not because they are mean or malicious, but who really have mixed feelings about school in general, it's very frustrating. The community college instructors have much heavier teaching loads, are expected to be on campus much more often than the other teachers are. . . . The community college instructors get paid more, and it's almost as if they are getting combat pay or something. But I'm not sure that ends up being enough to make you feel totally satisfied.

If you are in the community college, you're tremendously burdened; you are burdened almost as much as a high school teacher is. The college had it worked out so that if you taught composition exclusively and no literature classes, you taught four classes a semester. If you included literature in your load, you had to teach five, so you teach three writing courses and two literature courses. To get students to write well, you have to make a writing assignment at least every week and a half and ideally every week.

And that means you work all weekend and you work in the evenings or, as many of my colleagues have done—and I can't blame them for doing it at all—you cut corners.

The paper grading process: it's important at the beginning of a writing course, and I think I do a pretty conscientious job grading students' papers. It's a little bit discouraging to start out a semester anticipating that you are going to be doing that for four classes and that you are going to get a fat set of a hundred essays and often more than that, that you are going to have to spend all of your weekend and most of the nights for the next week and a half grading. It sets up the kind of situation that you begin at least a little bit to resent the papers, which is not healthy, because then that resentment I think is transferred a little bit to the student too. And at the community college there is a very, very high attrition rate, but there is no way to guess who's going to be dropping out of the classes. So for the first few writing assignments you're going to end up with many more papers to grade than you will have students at the end, and so you spend a lot of time and energy on those papers and then the students just simply disappear.

It is frustrating, it is very frustrating. Probably the most frustrating attrition problem occurs in evening college. At night students often overcommit themselves unintentionally and then get very strung out and have to quit and feel frustrated about that. You feel frustrated about it and there is nothing you can do. Somebody has a kid who gets sick and has been sick for two weeks, and that person has been trying to go to work and take care of the kid and go to school, and it's somebody who's been a particularly promising student usually, who's been doing very well and has been really improving, and you have high hopes for that student being the best student at the end of the semester. And then half way through, this minor tragedy occurs and the student has to drop out. In your evening courses you start out with thirty and end up with seventeen. And it is hard on the students as well because our numbers shrink as the weeks go by, and it is demoralizing to them too. So you are constantly dealing with a classroom whose dynamics are changing just among the students, and you're having to kind of be the buffer for that and fill in and it is hard. It is very hard. . . .

The first remedial class that I taught was made up of students who have never quite made it beyond freshman English in high school, and many of them told me they took the same course over for four years in a row. I went into that first class with high hopes that my class was going to be different from everybody else's. It was going to be Mr. Chips and they were going to make remarkable progress and be very enthusiastic about what they were doing. I spent hours figuring out these innovative ways to teach spelling and vocabulary and sentence structure and to get them to read and be interested in what they were reading. On the whole it was a fairly successful class. One particular day one student raised his hand and said, in the middle of a lesson on something entirely different, "Do we really have to take English after this class?" And I interrupted the lesson and explained, yes, that was the case. Somebody else said, "That's just not fair, that we have to take another English class, it's just not fair." And then a third person said, "Well, you want to know what happened to me?" and then all of a sudden they were telling these stories about what had happened to them and how they had been trapped into this class and how they really didn't want to be there. One guy who had just gotten out of the Marines and was a very angry young man said, "English isn't everything, you know." And I suddenly felt like the school marm who thought there was nothing more important than reading books and writing essays. I finished teaching that class and went back to my office and turned to my office-mate to try to explain to her what had happened and burst into tears. It was such a frustrating experience, and that was an extreme case of what often had a tendency to go on in those remedial classes.

On the other hand, the first eight o'clock class I ever taught was a class that turned out to be full of students who were just lovely. They were very interested in learning how to write better and even ones who were vocational students said that they felt the class had helped an awful lot. At the end of the semester they all got together and bought me a new, shiny, fancy thermos and presented it to me with a big card. That was a nice experience.

I spent the last few semesters at the community college working in the writing center. One of the writing center's main tasks was to reach out to the vocational programs on campus. I worked with a lot of vocational students. They often knew that in order to really get anywhere in the profession [that] they were training themselves to be part of, they had to improve their writing; but they were very scared of going up the hill where the humanities classroom is and actually taking English classes. They march out of the vocational building and up the hill assuming that they are going to fail yet once again. What we did instead was to go down into their territory and to work with them in their territory. The welding instructor was more than willing to say to his students, "If you can write, if you can write up a report, if you can write up a program or a design for a particular welding project, you're going to end up being a supervisor, maybe running your own company; if you can't do that, you are going to get stuck being a welder and it's going to make a crucial difference." Some of them made really quite remarkable improvement, and they were pretty enthusiastic about what they were doing. And that was very gratifying.

The administration has become very interested in machines and all that machines can do and how much cheaper they are in fact than faculty members. They have spent a good deal of money recently flying around the country studying schools that have converted to machine teaching in hopes of being able to convince themselves that it is in fact both cost-effective and student-learning effective. Introductory courses can be put into a machine and students can do a self-paced learning and earn unit credit for doing that.

And I have very strong feelings about that. I don't think it works. I don't think it works both because I have watched my students try to use machines and because I have tried to use them as well, and there is just not the interaction there is in the classroom. And particularly for students such as the ones who end up often at community colleges, who really need someone to sit down with them and say, "This is what you haven't learned, and we are going to try and figure out why you haven't learned it, and I'm here to answer any questions you have," as opposed to a machine that can only answer a few [questions]. The trend seems to be absolutely away from that.

They just spent a great deal of money installing new machines and carpeting in their reading center, in hopes that they could probably get rid of the paraprofessionals they have eventually and make that all machine-controlled. I don't think that's the way to go. And I don't think that's the way to go with writing courses, and there seems to be some push for that to happen with writing. I have seen tapes of sentence structure lessons and things like that which are cute and charming, most of them, and pretty ineffective.

From what I can tell, what it creates then is an administrative stance that seems to say, "We don't appreciate very much what you can do in the classroom; you know, we understand you are doing what a good machine can do. But beyond that, we are not so sure that you are doing anything much better." It's often an attempt on the administration's part, I think, to be cost-efficient; at least that's been my experience. They think that if they can plug a certain number of students into a computer and teach them whatever course it may be, Psych 1 or Typing Skills or whatever, then that's one less faculty member they have to pay salary to and health benefits.

You get a very distinct double message from the administration. On the one hand, you are told that you are to keep up the academic reputation of the community college and to really bear in mind that many of these students are going to transfer to four-year colleges. The classes they took at the community college should be comparable to the classes they would have taken at the four-year college. On the other hand, you are told, "We stay in business having full classes. So there shouldn't be a high attrition rate; keep students in the classroom." Well, one of the most effective ways to keep students in the classroom is not to work them too hard. I never made that choice, but it was a clear choice.

Other gestures are made which frustrate me an awful lot. The parole boards have begun sending convicts, even ex-felons, to the community colleges as their parole. They are to take twelve units, complete them successfully each semester, and that's the condition of their parole. And that places an added frustration on an already complex situation. The implication is that any ex-convict, with no matter what kind of education he or she has had, can certainly make it at a community college. That means they don't think that there is an awful lot going on there intellectually, or at least that seems to be the message.

In addition to that, a lot of the mental health patients are now living in half-way houses in the community. And they are sent to the community colleges as well. And many of them are people who really do not belong in a classroom. They disrupt them, they don't know what they are doing there. They are disoriented. And again the gesture seems to be, well, the community college is a place that will babysit people who can't get along anywhere else in the world. Those are discouraging gestures. I am very much in favor of ex-convicts being rehabilitated, and I think that mental health patients need places to go and things to do and they need to go out into the community much more than they have in the past, but tossing them all toward the community college I don't think is the solution to the problem. And it creates more of a problem.

Each semester it looked as if the next semester there was going to be a full-time opening. And I stayed down there in hopes that that would happen. The first couple of years I taught part-time it was fine; I didn't mind that and I didn't want a full-time position; I was also teaching at State. But then it had gotten to the point where I wanted to be making more money; I wanted a better teaching assignment; I didn't want to teach part-time anymore. I hung around for three years hoping that something would come up, and became increasingly more discouraged. Last year I took the fall semester off down there and only did my graduate studies. [Ingersoll had entered a Ph.D. program in Linguistics.] I finally decided what it was exactly that I wanted to be studying and I was taking some very, very good classes.

[Then] a full-time job came open at the college. And I was really being encouraged to apply. I had been there for four years and had done, I guess, good teaching for four years and it was clear that I was going to be a very, very strong candidate for that job. And I really agonized over it. I spent a month trying to decide really whether I wanted to do that or not.

I was feeling as a young teacher probably a certain amount of creative energy and enthusiasm that I wanted to throw at something and I had to decide which direction I was going to throw it in. I had at the time lots of ideas as to what would make that particular community college a better place and what would make the teaching a lot better, and how the administration and faculty ought to be dealing with each other as opposed to the way they are. And I think the choice came down to: Was I going to use that energy I had to fight a battle with the community college and hope to make some changes for the better? Or was I going to use it at the university, being a graduate student and pursuing a Ph.D.? My final decision was whether I was going to take the job that paid very good money and offered a certain amount of security or whether I was going to risk being a graduate student and living on peanuts for another four years.

I felt like the energy I was using, the reward I was getting for it, no matter what clever angle I figured out, the success rate at the community college would be a little bit greater but not all that much greater. The attrition rate would be the same because it invariably is. I felt like I was beating my head against the wall and running in circles, and it didn't feel that way with the linguistics and anthropology. . . . The practical part of me was fighting with the other part of me. The creative part of me was saying, "What you are really interested in right now is linguistics and anthropology. The teaching you like best is at the university; money is not really that important in the end." But it felt like a risk. It felt like a real big risk, and that practical part of me kept saying, "You are a fool. You know you are a fool. You are in a perfectly good place: why don't you stay there?"

The woman at the university who is my major professor shot up the tenure ladder faster than anybody in the history of the department. At the community college, the older women were very nice, I liked them very much, we had good relations, but they weren't people I necessarily aspired to be. I decided I wouldn't apply. I couldn't bear to tell them that I decided I wasn't going to apply.

I think maybe part of the reason that I was able to do that was being around people for five years who were in fact willing to admit that they weren't particularly satisfied with what they were doing. They were frustrated to a certain extent. They had dreams that expanded beyond teaching in the community college, but they got married and started a family and it was a good solid steady income. Then each year your pay goes up in a kind of impressive way. But the trade-off just didn't seem worth it to me. And I do think that it is true that I would have always wondered whether I would have been able to go on and finish a Ph.D. and get a different kind of teaching job, and that is something I would never have been able to answer if I had stayed. In that sense it is very, very positive, what I did. Sometimes it gives me the jitters, in the sense that I really am facing an unknown, but on the other hand, I think I made the right decision.

Profile: Cynthia Jamison

Cynthia Jamison, in her late thirties, teaches history and psychology in a New York state community college.

After I got my bachelor's, I worked at a large university library, which was a lot of fun but certainly no way to make a living. Then I got married and came here. The college was expanding rather rapidly at that time, and they needed people for teaching, and I came over and, lo and behold, they hired me. They were fascinated: I was the only person who had gone to a real preparatory school and to a fairly high-powered but rather bizarre college. I sort of fell into this job, rather than really coming to it because of design.

I did teach English composition until about three years ago. Although it might in many ways be the most useful course you can have, English composition is certainly not widely appreciated by anybody—students, administration, anybody. It is very hard to do because, of course, you are dealing with people who are just plain not interested. Especially when you start trying to talk about grammar and construction and order of thinking on paper, when people know they are not going to be writing that much; the society is not geared toward it. I don't think we really collectively as a nation give a damn about the excellence of writing.

Then the situation changed quite dramatically. I was given the introductory psychology course, two halves of a larger full-year course. I hadn't done anything with psychology for a long time. Somebody went on a leave of absence and they were short. What they try to do here is round up somebody who is presumably competent to teach something before they try to hire somebody new. They looked around and of all the people available, I was the only one who had enough training in psychology to take this course. I said, "What a wonderful idea," because I was definitely ready for a change.

So I had to retool to some extent for this other course. Because we still are under a system where we have to have what I call communal finals, I hold very closely to the book, and I tend to elaborate quite extensively on the text. I follow it, page by page, and I make that clear to them. The other preparation for it is that I do have to write multiple-choice tests. The multiple-choice test is the method of testing and we can add a short report or a paper or some such thing, but the actual testing is multiple-choice. Those are not easy to write, I have discovered over a period of time. They are difficult. I try to think it through, attempt to think of what would a student do with this question. If I were a student, what would I look at that would make me confuse the issue rather than go directly to the question. And that's not easy to figure out because sometimes they are so desperate for the answer they over-think the question. I don't even think the multiple-choice test is actually that bad. As a matter of fact, they prefer this type. They don't like to write, generally speaking, because this is not what is pressed on them in school very much.

I found it was very difficult to grade them all with a sense of absoluteness. And it was very hard when you are dealing with a bunch of people who have that kind of sliding scale of interest and organization. There are several hard places. One of them is do you grade them so harshly that they give up, which you don't want to do. But you don't want to be too lenient because then they won't try, so you have to hit that middle ground. Then, of course, you have to be more or less in tune with what everybody else is doing because students are not stupid—they are going to figure that out too. So they are going to start saying, "Well, so-and-so does much easier tests or grades easier." So you don't need that hassle, and you could possibly get it from the administration, who might say, "Well, you're out of step with the rest of the department." Because again they want to be able to pass this number of bodies through the institution.

I do point out to my students that a grade is crude; I say it is only an approximation. I also point out a job is always measured on what you see, rather than what's inside. But you never see the full aspect of a person's inner existence from what comes out. I mean in the best sense of the word, everyone has a sort of secret life behind their foreheads, so this is to some extent only an approximation. But neither am I the most lenient grader either. I am receptive to complaints, for example, about questions on this multiple-choice test; I say, "What I've got to do is review the whole question." If it seems ambiguous to them, I will say to them, "Well, let me check out all the tests and if it does seem strange, then maybe it is a bad question," which does happen occasionally and then I give it the heave.

When I first started teaching, I gave a test and the grades were kind of bad and you know sometimes you get some fairly rough joking out of students about it, but usually not too bad. One kid said, "I'm going to burn your house down if I don't get a good grade." And I said, "Now come on." And he said it again later on. So I told him he better can that kind of talk. It was hard to tell whether he is joking or semi-serious. You know, one hopes it was a joke, but nonetheless that kind of thing is unpleasant, although very rare. And they occasionally make some sassy comments which I don't mind; I mean some of them are kind of cute, and you can just say, "Same to you, Buster," or something like that. Sometimes they kind of mean the comments, because I'm sure school irks them a little bit. They have been in it since first grade at least, and they are kind of tired of it. But a real threat like that is not nice. And it has happened only once since in my entire career here. It was the same threat. This kid said, "You know, I want a good mark, or I'm gonna burn your house down." I was p.o.'ed, I was so irritated. I had a headache, I felt like hell, and I said, "This is it, I'm not going to put up with this garbage anymore," and just put a cork in his mouth and he never said it again. He was a sort of a big brash guy and I just buttoned him right up, which I thought was splendid.

I have had another course, a history course, a year-long survey of history from the very beginnings up to the present time. I've taught that when there has been an overflow because what I really wanted to do was history. And I finally inherited the mantle of the medieval history course, which is a tiny, tiny thing because it is an elective. I teach that in the spring. We have never been able to run it, for various reasons, both terms. It may be just plain scheduling, because a lot of these kids take technologies—people in dental hygiene, x-ray technology, criminal justice, and a lot of those have labs, extensive ones. These people have these huge block schedules and anything else is considered a service department. So we have to be, so the theory goes, stuck into the interstices of these people's schedules. The liberal arts department becomes the repository for people who have no idea of what they want to do, which, of course, doesn't make for very lively classes sometimes. . . .

I have had a bunch of interesting students. I remember one kid in the medieval history course. He had a shirt that said "Monty Python Freak" on it. I looked at that and I said, "Well, that bodes well." I mean anybody who likes Monty Python can't be all bad. Anybody who understands that somewhat bizarre humor has to have a brain. At least it is in gear. They all have brains, but some of them have never been put into first, you know. Now some of them take the medieval course because they want to, and then others take it because it is the only elective that fits into their schedule, and they can't stand history.

I don't think relevance is necessarily a big deal. I mean, really, half the fun of doing anything in this life is because it is interesting, not because it is necessarily going to get you a job, bring you money. This Monty Python kid was a good guy. He was a lot of fun, because he came up with all sorts of comments and he loved history; he just got a big kick out of it. The medieval history class in itself allows the people who really have strange interests or who are a little bit offbeat to shine or to open up because there is tremendous latitude for discussion of ideas, whereas this is obviously much less so when you are doing English composition or even, to some extent, psychology.

There are some people who think medieval history and psych are monumentally irrelevant to life. I said, "You can't avoid history; it affects you." I said, "Just the fact that they blew Sadat away recently has probably already bent your existence into an area that you don't know about." This place, although it's technically technological, there is a sense of broadening in the curriculum, and there should be. Like the fact that everyone was cutting out language. I think now they are beginning to realize they better stick it back in.

I don't want to lose that medieval history course, and I will be quite happy to stay in, say, a certain level of psychology in order to keep my mitts on that course. It is all mine and I make up the final and I can do anything that I damn well please in it. I don't want people meddling and telling me what I have to do, so I'm going to fulfill certain requirements that are going to make it look good.

I like psychology. I felt that there was more scope. Also frankly I felt it would be easier in the sense that students might like it better, because when you talk about psychology, you are basically talking about yourself, and everybody is fascinated in one way or another with their own workings, their inner selves. Even if they have low self-esteem, they are still intrigued by it. Sometimes they are very quiet. There are some classes that are absolutely mute. I will occasionally ask them questions. It's basically lecture, which is mostly what people tend to do; then I tend to elaborate on the text. I like to light a bomb under them; I hope to interest them so that they will be fascinated by subjects and have a more wide-ranging mental attitude. Life is hard enough. God, if you lose that, what the hell is there? There is all this crud falling in on you from taxes and people whose personal relationships are going to hell in a hand-basket, and your car's falling apart, and your plumbing doesn't work, and your clothes don't fit and you feel like you are getting sick—I mean you better be interested in reading, or going and looking at a sunset.

Just recently in one class—we happened to be in a room that sits high up so you can see out over the other buildings—I happened to look out the window and saw just astonishingly beautiful formations and I said, "Look at those things, look at the beauty of those clouds," and there was a little bit of snickering. "Gees, you lead one hell of a dull life if you can't notice the clouds," I thought to myself, but I let it pass over 'cause I didn't want to be derailed at that point into a discussion of whether or not you look at your environment and appreciate it occasionally just for, if nothing else, personal amusement and stimulation.

Sometimes I moan and carry on and mumble and look at the tests and watch people not come to class and I think, "What am I doing?" I feel discouraged and I tell them this. I will come in and

I will say, "I feel like I am talking to a wall." After I've said something five times, because there are five classes, I begin to think that I am talking to myself. But there is always enough interest that it seems rewarding. I do say one of the problems in this society is we have minimized the idea of education and curiosity just to the point where it only becomes a tool to wealth or power. So I said, "You've got to develop some kind of internal interest," and I say that's not easy. Then, I point out, one of the problems with aging is that you get tired because after you have lived for forty years or even thirty, things seem to fall short sometimes of expectation, even in terms of that kind of excitement of just waking up.

I really enjoy a lot of these students. I think they have a tremendous amount to offer. A lot of them are extremely fine people. They tend to be quiet, so you don't sense that at first, but when they begin to talk to you, you can sense a tremendous amount of quality. They want to do things well, and they wish to be functioning and contributing. They keep quiet and absorb and just think about things, so more of that kind of questioning goes on than one might suspect. So that is certainly one of the greatest things that keeps me going; it certainly isn't grading tests, that's for sure. The administration has a pretty firm stranglehold on what goes on in this place, and legislatures groove on tests and paperwork and stuff like that. In some respects, actually, there is a good thing to it in that it keeps the students on the straight and narrow. I think unless you are really inclined to study on your own or because you like it, you kind of have to light fires under people.

So many of these students hold jobs, they haven't time for anything other than going to class and doing a little bit of homework. As soon as people are through in their classes they split—boom, they are gone. The apartness that I sense occasionally is that, well, frankly, I think this country is rather anti-intellectual. In the sense that I think most people, and I can even sense it in myself, value knowledge as an end either to power or money or both, rather than something by which they actively engage their minds and keep from croaking off between now and their actual death; you know, keep their minds going.

Profile: Martin Brenner

Martin Brenner is in his forties and teaches
music at a suburban California community college.

Here at the community college now, my typical schedule
involves Choral Music and Vocal Music, Music Appreciation, a
Music Literature class. And also I direct an evening group as well,
a choral group. We are on a fifteen-hour schedule, and this is an
area which is hotly debated in terms of what is considered an
adequate teaching load across the campus.

I teach voice classes. The voice class is pretty classic, in that
it is taught around the country in various colleges. You have a
group of students anywhere from twenty to twenty-five to thirty;
sometimes the class is even larger. Since the days of full-time
equivalency, we sort of get entrapped in letting more students into
the classes than we probably ought to at times, simply because we
are afraid of ending up with classes that are too small. It is not a
choir, it's not music appreciation, it's not a class in sight-singing.
It's work with individual voices. I compare it a lot to a speech class
which has lots of lecture situations, demonstration situations, by
the instructor. But then, you know, everybody gives their speech.
Everybody sings their songs. Teaching a voice class is very frustrating in a community college in many ways because on the one hand,
you have got some students who are capable of learning their own
music. They can go out and take a piece of music and sit down at
the piano and work it out, because they are musicians. But you have
a lot of students who don't have that at all. They don't know a
whole note from a rest, so they don't really have any way of learning
the music on their own. We used to use a regular textbook with
music in it. But they just couldn't learn it.

I had been teaching my voice classes like a product of the
sixties: everyone can do their own thing kind of approach. And that
works for some people fine, but for a lot of people it's not very good,
especially in a discipline like music where you just have to develop
certain skills. So I finally decided, rather than just let them learn
any material that they wanted, to get them into good vocal
technique. I say, "I have this song material that you are going to

be using during the semester. You will pick from these. There are about sixteen or twenty different pieces of music all the way from folk music to classical songs to Italian songs to some German and American folk songs." This has worked out very well. It becomes like a seminar class in which everyone performs for each other. I am the accompanist and they work on their materials. You just never get through it all in a given class period. They make a list on the board; you get ten or twelve students who want to sing in a day and there is no way that you can get through them all especially if you're going to talk about each situation.

I tell them that in order to get an A in the class, they will have to have performed in another language. They can't get an A just doing the folk songs because those are a lot easier to learn. If you want to get an A, you have had to work at a couple of more difficult songs. Grading is very difficult for that class. The administration wants us to write up a sheet and say this is how the grading will be done and by the time I finish explaining all this I have got pages. It is difficult to put that down on a piece of paper.

Music Literature is the basic course in listening, developing skills in listening to music. We have another course which is Music Appreciation, more of a history of music designed for the nontechnical approach, for the nonmusician. The whole approach is for developing the ear from the beginning. In the old days, teachers of music appreciation put a piece of music on and they'd tell a story about it. I try to immerse them in the whole idea of listening. And that is difficult because most college-age students come to music with rock and roll in their background. It makes every other kind of music sort of pale next to it. To sit and listen to Mozart after that is difficult.

The a cappella choir is the typical college choir. The last few years the choirs all over the state have gone down in size in all of the community colleges. Students aren't taking them. The average student-load in community college is under six hours a week. Most of them are working, so there are a lot of things that they are not taking. The community college situation [has] changed in the last few years. We used to be wealthy with students and wealthy with money and those days are gone. Most of our students are not music majors. We have a lot of community people, older students, who

come in. A lot of our students are very gifted musically, but they are
not applying to be music majors. We do have that certain group
that are music majors taking music theory and taking the regular
sequence of courses. They'll transfer on after one or two years to
another college.

Presently all the energy seems to be going into areas of
sciences and computers and math. And I don't think that is enough
to make a well-rounded person. In some ways it is kind of
unfortunate that education has now got to mean totally that when
you graduate from college, you should at that point have a job in
a computer field or whatever it is. You are going to go right to work
because you have been prepared for that job. I'm not sure that is
what education is for. We at the community college have some of
our greatest wealth and success dealing with students who are now
coming back to us who have missed out on all these things because
they have been so busy making a living and learning how to do a
job.

I think it is unfortunate right now that for students at our
community colleges, their average load is less than six hours. It used
to be about twelve, so consequently areas like the arts are suffering
in terms of enrollment. Now when our teachers retire from the
music department or die, they don't replace them. Sometimes you
wonder when you see areas that are much more fertile in terms of
students, like the areas of science and math, computer technology
and those kinds of things, where everybody seems to be gravitating,
and you sort of hold on for dear life in the area of the arts.

Our department head kept coming to me this last year
saying, "What if you have to give up your Music Lit class? And
maybe teach some beginning piano?" I don't want to teach beginning piano. "Or you may have to teach five sections of voice." That
may be a way to go crazy. I'm really not too old to try something
different, if I really set my mind to it. The way things have gone
in the state all over in community colleges, we are being told that
we may have to teach a night class as part of your day load; there
have been a number of members of the college who have been really
upset by that. It's a discussion that goes around all the time at the
college. I think everybody just sort of accepts the fact that it may
be inevitable. You say, "Well, I'm just glad that I have a job."

Sometimes you ask yourself the question, am I really doing anything worthwhile? So you try harder or you feel more frustrated by the fact you don't always seem to get all the best students or as many as you want. And then you sort of yearn for greener pastures. I suppose everybody does that a little bit. You think about how much better it would be at the university. I wonder what would have happened had I taken a couple other turns and got my doctorate, maybe even gone to teach at a university. I think that I am capable of doing that, but it's just not the way the directions went.

The community college is a little bit [of a] different animal, I think, than the state college, because we have a lot of programs that a typical four-year school doesn't deal with. We accept the fact that a lot of our students in the music department are students who are there for two-year programs for jobs—in, for example, dental programs. I think music is more important than sheet metal, and yet I know the instructor who teaches welding. He is a master welder and having come up from a working family, I can respect that kind of a thing very much. But I think of college as being more the kind of thing that I went through. A lot of these programs are very successful, and we know that's part of the community college that we all accepted when we came here.

We're contemplating creating a number of career programs, one in the area of recording. The community college is a perfect place. We've had to rethink in our own minds what music should be at the community college. All of us who teach there have come out of pretty traditional music backgrounds. Some of those areas and aspects of commercial music require skills and preparation which many of us don't have. After all, I came out of a church music background and I am more interested in choral directing. I was never an active practitioner of popular music. A lot of us have had to do a lot of retraining of ourselves. For instance, a few years ago I started a jazz choir at the school. I didn't have the experience in the area of jazz choir, and I was learning with the students at the time. There are many schools in which they have almost given up on all the traditional programs and have gone almost exclusively to the popular idiom, rock and roll and jazz. We are trying to keep a balance. It turns out that some of the most exciting aspects of commercial music are taking place in the community colleges, in the teaching of jazz and in the area of jazz choirs.

I like to write when I get going, but I just never took the time to do it. I'm always busy looking at music or directing a choir. I'm always going to some rehearsal. My wife encouraged me to write. I don't think the community college encourages it enough. Various people do it just because they are committed to it themselves. One thing to me that has always been lacking in lower-division college work is a successful text for voice classes, one that has flexibility, has certain materials that students can use. I have always wanted to do that.

It's almost kind of a byword in community colleges that we haven't been trapped into the publish-or-perish kind of approach to education. There was a period of time when there was a kind of anti-intellectual attitude, and that may have been also in the four-year schools. As if it was better to use all your experiences in your classroom rather than what you have studied. I have always had a feeling that to survive in the music business, even as a teacher of music, you have to prepare yourself, you have to work at your technique, and you have to spend a lot of time to get to that point where you can play well or sing well. I always got that feeling even at this community college that those things weren't that important. They aren't nearly as important as how you feel. But I think it is different now. I think everyone has a more traditional approach. There is much more concern about grades again.

I think it's easy to get trapped, I suppose, in a series of situations out of which you can't get yourself. You have a certain standard of living and you don't want to change that. One of my colleagues has a yearning to find a small four-year college somewhere where he can just kind of finish out his years. He wouldn't even mind taking a pay cut to do that. But I don't think I want to. I'm not sure that I want to leave this area. I wouldn't want to go out to some place in Idaho or a small town in Oregon; it just doesn't appeal to me. I don't really have any illusions about who I am. I'm not the greatest choral director, I'm not the best teacher, I'm sure. And yet if an offer came, I would sure think about it. I know I don't have the best job in the world. But I have a fairly good thing where I can kind of branch out and be creative and feel that I have accomplished something.

Math and Science Faculty: Making Up for Students' Educational Backgrounds

When community colleges promised to democratize American higher education (Medsker, 1960, p. 20), they held out the promise of providing education in, among other areas, mathematics and the sciences to a wide range of students, many of whom had not previously been successful in those subjects. Ironically, the very fact that community colleges exist to give students a "second chance" may contribute indirectly to the complex factors that lead to the lack of previous success some community college students have had in math and science. Knowing that community colleges will admit them no matter how much or what kind of previous success in math or science, some students persuade themselves that there is always the hope that if they must, they will contend with math and science in the community college. They make choices in high school about math and science that seriously affect the paths that they must take later without really understanding the consequences of their choice.

The problem is that math and science, perhaps most of all subjects, are cumulatively organized. Progress in math and science at one level rests on having achieved a solid foundation at earlier levels. The further one goes up the hierarchically arranged math and science curriculum, the firmer the foundation of basic understanding and skills must be. The hope that a shaky and incomplete understanding at introductory levels of math and science can be compensated for by courses in the community college may be illusory for many students who take science and math in the community college. Remedies for problems that most often develop over the course of twelve years of schooling in those subjects are not easily found at the community college in two years.

Faculty in math and science in the study spoke of a willingness to take almost every step possible to compensate for inadequate preparation on the part of their students and to help students fulfill their hopes. Where tension arose, it sometimes centered on the level of expectation and understanding the students had for themselves and for their future in the subject area. The faculty in math and science and in many of the career programs know that a great deal is at stake for the students. They know that in any technologically related career, the scientific underpinning of the technology is crucial if the student is to have a real sense of opportunity in the field. Furthermore, they know that progress in science is to a considerable degree dependent on mathematical skill and understanding. They know that whether a student trains to be a repair person or is educated for a career in engineering depends significantly on the level of mathematics the student has mastered.

At the root of the matter is that in scientific and technological fields, mathematics holds a key to the historic division in western civilization between intellectual and manual labor. The Egyptians used a rope for problems of measurement. Using the rope was a manual skill and it was specific to the place where the measurement arose. The Greeks, however, as Sohn-Rethel has described the development, "invented a new kind of geometric demonstration. Instead of stretching ropes, they drew lines by ruler which remained on the sheet underneath, and together with more straight lines, formed a permanent figure from which could be recognized geometric laws. The combination of lines were tied to no particular location, and their size was infinitely variable. The geometry of the measurement thus became something quite different from the measurement itself. The manual operation became subordinated to an act of pure thought. . . . An essential point regarding the 'pure mathematics' of the Greeks is that it grew to be

the unbridgeable dividing line between mental and manual labor"
(1978, pp. 101-103).

The profiles of mathematics and science faculty that follow
highlight the possibilities, complexities, and tensions in their work
as they attempt to provide the basis for their students to move across
the divide between manual and intellectual labor. Their words offer
administrators and faculty leaders insight into particular
difficulties of math and science faculty and into those they share
with other faculty in the community college.

Profile: Jesus Lopez

*Jesus Lopez, in his late thirties, teaches
chemistry in a California community college.*

The teaching pace here is very hectic, it's very demanding. I
know from talking with other people at other schools that they're
sometimes amazed at all the things that I'm expected to do during
the course of a day. They're sometimes amazed at the teaching
load—it's very high-paced, very frantic. I don't as a rule notice it
much, because I do have a keen interest in teaching and that seems
to absorb a lot of the wear and tear that I might perhaps accumulate.

As much as possible after class, depending on whether or not
I have a break, I'll usually just come up to my office to do some
work. The physical setup of the school, with the study areas in the
center and offices around the periphery [and] the glass doors,
precludes anyone hiding. Normally what happens is I'll go to my
office and do some work, but students will see that I'm in my office
and will come in, and I will spend usually a great portion of the
time talking with students, handling questions whether they be in
my course or someone else's course. We sort of have a "teacher's fair
game" policy around here. So even if they're not in my class, they'll
wander in and ask me a question concerning another one of their
chemistry courses. So I spend a great deal of time doing that, and
I squeeze in the basic work that I can in terms of grading papers,
recording scores and that sort of task in between students. To keep
my sanity, I occasionally flee to the cafeteria for a cup of coffee and
stay there til a student finds me and we come back to my office.
They're pretty persistent once they realize that you're willing to
spend time with them. I try to make that a commitment. I tell them,

as far as I'm concerned, when I'm at school my job is to interact
with them, to convey any explanations or knowledge that they may
want to pursue. They take me at my word. Peppered in between,
there may be various committee meetings. Lately the meetings have
been more frequent than I would like them to be. I have a bad habit
of not saying "No," so as a result I end up being on many
committees.

I'd served for about three years as the Mexican students'
advisor. They have dances, fund-raising events, bake sales, and
things of that nature. We as faculty will participate in terms of
helping with the planning and logistics, and helping them understand the mechanisms of the institution and how to get their events
planned, so that they know that if they want to put on a dance,
they've got to plug into the maintenance system, get the event
approved by the board, and so forth. We also help with the events
themselves. I guess we try to serve as role models and encouragement for Mexican students. We also advise in terms of political
issues. We encourage them to become aware of these things and
pursue them, and not wait until they come to a crisis situation.
We'll work in terms of making them aware, making sure they're
aware of the various programs that schools offer, be it a scholarship,
financial assistance, job opportunities, whatever. I don't know, I
guess maybe it's a big brother, big sister role that we play. It can
be very time-consuming and can be a major factor in your life if you
allow it to be. I find that what usually happens is that we'll burn
out after two or three years of being very, very actively involved with
the students, and then take a sort of backseat for a while, still active
but not as active. Someone else would then take on that primary
role. I'm sort of in that position now.

If people aren't careful they can burn out here very quickly—
literally burn out as a teacher. I've come to the realization after six
years that the sort of pace that I started with, after two years I knew
I couldn't sustain. That's why I said that I was trying to withdraw
a little bit. I've done that because I feel that there's enough work to
do just to be an instructor here, because of the high interaction
that is expected of you, in terms of student interaction. If you're also
doing the semi-administrative, peripheral tasks, that can lead to
wearing you out in a big hurry.

I don't have as much interaction with other instructors as I would like to. If one could sit down and talk about what's happening in our area, what's happening in their area, curriculum matters, maybe two to three times a week—it would really be great if you could do that. I find that more often than not, I'm lucky if I really sit down and have a talk with someone once a week, but the interactions I have are very positive.

When I first started teaching and people dropped, I tended to personalize the students that dropped in terms of well, maybe I'm not really doing as good a job as I think I'm doing. As I got over that first year and began to have more interaction with not just students in my class but students in other courses, and hearing why they had dropped a course, it turns out that the picture that begins to emerge is that students drop their courses not because of the teaching, in many cases, but because of circumstances outside of the classroom. Their life schedules would change or their work schedules would change. Pressures from the outside kind of bear [down] on them, which they didn't visualize when they first started. Other students simply drop because they all of a sudden realize that they've too many courses, and they have to make a choice, and your course is the one that they've deemed to be expendable. I think after that first year I stopped taking their dropping as a criticism of my course. Now I deal with it in terms of what can I do to help the situation. Some kids are literally forced to drop my course. Can I make some adjustments that would be accommodating enough so that it will fit your needs, but not to the point where it compromises the course?

I think one of the key frustrations that I have is when you have students in your course you know have potential but they don't have the motivation. I see, for whatever reasons, a lack of motivation, a lack of concern or interest in what they're doing. They're completely happy to do as little work as possible—just barely get through. I guess it really bothers me to see people not utilizing their potential. They sometimes will come in and have a discussion in terms of "You know, there's a lot of work to your course and I'm not doing very well. I don't think that there ought to be this much work for your course. I think that you ought to ease up on it; too much work involved in it, too many assignments, things to do."

I explain to them that they have to realize that the course they're taking, especially if it's a college chemistry course, this is a course that's going to transfer to a four-year institution. It ought to be at that level, and my course is no more rigorous than I feel it would be at a four-year school. I think that's my responsibility to you. They don't always agree with that rationale. They feel it's a community college; one ought to perhaps compromise the rigor of your course because it's a community college. So I guess I get frustrated and sometimes offended by that because I'm expected not to have so rigorous a course or not be as demanding. Some students have come in and said, "You know, if I wanted to do this much work, I would have gone to the university" or "I would have gone to some four-year school—I wouldn't have come here." And I say, "Well, I don't know what your conceptions were of what a community college was, but it's essentially a college. That's the first two years of your undergraduate work. Academically there should not be any difference. We are expected to be, at least in terms of conceptual and academic rigor, on a par with the university, especially in transfer courses." That sort of frustrates me at times because I guess they expect the compromise. That bothers my inner sense of the way things ought to be, what people ought to expect from a community college. Most other things I can usually just pass off right after they occur. It's not a lasting thing. That one particular thing does, I think, provide a source of frustration.

Usually students will either walk away thinking the course is not worth their time and effort, and will at a later point come back to me and tell me they're not willing to work, and drop. Which I guess is always their option. Other times they're able to see that I am not purposefully trying to work them to death and that if they're successful in my course, then they certainly ought to be successful in any other courses at any other place. We normally have one of two outcomes: the student will walk away pretty much satisfied that he's not being overly worked; or he'll walk away with the idea that, well, if this is the work that I have to do to take a chemistry course, then I guess I'm not going to take any chemistry courses here or any other place. They'll come back and tell me they're not going to take "your course." "I thought I wanted to go into the field, but if I have to go through these courses to get to it, it's not worth my time and effort at this point in my life. I'm going to try something else."

I try to talk with the student and have them realize that the decision ought not to be made as a result of some frustration. I try to point out to them that you might have to suffer through my course, if that's the way they want to look at it, but the payoff is that you'll be able to go out into a field that you're interested in, you enjoy working in, hopefully, and that you're going to be doing that for thirty to thirty-five years. I try to get them to look at things in bigger scope. I don't get involved in it personally one way or another because I feel that that's their decision to make. All I can do is try to point out different factors.

As I talk with students, the picture I get of high school education is one in which they never had been asked to really extend themselves. They're not used to being challenged and asked to do things. They're used to sliding by, with a minimum of work and still being granted a grade. They feel that if they show up to class every day, that guarantees them, if nothing else, a C. If they turn in a homework assignment too, that should be a B. If they do anywhere close to respectably on any one exam, that's an A. And they're very surprised when I tell them that's not the way it works, not the way it ought to work. I say, "If you get an A in my course, I feel the responsibility that if you go to another school someone can talk to you and get the impression that yes, indeed, you are an A student; you do have good enough mastery of the subject matter so that they're not surprised when you tell them you got an A in my course. If you go to someplace else and someone talks to you and they begin to wonder if you ever had a chemistry course, and then you tell them you got an A in my course, I don't think I could tolerate that. That tells me I'm not giving you enough chemistry in the course. I'm giving you something else under the guise of chemistry. That's a disservice to you. I guess it's a disservice to people who are going to be involved with you in another institution where you transfer."

You get people that are high school graduates and you just simply have to tell them, you know, your problem isn't that you can't understand chemistry; your problem is that you can't do math, your problem is that you can't read. For all I know, you're potentially the next great chemist, but your problems are not an inability to understand chemistry. Your problems are much more basic than that. Your problem is that you just cannot read. If you can't read a chemistry text, you're not going to learn the subject matter. I tell them because I don't want them to feel that it's chemistry per se that is their problem. I would like them to be aware of the fact that they have a much more fundamental problem that's going to affect every class they take, not just chemistry. The lack of success in school isn't tied to any particular subject matter but rather their inability to do one of the very basic tasks in education and that's reading, comprehending what one reads. The fact that we're in the sciences—the area itself does a lot of self-screening. People are very reluctant, if they feel shaky at all, to enroll in a science course. I don't see as high a percentage or as many students that can't read or do math as, say, someone in the liberal arts area. You know, when I talk to other instructors, they say, "Gee, you can't believe it, I've got half my class sitting there and they just literally cannot read."

As I said, I think for me school has always been a setting where I have enjoyed success. I have derived a great deal of pleasure from just being involved in the process. I guess I just see this as an extension of that history. I can observe students going through that process. I think [that] about the second year of college, I became very interested in how people internalize knowledge—how do you finally come to the point where it stops being something that's just written or something that's just verbalized but something that's literally a part of you. That process became very interesting to me. It gives me satisfaction and enjoyment, seeing students reach that point. I think it's just some very basic emotion within me that is fulfilled by seeing that one moment that comes to you when you find that you do gain insight. I look at students as I'm explaining things to them. I think that the payoff for me is that one instant of time when you can see their expression change and their eyes change from a bewildered look to a very sort of enlivened look, and all of a sudden they look at you and in their look they are saying, "That's so easy! Why didn't I understand that before? Why did it take me so long?'' That one moment in time that I now share with students is immensely satisfying to me and keeps me coming back.

Profile: Eugene Bowen

Eugene Bowen, in his forties, teaches mathematics at a Massachusetts suburban community college.

The community college is like working in three worlds simultaneously, the world of the student, the world of faculty and colleagues, and the world of the administration; and the three are so different. You have people in your classes who are older than your father, people in your classes who are seventeen and very immature emotionally, and everything in between. You have people who carry such emotional baggage with them that it is very hard for them to do a simple thing like ask a question. The nub of the student world is really trying to find where the students are in their mathematical ability, and to find effective ways to teach that and get sufficient feedback so that you are in a true kind of emotional dialogue for the semester.

A lot of students have picked up a mental block that says, "Last week I didn't understand so I will never catch up." So I try to encourage them that they can catch up, and let them try one or two problems while I am in the office and see if there is any success, and if they don't, continue some form of dialogue until they do have some success. If a person asks for special favors, I try and give him the benefit of the doubt. Sometimes I have gotten stung. Kids will say, "I will be out of school for the next two weeks and I want all the lessons in advance. Can I make up the test?" I do it and then I discover the whole thing was a fabricated story. Some student says, "I can't possibly meet you until three o'clock," and I make a point of saying, "Yes, but if for some reason you can't make it, please call the office and let me know." And I check and there has been no call and I drive all the way back, sit down with my books and get my notes out and think of what the student's questions might be and wait there for a half hour, and he never shows up. The next day he says something like "I forgot," or "Gee, I was busy and couldn't get around to it." Most of the time the kids will come, but 30 percent of the time they don't and you get hurt.

A lot of times kids have been taught in high school, by unfortunately whoever taught them, that it was disrespectful to ever ask a teacher to explain a problem on the board that you can't understand. Some of them have been told the first day of class, "If you kids sit there and shut up, and don't bug anybody, you will get a C." About one-third of the students never had any algebra in high school. The whole idea of using a letter to represent anything is a total mystery. About the other two-thirds have had high school algebra and have failed it or it has been a long time and they have forgotten it. They look at the board, their faces wide open, and say, "What in the world are you doing?" I know how they feel and I stop the class and say, "Listen, some of you people are going to feel lost for the next two periods because you never had this before. The course is still designed for you. I will answer all your questions, and we will not go too fast for you, and you will not get lost, and I know how you feel." It usually helps.

I am a very, very energetic teacher. I come into class and ask if they have any questions about the homework and usually about a third of the period ends up being utilized in that way. I will work through some of the problems on the board. I never sit in class. I am almost always putting problems on the board. I am usually covered with chalk dust at the end of the period. I go through a couple of pieces of chalk every period. My classes are between thirty and thirty-five. Some of us get stuck with a little fuller sections. I don't like them bigger than thirty-five, but it doesn't make an awful lot of difference.

In the community college, every year there is less and less faculty involvement in the total daily operation of the college. When I first came here, there were about the same number of full-time teaching faculty as we have now, maybe five more. We had two counselors for the whole school, two librarians for the whole school, maybe four deans, one president, eight secretaries, and that was it. The faculty did everything. We counseled the students, we did this and did that, we were just involved in the whole mesh of things. It is easier to have that holistic view of the college if you are dealing with financial aid problems of students, if you are counseling students.

Now there is a structure. We have nine full-time counselors, we have librarians and I don't know how many deans there are in total—probably seven or eight; every dean has an assistant dean. Some of the deans have two assistant deans and an associate dean. All the directors have an assistant director—director of financial aid, associate director of financial aid, director of student affairs. Everybody has just compiled other job descriptions. There is far more structure now so what started to be a college of one hundred and five teachers, and eighteen staff, and a president and four deans is now a president and fifteen deans over one hundred staff members of the college. So that the staff has actually reached the point where, exclusive of the secretaries, the staff for the college is as large as the teaching faculty, and it [the college] has compartmentalized and pigeonholed job descriptions a lot more, and has made it harder to function as a team.

I guess I felt a personal responsibility to step in and be the department chairman. Beyond that, it certainly has something to do with my career plans. I am just completing a doctorate. If I should go on to some other level at a four-year college or administration or something else, I felt I needed the administrative kind of experience. Part of it is practical; I find it extremely difficult to live on the salary that they pay me. I feel that one of the options open to me is to move up in administration. I keep thinking through in my mind what I really enjoy doing. I enjoy teaching very much; I don't enjoy administrating too much. People tell me I am successful and I receive that feedback verbally from them. Internally I don't think that is a complete message. Maybe I am doing a surface job of being successful, but I am not too happy with myself.

Maybe that is just because I can't live with the high amounts of frustration that administration involves and the problems that can't be resolved. I guess maybe the problem is this: In my world of teaching, there are very, very few unresolved problems. No matter how screwed up they are—the learning problems—no matter how many students get jammed in your class, no matter how terrible the textbook is, I am able to turn that situation around and make a success and know that I have communicated with the students, look[ed] at their final exams, and [I] get letters back the next semester saying you are a fantastic teacher. And there are very few

things that I now experience in teaching where I ever feel a real
failure or an internal problem that I can't resolve. If the kid is absent
for two months or in the hospital, I know how to set up makeup
tests for him. I know how to tutor him; I know how to get him back
to where he needs to be mathematically. So I live with a lot of
successes in teaching and that is encouraging.

A lot of times in the administration there is a no-win
situation. You are forced to do something that is wrong or not fair
or inequitable or not in the best interest of the student, but it has
to be done because some administrator or some legislator has said
that it has to be done that way. I find it hard to live with. If I am
ever going to be an administrator as a permanent career, I am going
to have to learn to divorce part of my caring. It is a tough world
and some of these things can't be clearly resolved, as hard as you
try to be clear and satisfy everybody. In administration, sometimes
you can't and you have to find the best approximation in the
situation and not live with such idealistic views.

I intend to finish my doctorate, to keep my eyes and ears open
for other opportunities. I perceive that for me the next step of
moving upward to administration would be, if I ever did, an
assistant dean of faculty at some other community college somewhere. My dream would be to be in an area of curriculum
development and faculty professional development and that kind of
thing. I do enjoy taking a challenge and bringing order out of
chaos. I do enjoy accomplishing a mission. I do enjoy helping
somebody and knowing that the program worked out well. So that
kind of a motive is there too.

Two forces are very real in my life that make me strive to have
a meaning at my job. One is the force that, I guess, you call a social
prestige type of force that says: "Oh, you only teach at a community
college. You are about to get a doctorate; what are you doing here?
Is that all the level of math course you get? You only have kids up
to Calculus 2 for a semester? You ought to be teaching at a four-
year college." And that is perhaps a more significant force of my life
because of the track of my education through Harvard graduate
school and having a lot of colleagues that teach university and in
four-year schools and have a doctorate. They have an attitude of
discussing the community college as "down there," that it is trying

to help the underprivileged students and having watered down academic standards. That force was very clearly explicated one time when I had a friend from a local four-year school visit me for the day. He is also in math, and we returned to campus and at the end of the day he said, "Boy, you have really got to be committed to teaching to teach in a place like this." He was serious and that was his gut reaction. I catch that a lot from people.

So those forces really impact on me, and they really cause me to dig deeply as to why I am here. Is it really worth it, is this really the best place that I could be? The status system that says you are this quality person if you are in this kind of job, and if you are a university professor, you are in a different elite status plane. I don't become a better person if all of a sudden I resign here and become head of the math department at a university. I know that deep down, at least I know it intellectually. To honestly live that is sometimes a little tough. You have to think that through.

We moved from one neighborhood to another in the same town three years ago. Picked up a whole new set of friends. We moved to kind of a nicer neighborhood. A lot of them are rather well-off financially. Where we were before, when we got our first house, we were poorer than we are now, and we could only afford a modest home in a less desirable part of the city where the lot sizes were small, where there were a lot of blue-collar people. There were very few professional people on the street. The high school dropout who works as a full-time painter for a living will think that the community college teacher is pretty great. So I didn't get so much negative input from the neighbors then about my job in that environment. Where I am now most of the people are either college professors or they are the director of data processing, or editor of this, or the machine supervisor at some big company. Some of the comments that they make give me the impression that they think that the community college teachers are beneath them. They don't treat me as being beneath them. I don't feel personally treated that way, but sort of the way they discuss my job gives me the impression that they have that perception of my job. In retrospect, I didn't really realize that there was an absence of negative input about my job where I was before. I think a lot of people say that community college is wonderful and it is a wonderful job that you are doing, on the surface, but then they say little things with subtle hints and things come out that give you a deep-seated impression that they think your job is not really that great. My belief is that if I could physically take them through one day of my teaching experience, let them see every thing that I do, that it would totally erase, I think, their perception.

There are some limitations with this building. I will feel better about my teaching and I will be more looked up to if we get a nice campus. For several years I ran with the idea that hey, it does not matter what environment you are in. It really isn't important. You can make any grubby place into a learning experience. Now I honestly feel that a whole lot of learning that we want to happen here doesn't happen because we don't have a new campus. There is nothing magical about a new campus, but I think that a new campus would be an exciting tool that says to the student that learning is important, look at the environment we have created to facilitate it. And I know that some of the kids from the city want nothing more than to break away from their world because they live in the city, they work in town, and they walk up the street to this building and it doesn't seem very different. It is not too much of a place to study, and they go home as soon as they are finished. I have really come full circle to thinking that the most important thing that we can do in the future is build a new campus. It is really no longer for me: I think the kids need it.

Profile: Murray Green

Murray Green, in his thirties, taught mathematics at an urban community college in Massachusetts until recently.

My work here is vastly different today than it was three years ago, which was vastly different than it was six years ago. I come here most recently with probably less idealism and less patience than three years ago and certainly less than six years ago. Part of it has to do with the fact that I have been doing the same things for seven years. I like the students, I think, more than I did before. I get along with them really well, most of them anyway. The students are a lot better than when I first started here, so it is a more interesting job teaching. A lot of what I feel about working here is just plain frustration. It is sort of a personal frustration, and it is sort of an institutional frustration. The personal frustration, I think, is just because I have been doing the same damn thing for so long, and the institutional frustration arises from the fact that none of us here had any idea that any of this was going to be continuing. The school has been in a sense living on borrowed time ever since it opened. All kinds of major decisions regarding the school have been postponed. I can look back at the last six or seven years and say, "We have done a good job," and at the same time really having grave feelings about the future.

At the beginning it was a case of idealism: let us get this place off the ground, let us work like hell. Let us do everything that we can to keep it going. A lot of that enthusiasm has faded, at least in my case. I mean, I do my job here mainly in a teaching capacity. Quite frankly, the only joy I derive from this job, at this point, is walking into a classroom and talking to students, or seeing students in my office and explaining the subject material. What is still really good for me is teaching, talking to students. Everytime I go into the course, I know exactly what I am going to say. I know the examples I am going to use and probably over the years my teaching has gotten better and better. I think that if I started to actually dislike the classroom process, I would leave, almost immediately.

Most of the kinds of things I teach, except for the statistics course, are really sort of mechanical manipulative type of skills. I suspect that the majority of what we do is teach people technical skills at this point, how to manipulate an equation, how to solve an equation that is already there, how to draw a graph, how to remove a parenthesis, how to take a derivative. Something like that in preparation, not to be a mathematician, but in preparation to look at a formula in an economics book and be able to look at a graph and be able to read it. Quite frankly, when you have college quote freshmen unquote who come in absolutely unable to do the basic arithmetic computation, let alone algebraic computation, and who want in the space of two or maybe three years to get out of here with an associate degree, able to transfer to a four-year school, we do not have the luxury to sit around and talk about examples. We have only time to give an incredible crash course of twelve years of public education. So what we have to do is take things that normally people have an incredible amount of time to do and just cut them down to the absolute bare bones.

I encourage a lot of class discussion. I give them a problem to do and I say, "Talk to your neighbor about how to do the problem. If you don't know how to do it, ask questions. Let's just not get all heavy about what we are doing here." Let's face it, how many times have these students been told how to multiply fractions? And they still don't know. How many times have they been taught how to deal with a percent? And they still don't know. Obviously, there has to be some sort of different approach to this kind of education, this time around. Because if this is the tenth time you are going to learn it, this is the place of last resort. If you don't learn it here, there is no other place that is going to deal with you. Let's face it, you have already been through high school. You have already been through all kinds of community tutoring programs. You have already tried it at the state college, and it didn't work out. Well, let's do something different. Let us help each other. I am not just your teacher. I am somebody who is really trying to help you learn this. And if there are thirty people in this class and I give thirty A's, I am absolutely delighted.

So I try to make it very clear from the beginning that we are all going to work together, that we are not going to have this gigantic division—teacher versus student. It is going to be teacher and students. I have developed an intuition about students. I have developed an intuition about what that look on somebody's face in the middle of a sentence looks like and can stop and start the sentence again, in a different way. I have developed an intuition [about] where problems are going to arise and therefore spend two weeks on that instead of two days. I am just a lot more sensitive to intellectual problems, academic problems, personal problems, ego problems, health problems, but can also put them into better perspective. You know, Is this something that I should be sympathetic toward? Whenever you are dealing with a student in trouble, what you are going to do is always sort of a judgment call. I think that what has evolved is that the judgment has gotten better, the sensitivity has gotten more precise, and the intuition has just sort of started and been developed.

When I first came here, I was sort of aware that I was this color and they were that color. Coming out of all of the upheavals and guilt of the sixties, you know, I had all of the standard white liberal bull. Over the years, I mean it sounds like a cliche, but I really didn't notice which ones were white and which ones were black and which ones were Spanish. Certainly I have been up against all kinds of cultural disparities, in terms of [for example] it took me a while to realize that half of the women here had kids, and what that meant in terms of performing well academically. It took me a while to be able to sort of understand that a lot of the men were working at one or sometimes at one and a half or two jobs, and what that meant in terms of classroom attention, in showing up, in terms of being able to do any studying.

At the university where I was a TA, what interfered with academic processes were: "I couldn't come to class because I was up taking drugs all last night and just couldn't get up for it; I couldn't come because we drove to New York and stayed out." That kind of thing was interfering with academic processes. Here, you know, it was "I couldn't come to school, my husband died." "Couldn't come to school, my baby is in the hospital." "Couldn't come to school, they wouldn't let me off work." "I couldn't come to school, I was in the hospital with a heart infection." We are talking about just horrible things. It was a horrible shock for me. It is a whole lot different when you are going to college and your parents are sending you there. That is a whole lot different than "I couldn't come to school yesterday, my baby died, the ambulance wouldn't come, my house burned down, the fireman wouldn't come." So that was a shock. Something of that magnitude is not constant, but the kinds of things that happen in this community are just incredible, and the kind of suffering really that a lot of people have to put up with is just overwhelming. I am not quite as shocked about it anymore, and when somebody says so-and-so happened, I say, "OK, are you OK now? And can I catch you up? Do you want me to send you to the tutoring center?" You don't have to go beyond the fact that something horrible happened, and [you] deal with it on an academic level: "Do you want to drop the course? Do you want to take a week off? What can I do?"

One talks about going to class, and you are going to do this and that, and people finally learn something, but there is always a sort of nagging in the back of your mind that this person is going to get out of here, and what in the hell are they going to do? You know, some of our students do very well; some of my former students are making more money than I am, and they are doing all right. For a lot of them, though, you know they are going to struggle through here, and they are going to spend three years and they are not going anywhere; they are just not going anywhere.

I find it interesting because I find the people I teach interesting. If we are talking about an intellectual challenge, forget it. It is not here. We are talking about a teaching-method challenge, an approach challenge, personality challenge, a patience challenge, an ingenuity challenge. In terms of being intellectually stimulated, in terms of in seven years anybody asking the question I didn't know the answer to, no. In terms of learning anything new about my field, no. In terms of ever having a challenging conversation about any of the things that have gone on, no. I mean let's face it, I did an awful lot of mathematics at some point, and I knew an awful lot of mathematics. I probably have forgotten 90 percent of it. I was moving a year ago and came across my thesis, and I couldn't read it. You know, I don't get out of sophomore mathematics here.

The fact is that this job is in a certain sense limiting. At this point I am looking at something else. If I had been in a four-year school, it is a possibility that I could have continued in my research and I could have been teaching more challenging courses. The challenge here is of a different nature. I could now be a very happy associate professor with tenure at Amherst, Dartmouth, those schools. It is really hard to tell. I sort of came out of graduate school knowing that I wanted to teach. It just turns out when I got the job here, it was the job that sort of turned me into, you know, 100 percent teacher. You can do research if you want to, but the college doesn't give a damn. If I had gone someplace else, it would have been a different thrust. I also might not have liked it. I might have said, "I don't want to do this research thing. I just want to teach."

Or I could have gotten to it and done a whole lot of research, and for all I know, I could have been sick of that and be at exactly the same place.

You know, I am not preparing anybody to go to graduate school. I am not for the most part dealing with people who are going to be scientists or mathematicians, engineers. Who am I dealing with? I am dealing with a whole lot of people who have got to take six credits a semester or they are not going to get out of here. I am dealing with a whole lot of people who want to be history majors, sociology majors, psychology majors, and the program says they have got to take some statistics. I am dealing with a whole lot of people who want to go into business, who want to go into economics, who want to go into accounting, management, and the business department says, "Look, you have got to get all of this algebra and you have got to take calculus." What I talk about is not an end of itself. They sort of have to pass by my classroom to get someplace else.

Social Science Faculty:
Teaching Material
That Merges Theory
with Students' Lives

Among the tensions inherent in the work of community college social science faculty is the fact that their students' lives are reflections of the social inequities that the social sciences explore. On the whole, when compared to students in four-year colleges and universities, community college students are less wealthy, more likely to be a member of a minority group, more likely to be part-time students (Breneman and Nelson, 1981, p. 23). Furthermore, the faculty teach their students in a setting in which the emphasis is increasingly on vocational training and career education rather than on liberal arts education. For a student who may be attending the college for the short-term goal of acquiring a job, it is complicated to be faced by faculty who ask them to consider long-run social issues, especially when their own lives may be reflections of those issues. Attempts to raise consciousness about social issues in such a setting can be met at times with passivity or occasional sparks of anger, or at other times with genuine intellectual interest.

In the profiles that follow, the social science faculty are sensitive to the social context of their students' lives. The faculty see the problems they face in their teaching more in the system in which they work than in the lives of their students. These profiles reveal the frustration some of the faculty feel with that part of the community college movement's endorsement of vocationalism that they see as shortsighted and perhaps exploitive. They grapple with the implications of the tremendous growth of their colleges for the quality of what goes on within the colleges. They talk of increasing bureaucratization and of the increasing distance between those who fund, set policy, and administer the colleges and those who teach in them. They describe their diminishing ability to do their work the way they know it should be done, along with a continuing commitment to their work as they see it. In short, the faculty in this chapter, as in the other chapters, argue for the dignity of their students and of their work as college teachers.

Profile: Lawrence Bauer

Lawrence Bauer is in his fifties. He teaches sociology at a community college in a small city in New York state.

By 1966 I definitely knew that I was going to leave the parish ministry. I began going back to graduate school. I matriculated at New York University in 1967 because I wanted to go into college teaching. I really had the feeling that the church was not the place where I could express the kind of social concern I really felt. I started part-time teaching here as an adjunct at the time. I started here in January of 1972 full-time.

The Social Problems course that I teach is the largest required course in the college. It's required of every student who comes to the college for every program. We all try to follow the same syllabus so that the students get as much the same course as they can from whoever teaches the course. I am really excited by the course because it gets into the kinds of issues that I've been accustomed to being involved in over my whole life. I can bring so much of my own personal experience to these issues that I really never get tired of the course.

I also teach at a maximum security prison and at a minimum security prison. The one is a fortress-like structure fifty feet high, of solid concrete ten feet thick. No one has ever escaped from it. It has eleven rows of iron bars you have to go through to get inside to the school. The guards go through everything—your briefcase, your lecture notes. Every time I go in—I've gone in there for ten years and they know me by face—every time I go in there, they go through the same thing. The college, you see, cannot require you to teach in the prison; you have to volunteer to do it. The college, as a matter of fact, pays what it calls hazard pay for going into the prisons because of the risk factor of going in there. It's about a $700 to $800 a year difference.

I was teaching a class there one day when [across the state] Attica occurred. I remember I had taken in a cassette recorder and I was playing a tape, and right in the middle of the class, storm troopers came into the room with helmets and masks over their faces, and shields that looked like what gladiators carried in ancient times, and machine guns, and one man put a machine gun in my back and said, "Put your hands up." The other guards grabbed my notes, my recorder, my equipment, everything—just dumped them on a tray and said, "Don't say a word. We are going to get you out of here, and if you stop you are dead." The word had gotten through the grapevine in the prison system just unbelievably fast that there was going to be a riot. I held my hands up and went straight out of the prison.

You go into a prison to teach a marriage course or a social problem course to the very people who are supposedly the social problem and their feeling toward you is, "Don't come in here to try to change my behavior." They resent anything of that sort; they don't want anything in terms of indoctrination. Forty percent of the inmates are men who would be classified as sociopathic. They have no reason not to do anything to you because they are in there on, in some cases, triple and quadruple life sentences, which means that they will never get out. [When] I go in, the men are usually coming from the cafeteria, either from breakfast or lunch, because our classes start at eight o'clock and at twelve-fifteen. I have a nice, good feeling about the men. They are 90 percent black or Hispanic, most of them are right out of Harlem and the Bronx. Most of them are what I call kids, between eighteen and twenty-five, and there are a few older men, but most of them are young, black, and Hispanic kids. They size you up very quickly. They know and they trust me.

It is culture shock when I come back here from the prison. There are many times I will teach a class at the prison the same day on the same subject and I can't get a word in edgewise with the students at the prison, and I will come back to the college with the same presentation and they will sit there and look at me and I can't get a discussion started for anything. They can't relate to it or get involved in it or identify with it in any way. It is just two different worlds altogether. In some sense the prison work represents the real world more than what I see here. These guys are more informed on current events and current social issues; they are more interested in them than the community college student here who is taking a course because it's a requirement. They are a captive audience and you have to, you know, really provoke them to get them into a discussion, which I sometimes deliberately do. But I don't have to do that in the prison. On the other hand, I am exhausted when I finish [prison] class because they are just loaded with questions and they want to know everything: "Go on" and "Explain what you mean" and "Say more." It reduces their time in prison by going to the college. They go five days a week, they study all night, and all weekend. And so there is high motivation among them.

I think the community college, in the time that I have observed it, has become a college for a lot of people who see it as a training institution rather than an academic institution—being tooled up to do something—and that disappoints me. So they come into the liberal arts courses with a built-in resentment. I see that in my classes. Except for the Marriage and Family course, most people don't see the connection between why they have to take this course and why they are at the community college. That deeply disturbs me. That's not preparing anybody to live in the real world. That's preparing you to go out and do something but not be aware of a person's social responsibility.

It disturbs me to see the apathetic kinds of responses that students make to these crucial controversial issues that we are dealing with in this world. There are some who genuinely do catch ahold, and they get excited about it; they get turned on by the course, and that I like. But by and large, you can talk about an issue for fifty minutes and have a whole class sit there and stare at you with a blank expression and not say a word. And you can say things that you know deep down inside they utterly reject from their value system. I come out of the prison exhilarated from it, and I come out of the classroom here with a feeling that I have not been successful in accomplishing what I went in to do. It's depressing to me, the feeling that these students are going to go out into the world and virtually separate their intellect from their work. Only 20 percent of our student body now is in the liberal arts and languages. Maybe it is confronting them with something they can't deal with or don't want to deal with.

When I started, I used to require a term paper for every course and read it and spend great time responding to the paper for the student. Today I can't do that and, in a way, the student is suffering. I see my colleagues now resorting to testing systems that really disturb me. They are giving all multiple-choice tests, and they are taking them out of test manuals that are provided by the publisher of the textbook. They run it through a computer and grade it; the students never see where they missed a question, or whether they got a right answer. They don't know anything except a score. I will not give an objective test. I give essay questions, and I write answers to them, and I tell the students where they didn't give a complete answer, or where they didn't develop it as it was [developed] in the class and in the book.

When I got my doctorate, I was quite interested to see how that kind of change would affect my title, what people would call me. I thought that the Ph.D. would be a title that would immediately subsume the place of Reverend, but it didn't. I've never once been called a professor at the community college by a student. I get called professor when I go out to the prison by the students there because they look upon the status of the community college teacher as a professor, but the students in the community college don't.

It was really difficult to try to get a doctorate. I was forty years old when I started the program and by then most people are through and not even interested in further graduate study. It meant commuting to New York city twice a week, getting a morning schedule to get away, going to summer school every day for three to four weeks out of the summer. But I got up to the point of the dissertation, and then I requested a sabbatical to write it, and I got approval for it. The college gives real importance to people taking sabbaticals to pursue graduate work. They really regard that as the number one basis for granting sabbaticals.

My feeling prior to getting the degree was that this is probably the most important goal of my life. I felt that it carried a degree of respect that I didn't have before by my peers and by my students and by the administration of the college. I remember taking a copy of the dissertation to the president of the college. He made a point of congratulating me and having it filed and put in the library of the college. And I went to my department head and said, "I have my doctorate now, and I'd like to have a name plate that says Dr. B. on it," and he wouldn't approve it. He was very definitely threatened by all this; he didn't like the idea of someone under him having a doctorate.

I have a very strong sense of personal satisfaction from getting it as a symbol of my own ability to make that accomplishment at that age of my life. I would imagine probably 40 to 50 percent of the faculty at college have all of the course work but have not finished the research and the dissertation, have not made the effort to go that final step that you have to take to get the doctorate. It really represents something in terms of how you are perceived by your colleagues in terms of making that final extra push, that effort to do that research and buckle down to the nitty gritty of the hard part of the doctorate.

I am sort of jokingly referred to in the department as the guy that reads all the time. I try to spend at least two hours every day in reading-preparation time. I feel that it is imperative to the nature of the courses that I do to be updated, and I have at least three or four books going all the time. I will come in and shut the door. My students know that they are welcome to come anytime. I don't restrict it to the hours that we have to keep.

I think the administration and the trustees of the community college see the role of the faculty principally as one of being in the classroom. They are continually trying to increase our contact-hour load. When I first started at the college, I was carrying twelve contact hours a semester and working three extra for overtime pay. I'm now up to eighteen and all of that has happened in the ten years that I've been here. They're also increasing class size, and they jokingly talk about the fact that we only work fifteen hours a week.

That actually was said by a county legislator at the budget hearings of the college: that they are only working twelve hours a week in the English department. So they are continually pressuring us to get up to eighteen, and I perceive the days that are coming when they are going to get us up to twenty-one a week. I see my role as one who should devote as much time in classroom preparation and in study as I do in the classroom, if not more time. I think it is just crucial that I have myself as thoroughly updated and informed as I can be to go into the classroom. So the time that I spend here in my study at home or in my study at the college, on my own, doing my own reading and writing, is very important to me. And I consider that of utmost value as far as what I am in the classroom [for].

I don't feel that going to the community college from the ministry was a horizontal step. I lost status as far as my social role, and I did not become a professor. That's about as well as I can state it. I became a teacher. As an occupation, professor is seen as one of lots of intellectual work and stimulation, as opposed to a teacher who is seen as an eight-to-three job kind of thing. For example, I am told that I have to be on campus six hours a day. The dean has sent the message down that faculty should spend six hours a day on the campus. I see no reason for that. I don't see the occupation as one that is confined to a number of hours of work on the campus.

Profile: Samuel Berger

Samuel Berger is in his sixties. He now teaches in a university after a long career in community colleges.

I started teaching in September 1945; that was a month after V-J Day—very few people were back from the Army. It was during that semester that they really started to come back in numbers. I remember for example that most of the classes were eighty percent women students. But within one year the veterans started to come back. The institution was growing very rapidly. The minimum work load was fifteen hours a week in class—that is, five three-hour courses—and that was normal. When the veterans came back in

1946/1947 in very large numbers under the G.I. Bill and we didn't have enough faculty, we were offered the opportunity to teach overtime.

I not only was learning how to teach in a community college, I was learning how to teach period. My principal academic preparation was history; in fact, technically, European History, which I've never taught in my life. There was a great variety of courses. . . . I was learning a great deal since it was stuff that I hadn't taken—a course, for instance, in geography. So that was very stimulating, the first five or six or seven years. Many of my colleagues were in the same position. We started to hold meetings outside the department. And we had very excellent discussions with the people from economics, my colleagues from history and geography. Everyone was learning. There was so much energy, intellectual energy in that setting.

The veterans were extraordinary. Most of them wanted desperately to finish school and a number of them had not gone through high school [but] had been drafted. They took the GED and if they passed it, a lot of them would come into the college. I began teaching when I was twenty-four, and some of the veterans were older than I was.

We started to expand so fast in the late forties and early fifties. Everybody had to be a counselor. I wasn't against it. I had no real formal preparation, but nobody else did either. We had very few full-time professional counselors at the beginning in those early years. Later, when I left, they were more or less all of them counseling people, psych people mostly.

There was redbaiting going on. I remember when I was on what they used to call a trial period. It is a two-year period of trial, probation, and after you would pass it, you were on tenure [track]. In 1947 the Cold War was starting. . . . I had political differences with some people on the campus, and there was redbaiting. Any liberal statement was regarded as a red statement. I had that sort of thing. But my colleagues were fine. My boss was fine and very fair-minded, and when he probed for any kind of evidence, there was no evidence, just baiting. We taught the general course in social science. We dealt with some hot problems, you know, politically hot; I think that during the McCarthy period we pulled our necks in somewhat. You had to take an oath; you couldn't be fired, but you couldn't get paid if you didn't take the oath.

In terms of the union, forming a teachers union at a college, I was very active in that in these years. I have been a union person; my father was a union man. When I worked in a plant, I was very active in the UAW Local, and when I came to the community college, I guess the first day I wondered, "Where's the steward, why hasn't a steward come up to me to ask me to join?" Then I found out that teachers had no protection at that time. I am speaking of the whole school system, including the college teachers. It was extraordinary. The president of the union at one point used the term "crumbs" positively. He said, "I went in to the superintendent last week and I think there is going to be a few crumbs for us." That is the way it was. We had no protection at all.

I got out of it [teaching in community college] what I wanted. . . . got more out of it than I expected to, actually. I wanted to teach poor kids and I sure as hell did. A number of them were older people, especially mothers whose kids were grown. They were highly motivated people. The veterans were the most highly motivated of all. In the city college, very poor black students were highly motivated, because many of them had left school years ago and now really felt the lack of an education. They were coming back very intent on making it. Some did and some didn't; a lot didn't.

We could have helped kids much more than we did and more than we do. I regarded the community college as the only chance or the last chance for many, many kids, the only chance for black kids especially. Except for very few, the community college is the only chance that they will have to go to a college. Some few of them will go on, but very, very few black kids in that city will go directly to a university out of the high school. For those kids, the community college was the only chance they would have, and it is very important for a community to have such an institution. I was always proud to be part of it. It is not true that kids who were very poor, white or black, that they are somehow not intellectual, not interested in things intellectual. They are usually not given anything to think of intellectually. They are interested in fundamental questions as much as anybody else. There is no intellectual reason to cheapen or lower your level of interest. The problem is how do you meet them at a certain point where they are.

Very early in my career it hurt me to give a low grade to a student, but I got out of that very soon. I had to get out of it. I became known as a tough teacher. I found that the kids respected themselves and respected me if I demanded that they learn something. I also went through a whole development on what kind of grading system I ought to have, since the kids I had were on an enormously broad range. I had kids who could barely read and in the same class kids who were headed for a top university. Some teachers said they can't deal with that, they want it split. I felt like that at the very beginning, when I first started teaching. As I taught, I came to value the variety.

I always had essay exams. I came to the conclusion in my own teaching and in my own work that the multiple-choice exam was a terrible obstacle to the improvement of a course. In fact you couldn't change a course because you had to think of the common core. I got to react quite a bit against the multiple-choice exam. I have never used it in my own courses. The stuff that I want to get at, I don't think I can get at that way. I give them five questions to write on. They have to write on two of the five. I classify them by the best answers. Then I have each kid, maybe two or three kids who wrote the best answer, read them in class. I am proud that they did a good job, and it is so clear to the other students who wrote less satisfactory answers to listen to a really good answer. Very often a black and white kid would write the best or a black kid would write the best answer. I thought that was very important that the white kids in class should hear that and be able to judge it themselves. Here is a really top question written with balance and detail, with some idea of a thesis. You can't do anything like that with a multiple-choice exam.

When I began, I thought a kid, regardless of his background, ought to be told what the requirements were and just measure up to that, and if you can't do it, too bad. But that bothered me after a couple of semesters. I saw that was a way of getting rid of the problem instead of solving it—you know, just looking the other way. So I came to think we have to give every person a chance with some help. And it was on that point, and the questions of how much help and how do you organize help for such large numbers of kids who have such poor backgrounds, that there were just so many battles. Most of them I lost. I am very unhappy even now when I think of it.

You know, if I had a class at nine, I used to come at seven-thirty or quarter of eight, and I would sit. I would be available for any student who would want to come in for special help, and the special help turned out to be the most elementary help in reading an assignment. First I would ask the kid (many times not a kid, these were older people, in their thirties), "What does this paragraph say?" "I don't know." "What does the sentence say?" "I don't know." "What does this word mean?" "I don't know." "You don't know how to read. Do you have a dictionary at home?" "Yes." "Do you ever use it?" "No." When you work with people on that basis, say several times a week, if they come back—it is strictly up to them—many of them make headway. And I learned that [with] people who ask questions that seem so elementary, it wasn't that they were stupid. No one had bothered to teach them along the road before they came to the community college. But as soon as they understood what that long word meant, they could use it and did, and so it is worth spending the time. . . . The sadness of people being wasted—I feel sad about anyone who is wasted, who is not accorded the dignity that he or she deserves, isn't given an opportunity to show and to learn and to grow. That makes me very sad.

I remember a black student [of] about twenty-six or twenty-seven. I had him in Social Science 101, so I hadn't seen him for a couple of years. "What are you doing?" He said, "Well, I graduated and I am going to a technician school." I said, "Well, why don't you go into engineering school? What grades do you have in math?" And he said, "Pretty fair." "Well then, why don't you just apply for engineering?" "Well, I don't know." He didn't know why he didn't apply, but it was something that was distant from him. He had gotten the idea that he was not good enough to apply to engineering schools. That is what you have to work with: "I am not good enough to think about big problems. I am not good enough to go into medicine; I have got to go into a medical assistant program."

So being associated with a community college that meant so much to so many kids was worthwhile as far as I was concerned.

I don't want to give you the impression that I thought it was a haven of scholars, because it wasn't. In terms of the students, it was very rare that we got a real scholarly kid. Nor am I saying the teachers especially were scholarly, because they weren't. Very few of them ever wrote anything, and so I was sort of an odd ball in doing what I did. Most of them were damn good teachers. Many times our kids would come back and say, "You know, we never had it so good as we had it here."

If you ask me to look over my career, I think of it as a very positive thing, but it could have been more positive. So much of it was a struggle against inadequate thinking, you know, at the top. The administration seemed to be exceedingly interested in making the colleges primarily vocational schools. There were special payments that you get from the state for vocational education. I said to my administrator friend, "What if you didn't get special payments?" He said, "Then I wouldn't be interested." Cut-and-dried. It was a very, very uneducational reason and something done in contempt. I remember a black campus on the other side of town. They introduced an auto mechanics course. No black students took it. Nobody wanted to study it. That isn't what they are there for, but that was the whole tenor. Make it vocational. And the vocations were not so great. Auto mechanic! You can just learn more hanging around the station you know. There was such inadequate thinking of that sort.

I don't object to connecting up vocation with higher education. In fact, at the university every other guy is in a vocational program; he can't wait to go into teaching or medicine or law or some damn thing there—vocation, I don't object to vocation. If somebody wants to go into nursing, a part of their program must be a consideration of the role of medicine in modern life and an analysis of the industry, problems in medical care, the distribution of medical care, the economics, the history of medicine. In other words, I want to humanize the occupational interests. But they don't want to do that. When you ask me what I think about occupationalism, I don't say, "Down with it." If you come from a wealthy, middle-class family you don't have to worry about occupations. But if you come from a working-class family, you damn well have to. The struggle there is what occupations. So it is not occupationalism as such, but what kind of occupations and what context you put them in as far as curriculum and historical context. Because that is the way in reality they are. . . . I want a more complete conception of education rather than taking one aspect and saying that is legitimate and the other one is not legitimate.

I remember we wanted to rethink the whole social science program. I worked out a course in great detail. I worked out an outline and subject matter. So I was explaining it to my colleagues and I noticed two of them were asleep. That was a fateful day for me because I put away that outline and we never did anything with it and I have it here. I thought, "What the hell am I doing, I am putting these guys to sleep?" Some others felt that we've got our John Stuart Mill "On Liberty" and I am [we are] used to teaching it. The university still teaches John Stuart Mill, so it must be good. I think it was around that time that I first said to myself that something is profoundly wrong here. There was a hesitation to take a situation and think your way through to it. It was a disposition to take the easiest way out, the customary way, and that was diffused throughout the entire school. It was not only some colleagues and a few administrators, [it was] all institutional research people, the whole system. There was no interest to sit down and grapple with the problem, except let's say when black students occupied and you had an emergency and they wanted to know what could be done to get out of it.

To teach there, you have to teach at least four courses in each semester. That is one of the primary reasons that I left. In the junior college there is no publish or perish. You are not expected to write, to research. By doing research and writing, you are even allowing suspicion; that is to say, "What is this guy up to? He is writing, you know, what for? Doesn't have to. Something strange about it." The whole approach is that we are here in order to teach, and teaching is unrelated to the life of the mind, apparently. There is a cloud that descends and it says, "You don't have to do research."

I have faith that if we ever build a school system and a community college system and a university system that can deal with poor people, children of poor people, we will be amazed at how they take up the intellectual life. I want them to change the world. Our world stinks. That's it. Our world is not anywhere near the world that human beings can make for themselves, for other human beings, and I want them to change the world, I want to change the world. The intellectual life is related to changing the world, making a more just, a freer, society. That is, I am looking at a society that we live in, which is an unjust, racist society, that is both unjust to a lot of people that are not minorities and [also] it is a racist society. It must be changed; I want to do what I can toward it. Part of what I can do about it happens to be an intellectual job. So since I know there are so few others doing that part of it, I've dedicated my writing . . . [to] dealing with that.

I believe the more we try to separate the junior college or the community college from the whole domain of higher education, the worse off it is. Now we have this awful phrase "postsecondary education." It isn't even a commitment to a college. It only says there will be something after high school, not beyond but after high school. At least "a community college" has the word "college" in it. The more we draw distinctions within the realm of higher education or certain parts of it and say we have "a community college" and now we have "postsecondary education," I think we make it meaningless. I think it is pernicious, although it is quite popular.

A junior college occupies just about the lowest rank in prestige in the academic world. But I really don't know a difference between a community college teacher versus a good university teacher. I remember I was told that there is a distinctive aspect to community college teaching, that you are interested in the individual student and you sort of nurse that student, sort of like little children. I had a colleague, for instance, when he would teach in Soc. 102, he would give them a virtual outline of the book. I never did that. He believed that that was a distinctive kind of thing in a junior college, that somehow you have to baby the kids along. I don't believe that. I find it hard to distinguish or single out any specific respect in which a community college teacher should be a different kind of a teacher or a different kind of human being than a university teacher. I just can't conceive of one. I have been told that there are such differences, but I just don't know them.

Profile: Richard Young

Richard Young, in his forties, teaches econom-
ics and government at a New York state community
college.

I teach Principles of Economics. It's the basic economics
course. Until last year, actually, I spent a lot of time teaching a
combination of economics and government. The other course I
teach is Consumer Economics, and I started that course in the early
1960s when there were very few of them in the country. It's required
for commercial art students and that gives me a lot of enrollment.
Most commercial art students go into advertising, and I think the
art department chairman at the time thought they ought to hear the
other side of the story before they go out in the world, and I think
it is a very wise choice.

When I started the course, it was seen by the dean who gave
permission to start it as a course for the terminal students. It was
not supposed to be too rigorous. Now I wasn't too happy with that
description, so we negotiated and it was agreed that it might be a
combination of the relevant parts of Economic Principles and some
concrete how-to-shop, how-to-buy information. And that's what it
is now, a hybrid course, basically: the market system; sociological,
psychological influence on buying; ceremonial consumption;
credit; funerals, weddings, gift giving and that sort of thing;
advertising; pricing system; budgeting.

Each class seems to have a personality. Sometimes the
personality is just to sit there and take notes, and other times they
have the right combination of people who speak up. Usually if
there is a lot of talking, it's often because there are some older
woman students in the class, and they tend not to be afraid to talk
up and they express themselves. I always like to have them in class.
By older I don't necessarily mean elderly but maybe beyond the
normal student age; that could be as young as late twenties or early
thirties. But they are not shy and reserved. They speak up and they
are a real asset to the class usually.

Most of us recognize older woman students as serious, good
students. And most of us try to get them if we can. We have a

program that is designed specifically to bring women back to campus, and there is some counseling; there are some courses in which they are concentrated so they will feel more at home. We put a big emphasis on that. I guess all colleges now are receiving what they call the nontraditional student. And these women make up a good part of that. They are serious. They are good additions to every class. I had an older woman auditing my Consumer Economics class this year. She was wonderful. We have a policy where senior citizens can audit for free and several of them take advantage of that. It's just refreshing to have someone who has had some experiences and who isn't afraid to speak up about it, and they are good students. They prepare, they study, they usually write well, express themselves well.

I don't give that many A's. I don't really think I'm a hard marker. I give all essay tests and that's pretty rare these days. And students are not used to it and they don't like it. And some of them for very good reason, because they can't write. The reason that I stick to it is because I think you can test concepts a lot better with essays than you can with multiple-choice exams. Essay tests take a lot of time to grade and sometimes I take a long time to hand the papers back, which I'm not awfully proud of.

There is a very wide range of students here, including some people who clearly don't have the language skills to work effectively, and probably a lot of them don't have a lot of motivation. Some of them have serious educational liabilities, primarily language; they don't write well or read well. They don't understand what you are saying. On the other hand, some of them are great students, particularly in the Principles of Economics class. I remember a few years ago I was reading an announcement about the dean's list and then I said, "I better not bother reading the list because nobody here is dean's list," and they said, "What do you mean?" So I asked them seriously, "Who's on the dean's list?" There was about two-thirds of the class. It stunned me. I mean I knew they were pretty good, but I didn't know they were that good. I had a girl last year, amazingly good; she was valedictorian in her high school. I used to use her papers to grade the test. She wrote a better answer than I could. One of my ex-students who worked with me at camp went on to a big university to get his doctorate and the last I heard he was the assistant to the president at that university.

But the other impression I have about our students is basically they are very decent human beings. They are just well behaved, considerate, nice to work with. The campus is exceptionally clean because they take pride in the campus. When we go on a field trip, I don't have to warn them to behave or anything. I just turn them loose and invariably someone will come to me and say this is the nicest group that we have had.

It's the liberal arts students that take more advanced social science courses. And our liberal arts enrollment dropped from over 50 percent to somewhere around 25 percent. It's a question of numbers; I don't take it personally. We just have eight people interested in Comparative Politics, eight people that are interested in European History, eight people interested in Labor Relations, and that's not enough to teach any one of those. We have to accept the fact that we don't have that many students. And it'll come back, it's coming back now. I guess maybe the reason I take such a tolerant attitude is because it really hasn't affected me that much. Economics is required. The enrollment of Economics didn't go for a few years and all of a sudden, unexpectedly, there was enough this semester; and we are going to try Labor Relations again.

I can't dictate what I would like to do here. I have to do what needs to be done. I'm teaching a lot of the things that I like. Now some of the people in my department were justifiably annoyed and frustrated. Our work load has just been increased in the last contract. Now we teach five courses every semester and I think there must be more of a chance that I will be teaching three preparations. I have never taught four, and some people have.

I don't sense a great deal of power; I do sense a fair amount of freedom and flexibility. I think it's a good place to work. I'm very happy that I came here. My department, I think, is the best in the school, the best one to work in certainly. I have a choice of schedules to a large extent. I really would dislike eight o'clocks and I don't get any. I return, of course, I get a lot of four o'clocks. We get choice of textbooks, method of instruction, method of testing. So I am reasonably happy with that. I've gone to other places and I hear about having to submit exams to the department chairman and not having a choice of textbooks and being told how much to lecture and how much to have discussion and that sort of thing, and we have nothing like that. I think it's a good institution, and every time I go to a conference and talk to other faculty, it reinforces it. Now as I think about it, I sound like a Pollyanna, like I'm just tickled pink with everything here, and that's not how I feel all the time.

I like to control things. I like to control what I do, and I certainly don't want anybody controlling me. There was that phrase that Lorraine Hansberry used in *Raisin in the Sun*—an "exhausted insurgent." That's me. I'm an exhausted insurgent and I've had it. How did I get that way? Age. As you get older, you don't have as much energy after a while. And you don't think that it's worth fighting for. I look for things that are relatively peaceful. I think of myself as having been an activist and one of those on campus who was pushing for an organization, and after a while I just stopped. I think it's something that I chose rather than the clock just stopped. A lot of the things that we fought for were accomplished. When the institution was young and new, [there were] a lot of things we figured we would get done, and some of them worked out and some didn't. The institution is a lot bigger now; it's much harder to get things done. How could you sustain that level of intensity if, in fact, you find that it is not being productive, or that it seems so difficult to do and doesn't seem likely to be successful? That's why mostly the insurgents are younger people and I don't know whether it is because they have more energy or they haven't been disillusioned or what.

I had a feeling that we needed faculty governance here, that the decisions were all made by the administration. And at one time I thought we ought to have a rankless college, no faculty rank at all: control by the people who are doing the work on the firing line. Presumably they have a better idea of what's going on. I guess it wasn't that important.

I think the power structure in community colleges is not exactly the same as in the four-year college and yet comparisons are always being made. Everyone doesn't necessarily see us as bona fide faculty. They think, "He is just a community college teacher, and he is different, and he is not really among the educational elite. He's not research-oriented, probably, and the students are not as good," and they see us as a kind of a halfway step between high school and real colleges. And sometimes we hear that phrase, "It's not a real college. It's just a community college." I think a lot of our work situation represents that position, in terms of work load, in terms of pay perhaps, although I don't think our pay is really inferior, but in terms of support services; for instance, we really don't have as much secretarial help as we might have. Our department is virtually unique as I understand it in giving us any secretarial help at all. We still get sent to conferences with the bill paid by the school. I went to an economics convention in San Francisco and I met a teacher from a nearby, prestigious four-year school and he was really surprised to see me there. He asked me how much of it did they pay, and I said, "They paid it all, of course," and he said his college doesn't pay it all.

There are significant differences. It would be foolish to try and pretend that they don't exist. You don't get a chance to teach on a very advanced level; many of the students are not as good as you would hope, and that affects the nature of your teaching. The work load is heavier; you have less time to spend on other things— research, reading. Certainly the public doesn't perceive you in quite the same way. For instance, some of the politicians have been talking about the budget; they'll indicate that this is not a college like a nearby, prestigious four-year school, you don't have doctor- ates here, so why do you deserve as much pay as you get? Why do you need the kind of support services you get? Sometimes we hear ourselves referred to as a thirteenth grade.

I was talking to a girl last night in swimming class about where she is going when she gets out of high school and she didn't know that I taught here. I asked her if she had given any thought to the community college. She said, "Oh no, that's just like high school." Then she was embarrassed when she found out that I did teach here; she said "Oops." It's a little bit of a blow to your ego. It's as if I worked in a restaurant that wasn't a five-star restaurant and someone said this is not a first-class restaurant. That doesn't mean that it's a bad restaurant. It's just not structured at that level.

I can remember when I came here, I taught my first course in Principles of Economics. I taught it basically the way I taught it at graduate school. This is something that we talk about among ourselves quite a lot. Whether we "water things down," that's the way it is usually put, and then the whole problem of grading inflation. I don't think anyone could consistently teach without regard for the level of the students. There is just no way you can continue to talk as if all of the nuances and subtleties were being picked up by students. I don't like to use the term "watered down," but I do certainly think that the subject matter has been "adjusted"—a crazy euphemism, but it has been adjusted.

One of the things that I tell my advisees is never to take a teacher who is teaching here for the first time. For a very good reason. They tend to be very, very severe, very strict; they perhaps have not adjusted to what a community college is all about. . . . Many teachers come directly out of graduate school where they have been eating, sleeping, breathing that one subject for two years or more, and they just have forgotten what students are like who don't necessarily care that much about that subject. I recognize, when I mark an exam paper, most of them are not going to be written very well. Some of them are not as good as you would hope. They don't necessarily catch the concepts. They are long on examples and short on principles. Some of the better students are just as good as any student would be anywhere, and when they leave here, they do well.

We call ourselves a comprehensive community college, which means that it is supposed to serve a variety of purposes. And it's supposed to be able to serve people who have a limited ability and still be meaningful and appropriate for those who have more ability. Now that fellow that I told you about that became the assistant to the president, his record was incredible. He was thrown out of high school. When he came here he was on academic probation, and then he did a little better and by the time he graduated, he was president of the student body and he had a 3.5 average. And then he went to Colgate, I think, and there he was magna cum laude and he went on to get his doctorate in a short time. I had another student who was my advisee who flunked out of here, went into the Air Force, came back four years later and got virtually straight A's. So I realize that the level of performance at any one point does not necessarily fix it for all time.

Hopefully, I will be a catalyst for some more serious application, some change in their life. One of the rewards here is that we see people who show a little promise initially and by the time they leave they are quite different. Some of the women that come in want to be a secretary. And before long they switch to the business curriculum and now they are thinking in terms of becoming a part of management. When you have a really lively class, a lot of discussion, a lot of interest, high level of energy, now that's a kind of reward, too. Or if you give an exam and the exam seems to show that they really caught the notion that you were trying to teach. That's rewarding.

Some students I keep in touch with long after they leave here. They come around to talk. I taught one course at a nearby liberal arts college, I student taught in high school, I was a teaching assistant when I was in graduate school—and the students weren't as nice. On this campus there is a kind of a mutual respect, and I get a lot of this when our students come back after they have gone somewhere else. And they say, "I really didn't appreciate what we had here." There is a different feeling, there is a kind of a community feeling here. I do like our students. They would be absolutely perfect if they were a little better prepared.

⌒⌒10⌒⌒

Career Education Faculty: Bridging Vocational and General Education

⌒⌒⌒⌒⌒⌒⌒⌒⌒⌒⌒⌒⌒⌒

Community colleges have participated wholeheartedly in the vocationalization of higher education in the United States described by Hurn (1983). The split between career and academic programs seems to be deepening in community colleges; yet the stories and experiences of men and women who are career education faculty touched on many of the same themes that their academic colleagues spoke about. Career education faculty stress the importance of reading and writing to their students, lest they consign themselves to dead-end jobs. The career education faculty were concerned about standards and dropouts. They were sensitive to the stigmas attached to their students who would be perceived as "dumb" because they work with their hands. These experienced faculty knew that students who were good with their hands must be—and were—good with their heads also. Career faculty recognized the false dichotomy between head and hand that is conventional in our society. The career education faculty in the study stressed to their students the importance of understanding the theoretical underpinnings of their fields and the critical issues within their occupation. Like their academic colleagues, they urged their students to get an education and not just training for a job. But in doing that, they were, like many of their academic colleagues, working against a strong countercurrent that tends to separate such broader questions from the so-called practical issues involved in job preparation.

While they shared many of the concerns of their academic colleagues, and while their programs were much in demand, career education faculty often communicated ambivalence about their status in the community college. Thus although Ed Thompson, who teaches small machine repair, insists that he will match his wits with anyone on the faculty, other career faculty who have come to the community college with long experience in their occupational fields see their academic colleagues as the real "professors" in the college. The sense of status, power, and opportunity that career education faculty convey often reflects the relative status of each occupational field. What is more, women among career education faculty must contend not only with the place in the college hierarchy of their occupational fields, but also with their position on the totem pole as women. In their own words, the five career education faculty whose profiles follow tell what it is like for them to work in a community college as they face these interlocking issues.

Profile: Linda Donovan

Linda Donovan, a woman in her thirties, teaches business and secretarial subjects at a community college in New York state.

Teaching at the community college in the evenings, in the years that my children were babies, was a positive experience not only for myself but for my family as well. My husband and children developed a very strong bond with each other. I worked part-time. Whatever courses happened to be available they asked me to teach.

The first year that my second son went to school all day, full-time days, change started occurring. They needed a full-time business teacher and they had been pleased with what I was doing in the evening division. So I was invited to become a part of the faculty.

It was really dramatic to go from part-time to full-time. Most of the faculty with whom I had direct contact [in the evening] were not very conscientious. They generally had an attitude that it wasn't all that important to teach these courses. When I came to teach in the day school, I found that in the secretarial department, the teachers were extremely conscientious and rarely were out, and had a very positive relationship with the students, and I found that I started to really think about pursuing a career.

When I first took the job in the day school I just thought it was something I would do for a while because, of course, the extra money would be very nice to add to the family pot. Secondly, I kind of liked the feeling of doing something productive, and I just figured that I would work for a couple of years. Then I became very much immersed in the excitement of it all. I really loved the students. And I liked the challenge of always teaching and learning different materials. I would have different courses to teach each semester. The first five years that I was here, I taught a total of fifteen different courses. Now I'm teaching Business Communications, Word Processing, Business Math, and Medical Office Procedures. Business Communications is concerned primarily with the art and psychology of writing an effective business letter. We also deal with how to communicate effectively. I get into some time management, teach them how to use their time in the most efficient ways. Then we spend a lot of time working on the resumes, strategies, what kinds of things they should accentuate in the resume.

I consider the Business Math almost a preparatory course. It prepares them for some concepts in accounting, some concepts in statistics, insurance. We do trade discounts, how to figure out sales tax, property tax, basically dealing with any kind of percentage problems. Before we can get into any specific topics, I have to spend about six weeks refreshing their memory on how to deal with fractions, how to deal with percentages. It's incredible what they have either forgotten or never knew, and we have such a broad mix in the classes that it's almost overwhelming.

I was beginning to see that I was being held back professionally because I did not have a master's degree. I began to see notes in the promotion literature that would come out each year outlining the criteria that were to be considered for promotion. Among those criteria were always advanced degrees. It seemed that although it hadn't been that important before (people had been promoted to assistant professor without a master's degree—as a matter of fact we have people on campus who I think are probably either associate or full professors who do not have master's degrees), that wasn't going to be something that would happen easily in the future. I had approached my division dean and requested that I be considered for promotion to the next rank at the beginning of my third year. They did not feel that it would be a good idea for me to apply because I didn't have my master's. I thought that I'd really better get going on this whole issue, and I investigated the programs that were available and felt that ed psych was probably about as close to what I really wanted as I could get, at that point. My first choice was psychology, but since I had no formal psychology background the admissions director of the psychology department said that he felt my chances of being accepted were pretty small.

As I began to progress through the program, I became more and more disenchanted with the whole routine. I considered very seriously, last year, changing to something that I felt would be more interesting to me as well as make me more marketable. Because, you see, at this point in my life I realized that work is not something that I am doing because I want to pass the time; work is very important to me. If I were a male, I would probably love staying in the office from nine in the morning till seven o'clock at night, and call home and just say, "Please throw something into the oven fast, I'm on my way," but I don't feel that I have ever had that luxury. I feel a real sense of responsibility to my children first. I don't want them coming home to an empty house. I don't want them looking for something to eat on their own. I don't want them to ever feel that they have suffered because their mother chose to work.

I investigated other areas. The area that I felt would make me more marketable, and I would be interested in, would be an MBA program. When I went to discuss the possibility of getting into an MBA program, I became a little bit discouraged because I found that the first program represented sixty hours of graduate work, which to me is, you know, a little bit staggering. Because it's difficult for me to teach all day long, run home, prepare dinner, clean it up, and then race off fresh and awake and alert to sit in a three-hour class. I am still in the ed psych and statistics program. Realistically, I thought, my goal in getting my master's is two-fold: making me more marketable but also to get me off the instructor-level here. It really annoys me to be an instructor. It annoys me to see people who are not as effective in the classroom and not as conscientious and who don't really give a darn about their students, or do anything special for their students, be promoted because they have an advanced degree.

Last year there were three people—males—who were promoted who did not have their master's degrees. Not to the low level of assistant professor, but to associate professor. One in fact had been here fewer years than I and that made me angry. You see, if I were treated identically as everyone across the campus, then I could live with it or not be quite so angry, and say, OK, that's just a bureaucratic fact of life. I felt that, in many instances, some of the faculty might perceive their job as more important than mine because they were teaching courses that they considered more important. I had to demonstrate that my skills were just as good as anyone else's in order to have the same recognition.

The business division meant males; they were the successful business people in America. And, of course, in the secretarial department we could have some females who would be very good but who would always be considered just slightly different from the rest of the faculty. We get more exams to proctor because, of course, we don't work as hard, and we would have typically more preparations because our courses aren't as difficult to teach. You know, that kind of attitude. Well, with affirmative action becoming such a fact of life, about three years ago I started seeing some women being hired in other departments and decided that this was my opportunity to start mentioning that if an opportunity was available, I think that I would like to change, because, of course, I had already been teaching out of my department at least six hours every year. When the position became available, I was hired.

So I am not a member of the secretarial faculty anymore. I'm in the business administration faculty, and over the years I think others' perception of my role began to change. I felt that I was beginning to emerge as an equal in other people's eyes.

I would not have applied for promotion last year because I didn't want to put myself into a position of being rejected again, but my department chair very strongly encouraged me to do so. So I went through all of the proceedings again and was really very shocked when the person who was in charge of either turning it on or dumping it in the garbage indicated, through his secretary, that I was not going to be promoted. Then when I saw the published list of who, in fact, did receive promotions and found out that the criteria that had been applied to me were not applied campus-wide, I became more angry.

Then I saw the person who I felt would be in charge of giving me some advice on how this issue should be handled. Was I being treated fairly, was this a sexist decision? I do feel there are different standards that apply to the females in the business division and the males in the business division: two standards in terms of salary and promotability. He said, "Calm down, you don't have to worry about a thing because with the new contract that we are now negotiating you will receive a promotion automatically. Anyone who has received tenure will be automatically promoted to assistant professor." On the one hand, I thought, "OK, good, I don't have to confront the other individual with the anger that I am feeling because I don't feel that I've been treated fairly"; on the other hand, I was even angrier because I thought, "Damn it, they've taken away our personal motivation again. I don't want to receive something merely because I have been here five years. I want to receive it because I deserve it, I feel that I worked for it. I really would like to be rewarded for something that I am doing." Just because you have a degree doesn't mean that you're doing the job that you're hired to do. I guess I feel a lot of personal frustration because of that.

Related to the issue [was the fact] that I did not expect my job to be a career; it didn't really matter what I made. I trusted the person with whom I was dealing on salary issues [when I switched to full-time status]. There were no printed statistics. So he had said to me that I would be earning $1,400 a year more if I accepted the salary figure than if I were being paid on a part-time basis. And I said, "Well, it sounds to me like you feel that they're offering me a good settlement," and he said, "Yeah, I think that it's pretty good." I guess what he neglected to add was "for someone in your position who really is using this as a second income." And I, of course, being as naive as I was, felt once I get there and they discover how wonderful I am, there will be some way of upgrading and equalizing. I am finding that, in fact, it gets worse every year. I was much closer to the mean salary with the last contract than I am now. I will be even further away with the new salary because the contracts keep giving an 8 percent or a 10 percent increment to everyone.

I feel that I'm contributing something to society, both in terms of being a role model for many of my female students who may perceive success in the business world as rather intimidating, and also because I'm giving the students a sense of direction, particularly for the girls, to be able to consider combining having a family and being a responsible member of the community as well as having a pretty substantial professional commitment.

I felt very guilty about working in my initial times because my parents considered it inappropriate and my husband felt the same way. I'm slowly but surely indoctrinating people to believe that it is possible to balance the many roles that we have. I kind of identify with women who have chosen not to work and I see their lives as not having quite as much meaning as mine, not as much variety. You know, they go from one tennis match to another, to luncheon dates and bridge dates and golfing and they have a lot of fun. But every year is just like the last year and I don't feel that my life is like that.

I feel that I'm a lot more assertive than the average individual and sometimes I think that, particularly with males in our society, they're not really ready for that kind of assertiveness in females. For instance, many times after work if, for instance, my children are not coming home and my husband is not going to be home until five-thirty or six, I would not feel comfortable walking into one of our local restaurants that has a cocktail lounge and just sitting down with many of the male faculty who I know gather there all the time. I know that they would welcome me, but there would always be [the thought] in the back of their mind, "Why is she here, is she trying to pick somebody up?" Can't I just go in for the very same reasons that you may go in, just for the companionship and the camaraderie and to relax and have one drink before I go home? I don't want to have to justify why I am here. Can you understand that?

I was aware in my childhood that I was more assertive than the average female, and I always tried to tone down those characteristics to make me more acceptable to my female counterparts and to not intimidate the males as well. And at some point in my life I decided the hell with them. This is what I am and if they don't like me, then I am never going to be able to be myself with people.

The committees are male-dominated. A lot of the women who are a part of the faculty are almost considered part-time in that they do their thing and then they leave because they have family commitments. They don't become involved in a lot of the committee work. The men seem to have more of an interest in what's going on on the campus and seem to be more verbal.

I've been on a number of committees where problems have been thrown out—how shall we deal with this issue? And a lot of the men have offered some solutions to the problem. I think that one of my skills happens to be the ability to see a problem and then put it in its proper perspective, and then offer a solution. I've offered these solutions and I don't get credit for the fact that that was my suggestion. Somehow it gets buried, and sometimes it was a little bit frustrating to me where they wouldn't say to me, "Oh, yeah, that was a good idea." They would brush over it and just kind of incorporate it, and the suggestion that ultimately was used was mine. But nobody said, "Hey, that was really a good idea." Men in many instances do not like to admit to the fact that women may have ideas that are as good as, if not better, than their own. You know they sometimes feel that in order to maintain their own self-image, they have to keep women at a slightly reduced level. This is a very real thing. Initially this made me feel very frustrated and very angry. I don't like it at all. I don't like to have to subconsciously apologize for the fact that I'm a woman. I like being a woman.

I had a problem in my department that was crucial: getting the right room for our word processing center. The administration wanted to put us in a very, very small room that would have been totally inadequate. In order for me ever to use the chalkboard, I would have had to stand on a desk. I could not have had any overhead projector or any extra teaching materials in the room. Students would have been uncomfortable. In order for me to get what I wanted, in order for me to not alienate the people—the men with whom I had to deal to get the decision that I wanted—I had to make them feel that the outcome was their idea. Once they decided that it was their idea, they would love it and present the idea to me for adoption. Ultimately it came out just the way we wanted it. They really did feel that it was their idea, and they were just patting themselves on the back.

I am under a great deal of pressure, both professionally and personally, but I create that pressure myself. I mean I have a certain standard that I expect of myself. I don't want to fail with my children because I feel that my parents would blame me, but I don't want to fail because of me either. Because I feel that being a parent is an extremely important role. I feel that it is a responsibility that I chose to undertake and there aren't that many really important roles that people have in society. One of them is being a good parent, and it's a lifetime thing. If I felt that there was something that I could have done for them that I didn't do, that would nag at me, that would really bother me, that would probably even destroy me.

I feel a certain amount of respect in the attitudes of most people toward me when they discover that I teach at a community college. I don't think that I would have the same feeling of prestige if I said that I were a secretary. Some of my friends are secretaries and they are earning $25,000 a year. I find that in a social context they are not perceived as having the same intellectual caliber as I do—you know, good at the keyboard, but perhaps a little bit limited intellectually.

If I had not gotten married as early in my life as I did, I probably would have made all different choices. I probably would have gone into private industry, management. I expect that I probably would have gone back to school, or continued in my education, and been one of the pioneer women receiving their MBA's. I may have been a career person, I might not. I think I would have married. I kind of always liked the idea of being married. I think that initially in our marriage, my husband was much better with the idea of having a child than I was. I worked at becoming Linda Donovan, the mother. It wasn't a natural thing for me, like cleaning my house, not a natural thing.

I'm at another turning point in my life. I think that I'm through another passage, where a career began to become important to me. Well, now a career is not only important to me, but a full-blown, exciting, lucrative career is important to me. And I have to investigate where I can best fulfill those goals.

Profile: Roberta DeVane

*Roberta DeVane, in her forties, teaches nursing
at a small town community college in Massachusetts.*

When I came in, I had this feeling that, you know, I was just a nurse and therefore I wasn't quite as good as the rest of the people that taught here because they were English professors, they were college professors. They had their master's. I had a master's, but for some reason it took me a while to get used to the idea that I was just as good as they were. I've got a master's degree. I've got a lot of years of experience in nursing. But it took me a while to come to that realization. I didn't want to talk in faculty meetings. I just kind of did my job, and I really didn't feel a part of the college at all. That's changed over the years. I guess once I opened my mouth in faculty meetings, I found out that I could say something and I did know something.

It's hard as a nursing faculty here to get involved in a lot of things that are going on in the college because our clinical time takes us away from the place so much of the time. I'm only here on campus two days a week. Plus, we are responsible to the State Board of Nursing; we are responsible to the National League of Nursing as well as the college. Other faculty members don't have that kind of responsibility so it seems we are always involved in paperwork that a lot of the rest of the faculty don't have to get involved in. The state says that the ideal ratio in a clinical area is one instructor to ten students, and so therefore we have more faculty per student body than the rest of the school, and some of the faculty for a while were a little bit resentful of that. The nursing program started after the college was started, so it was new to a lot of people. They weren't aware of nursing programs, what they were like, what they entailed,

and I think through the years they have become more knowledgeable of what goes on.

I enjoy getting up in front of the students now, and they
don't threaten me anymore. If I don't know something, I'll say I
don't know it. Before I got all embarrassed. The last few years I've
had the same group for two days on Tuesday and Wednesday. I take
the same group of ten students into medical surgical nursing. I put
on my uniform and I go into the hospital and assign them patients
to take care of and I supervise them. You are right there with them
as much as you can [be]. When you get ten students in a clinical
area, it's a big responsibility. There are four clinical instructors all
doing the same thing. So we group them into four groups. It seems
like they're my own children at this point because I've had them for
a semester and a half, the same group of ten students. I know how
many children they have, what it's like for them at home, what
problems they are facing where they work. You know, at coffee
break you learn a lot of things about your students. You really get
to know them well.

That gets to be a problem sometimes when you have to fail
them. I've had one just about every year I guess. The most recent
one was a married woman, probably a little bit younger than I am,
several children, very much wanted to be a nurse, and when we
discovered that she had failed her final a second time, we knew that
we had to fail her. This was just before Christmas time. I called her
into my office and I said, "You know you failed both exams and
there really is no way we can pass you." And she, of course, started
to fill up and she started to get up and leave, and I said, "No, sit
down." I said, "You know, this isn't the end of the world. I know
it's devastating to be told that you are not going to be able to come
back, but I really think you can do with repeating a semester and
trying it again." And she said, "I just can't do that." And I said,
"Well, right now I know that it looks like you can't do it." I said,
"You go home and give it some thought, and after you get over the
shock, maybe you'll think again about it and you might be willing
to come back."

You know I just felt myself filling up because I felt so badly
for her. She said, "I've blown everything." And I said, "No, you
haven't. Your goal is to finish nursing, but you know sometimes

things get in our way and we can't accomplish it in the time that we would like to, but that doesn't mean that you can't accomplish it at some later date."

She is coming back. I felt so badly for her but yet I've got a responsibility to my profession and I've got a responsibility to patients out there, and if she is not capable of doing it, I have to fail her. And that's a very hard thing. They really have to work hard to get through the program. And when they have got families at home and they have trouble with studies—it was just kind of overwhelming to her.

In terms of the nursing itself, clinically, you have to write evaluations on students periodically, which involves a lot of work, and then see all those students individually, going over their evaluations with them. Making up exams is one of the worst jobs, one I don't like at all, because we go mostly with multiple-choice exams and those are difficult to make up so that the student can understand what you are asking. There are nursing faculty meetings all the time trying to revise philosophies, revise objectives, and revise the syllabus; trying to read some of the current material so that you keep up-to-date; trying to attend seminars that focus in on certain conditions so that you get updated from specialists so that you can pass new information on to students. We are supposed to keep five office hours during the week, which kind of gets to most of us. As nursing faculty, we put in an awful lot of hours anyway and we see students all the time, and I can almost say, except for maybe two to three students that are out of our program, that no students ever come see me during my office hours.

We have to be part of some standing committees. Each year we choose which committee we want to be on. I was on the admission committee for this year. We have to review students that are applying for the program and make some decisions about whom we are going to admit. You've got somebody's life in your hands because they want to come into nursing and you are saying yes or no. Somebody has got to make the decisions, I realize, but I don't like doing that. A few years ago we used to interview every student that applied. We had two hundred and ten applicants this year and we only had fifty spots. Seeing all those students would tie you up half a semester. Then we decided we would do it through an admission committee. We look through these folders and admit people, put other people on the waiting list, tell others that they should take some sciences so we can see how well they do.

In this class we have thirty-four students and two of them are male. We have two men on the nursing faculty and five women. That's unusual to have male nursing faculty and we have had two right from the beginning which is, I think, great for our male students. I've had one fellow in my group for most of the year. It's hard talking in class because you keep referring to the nurse as "she" and you have to catch yourself because he's in the class. All the textbooks are written with "she" in them. It is still very noticeably a woman's career, and it's difficult with patients too. Patients, if they see my male students, right away assume that they are a doctor.

It's particularly hard in this area dealing with doctors because they have been around for years. They are mostly of the old school; many of them still have the idea that nurses are to do what they are told to do and they are not to think. And we are trying to educate nursing students to use a lot of judgment and question, without getting the doctor's back up against them. They have to be a patient advocate. And if you can't deal with a doctor, then you are never going to be an advocate for your patient. The whole area of nurse-doctor relationships is pretty tight right now. And that's been a hard thing for me because, in the era from which I came, if a doctor came on the ward you stood up and you gave him your chair, you opened the door for the doctor. A doctor came into class and you all stood up, and you didn't dare speak to a doctor unless he spoke to you. You know, I still have trouble sometimes speaking out to a doctor and standing up for what I think is right, and yet I have to teach my students that; so it can be a battle some days.

Nursing has become more of a separate profession than it was years ago. Years ago it was follow the doctor's orders and that was your job. You didn't do too much thinking on your own. You just did the procedures, and you gave the bath, and you gave the medications the doctor ordered. Now nurses are being taught a lot of things that we weren't taught before. Assessment of patient needs, assessment of symptoms, and looking at what the drugs are doing to the patient. Years ago we never could tell a patient what they got for medication. Now we go in with a pill and say, "This is your heart pill," and we tell them what to expect for side effects and if they want to know their blood pressure, we tell them what it is. We do a lot of teaching which we didn't do years ago.

So nursing is really changed remarkably since I was a student. For the better. We are not just robots that walk along and follow what the doctor orders. And we don't look at doctors as gods like I used to. For instance, up at the hospital where I am, a patient was distraught because the doctor had not been in for four days to see her. I know that's wrong. If that doctor doesn't visit for four days, he is negligent. If I were a nurse on the floor, I think I would get on the phone and say, "You should come over and see this patient." But I don't have the clout as a guest in a hospital to get after a doctor for something that I feel they are negligent about. I say to my students, "You know that it's not right, he should be here. If you were in the position as a staff nurse, what would you do about it?"

Back a couple of years ago there was one doctor over there that was always hollering and screaming at the nurses. I felt it was very degrading. I went down to the emergency room one day. They needed some help and so I went down with the stretcher and I brought the patient out, and I heard this doctor hollering at somebody and I didn't pay too much attention to it because I was doing my thing, and all of a sudden I realized he was looking at me. And he said, "The next time blah, blah, blah," and he goes on and on. About fifteen minutes later he comes up on the ward and I got him down by the elevator door and nobody else could hear. And I said, "You know, doctor," I said, "I really don't appreciate being hollered at." And he said, "I didn't holler at you." I said, "Yes, you did." He says, "Well, I was trying to get your attention." I said, "Well, I've got a name, and if you want something just talk to me, and I'll find out what you need." And he never gave me any trouble after that. I was shaking in my boots, because I had never confronted a doctor like that. I'm just as much a professional as he is. We are in different fields, but he doesn't need to speak to me that way. I respect the doctors for what they know. I think they just get very careless with their care. And I'm very much concerned about my patients and I want them to get the best.

The hospitals accept us in to have our clinical experience there. We do not pay for that at all. They are ultimately responsible for their patients' care, so they have the right to say, "We don't want your students here anymore." You are not employed by the hospital; you are a guest there. You do give a lot of help, but on the other hand, they are ultimately responsible for those patients. If something happens to the patient, the patient is going to turn around and sue the hospital and probably not the student. Some enjoy the students and really enjoy having them there, and others feel they are in the way, and they'd rather that they weren't there; but they'll comply with what the administration wants and keep us. It's a lot of responsibility. If they weren't as good students as they are, it would be even more stressful.

I've been sitting in the same position for nine years with no promotion. I've been recommended for promotion every year since I've gotten here, but because there are no positions to put me in, I just don't get it. Every year I apply, but I think one of the problems that I have as a nursing faculty member is that because I am so tied up outside the college with clinical work, I don't have a really good opportunity to give much of a contribution in terms of some of the committees. And that counts very heavily it seems. I guess it's that old thing: we still feel kind of separate from the rest of the faculty because our job is just so different. We just don't get a chance to even attend some of the committee meetings that we are supposed to attend. We just can't do it. It's hard to feel yourself a total part of the faculty. It's kind of unique to nursing, I think.

I could go to the local hospital and work as a supervisor or nights and make more money than I'm making now. But there are a lot of reasons why I would not want to do that. What I'm saying is that, yes, I'd like the promotion, the extra money would be nice, but on the other hand, I wouldn't think about leaving because I enjoy what I'm doing. I mean, sure, we all like the extra money and I'd like the status of being able to say I'm an associate professor instead of an assistant professor, but I know what the state system is like; I've worked in it long enough. I just feel very good about what I'm doing. I like my students. You know, it's convenient for me, it's in the community. I like the people that I work with; I get my summers off with my kids. And I've got a husband that has a full-time job, so that money is not the big thing that it might be for somebody who is a single parent.

I look at the people that get promotions and I know the contributions they have made or the advanced degrees they've gotten, so I kind of assume that that's why they are getting them. Maybe it's my old passive self and my feeling that if there are fifteen of us lined up for this promotion and we are all eligible, that they are going to be fair about it and they are going to pick the right person out. Perhaps that's not the way it is. I don't know how to fight something like that, I guess. I know the medical field. I know what I know in terms of nursing education, but not education. I don't know how to get at them like I do the doctors because I'm out of my familiar setting. I guess I'm more of a nurse than a teacher, really. I've combined the two, but I think, you know, my basic instinct is that I'm a nurse and so therefore it's hard to take myself away from the nursing and say, "Now I'm going to go and deal with these administrators over here," when I really don't know what goes on in that office. I guess I just wouldn't know how to handle going in there and saying, "Hey look, I've been sitting here for nine years."

I feel like I have become an educator more. When I meet somebody at a party, I usually say, "I teach at the community college," and then they'll say, "What do you teach?" and I'll say, "Nursing." I guess I am identifying myself as a teacher at this point then. I don't know. In a sense what I'm doing is fulfilling my original mission of making sure patients get good care. I was just talking with one of my graduates yesterday, and I said, "When I know you are out there doing a good job, that's kind of an extension of me. You are out there doing the job that I want to see done." I kind of feel good about being a part of a community college. You live in this town, and it's a community college in this town. Some of my colleagues at the college will say, "You know, you people are really doing a good job in that nursing program. Students did well on boards this year; you must be doing a good job." I think they really have begun to value us as educators too.

Profile: Edward Thompson

Edward Thompson, in his mid-thirties, teaches engine technologies at a suburban California community college.

I teach several different classes. We teach the industrial engines, which are the smaller ones, two and three air-cooled types of engines. We do the motorcycle stuff, and then we do the marine stuff. My approach to these is pretty much the same. It is lecture-demonstration and then laboratory. I spend a lot of my time thinking about my lectures. I don't write them down on paper; they are all upstairs in the brain. I figure out exactly what I am going to say in the shower that morning before I get here. I have a format that I follow. I am constantly trying to figure out ways to make it better for the students. Just because I understand it does not mean that they are going to understand it the same way. We do some pure theory and then that is usually followed in the lab by a demonstration, by me actually doing it or showing them how; and the lab part reinforces that. I am also responsible for trying to keep this place clean and updated. I have to order all the equipment and supplies, and figure the budgets, attend the meetings that they have around here, keep office hours. I do the normal shop thing and maintain things, and correct papers, and grade papers, and do handouts, give assignments.

I am also responsible for a lot of stuff that has to run. In other words, it is not like a biology class where you screw the frog up and you throw it away because it is no longer any good. You make a mistake around here, this is very expensive equipment. A lot of the students working on it are beginning; they are learning and they are going to make mistakes. I have to be very careful and know what I am doing; otherwise, they would tear this stuff up right now and then you have nothing to work with. I also run this as a live shop, which means that we take in a lot of outside work—these boats and these cars that you see, they are not playthings, they are real things. My students will work on them and put them back together, but they have got to do it right. So there is a responsibility on my part, to make sure that the things they do in this type of situation are correct. I figure that sooner or later, they have got to take that responsibility and they had better take it in here. We try to make it as close to a working situation as we possibly can without getting the people in the community all upset about competing.

The students coming to me do not have the academic preparation. I find a lot tend to come into it because they think that they can do nothing else. They find out different. They have to pass reading and writing requirements in this class, plus mathematics, if they are going to stay. I spend a lot of time working with my students, reading and writing especially, to bring them up to a level where they could succeed in this business. I am not trying to put them through a four-year institution, but there is a certain minimal requirement.

What I am saying basically is the young students coming here are not in my estimation where they should be. The other clientele that I get are the older people. I get a lot of older people either that came back for retraining because of injury, or I get a lot of retired people who have put twenty years in service and are not thirty-eight. They are getting some kind of pension but they need something to back that up. These guys know exactly what they want. The kids sometimes can't see the rhyme or reason of what you are trying to do. But that is part of it and that is what I am here for. You know, not everybody can be a mechanic. How do you know unless you get involved in something and this is the place to do it. So it is a really crazy cross-section that I get. I got one man now who is seventy-eight years old in my night class, and he is sharp as a tack. Slow, but he gets things done, and he gets them done right. The youngest would be seventeen, still in high school, trying to get some advanced training.

The first of every class, I give an examination that I developed, and I determine the ones that are really having problems. I get some people that can hardly even write that are twenty years old, been in the service and back out. I have to take them aside and level with them and tell them that they are not going to make it. Most of them know that they have that problem. We have a tutoring program where tutors work with the students right outside this room on their assignments in here. They help them with reading the textbooks here. The same is true with mathematics. I identify the problems, and then the math lab is set up to help.

I tell all the students that the amount of money that they are going to make is going to be directly tied to responsibility that they are willing to take, and that is going to be directly tied to the amount of education that they have. Don't get me wrong. I would like to see all of my students go through the academic stuff. I push for that and they won't, for whatever reason. I get a lot of guys that you give the first test and they are gone. I know pretty much what is happening and I say that we have to talk. So we will go in here and shut the door. The student says, "I didn't show up for the test yesterday because I have not taken a test in five years, and I don't read very well and I don't spell very well." And I try to calm their fears and say, "Hey, that is OK. I still want you to take the test and give it your best shot," and then we will work and see what we can do about that, and I will inform them of the tutoring program. I tell them that somewhere down the line, they are going to have to bring up their reading and writing. It is imperative. You go work as a mechanic, and the next step up is the service writer, and above the service writer is the service manager. I say, "I am the only one that sees this stuff," and I say, "I am not so interested that you spell everything correctly right now or that your sentence structure is not good, but I want you to give it a try because what I am looking for is your thoughts, if you are getting the mechanical aspect of what I am trying to put across. We will work on the reading and the writing later." I can usually get them to do it, and in most cases the fear will go away after a while. And we will get them involved with a tutor. All my tests are not true/false—I make my students write. The stigma that a mechanic can't read or write bothers me, and so I really make that thrust, and you have got to be able to read. Our books get highly technical. Some students you never get to. They just disappear, especially when you have a class of forty. Maybe they didn't want to be a mechanic. We get a lot of kids that come and sign up because it is what their parents told them to do after high school. It is a kind of natural step. They are here for a while and decide this is not where they want to be and so they leave.

The person that is in here that can't read or write very well and who would never make it in a four-year institution, unless they could bring those skills up—I lean on them a little bit heavier to develop more of the actual skills for flat-rate time. I make them work harder because I know that type of individual, as soon as he gets a phone call for a job, is going to want to leave the program. So while I have him, I figure the best thing that I can do for him is to teach him as much as I can.

I have very few people complete the two years in my program. The people that come to me are striving for a job, just a job in general, maybe the first one that they have ever had. Or they have had a series of jobs that never lasted more than three or four months. They are looking for some kind of a skill to get them a little bit more stability in their life. Some people learn enough in a year that they can land a job. If I feel that they are good enough and an employer calls me, I will send them. They get the job and they are done with me. They may come back at night or later for further education, but I see my particular function not to try to keep them around for two years. They get a job and they are gone. They go lots of places. Basically, they go to work for garages, and they go into automotive parts houses.

You get that September rush. I would say that initially, out of forty that begin this class, probably at least twenty are enrolled in other types of classes, not a full load maybe, but they may pick up a math or an English. Midway through the semester, the number is probably down to about twenty-five. From that original forty, we are about down to twenty-five. Forty in here is unworkable, but we load it up that way because we know what is going to happen. After it stabilizes, about halfway through the semester, out of that twenty-five to twenty-eight, maybe eight of them are still taking other classes. Only five out of that eight are doing general education. I try to get my people and enroll them in the welding or electricity, so that puts them into other classes; but I don't term that as general education. The young man that was just in here is going to transfer on to State. He has been through my program, and he is smart enough to go to a four-year institution. I have those people, and I do treat them a little bit differently. Only about five individuals like that. The other people are picking it up for some type of survival background.

The ones that stay are highly motivated to learn. They get so much information and so many technical aspects that they sometimes get frustrated. There is so much to learn in this business in two years, and I tell them that they can't learn it all, but at least they can get a good start. They are eager and they want to know because they have a real need to know. They listen and ask questions. . . . Around here I tell everybody from the first day, "If you don't like it, you can leave at any time. Here is the door. If you want to stay, you know I will do my best to show you what I know and to teach you." We get it straight from the start.

Part of the function of education is more than just an academic type of thing. We need a lot of technicians, and there is really nowhere to get this level of training other than a junior college. A person goes to apply for a job, you know, and they say, "What experience have you had, and what schooling?" And they say, "No, I have not had any." And they say, "Well, we are sorry." So where do you start? I think part of the function of education is not simply teaching people how to read and write, but it is also teaching those people that want a specific trade or a specific skill. We can't all be brain surgeons. We need mechanics, we need good mechanics. We need good service people.

My enrollment has never been down since day one, and we are a small school. This is a small area. I thought that maybe we would saturate it with small-engine mechanics and people taking these types of courses. It just amazes me. I think that is a very important part of this school, and I keep telling the president and everybody else every time I get a chance. Because in many cases, they water down voc-tech, and they like to kind of hide that out back somewhere, as somebody's ugly stepsister, so to speak.

When they started this school, everybody thought that because of the geographic boundaries that this was going to be the vocational-technical school, because here we are where there is industry. The word started to spread: You know, there are great vocational classes over there. The president has fought for the last five years to change that image, but it is hard to erase that stigma from within a community. It is starting to work now, as we have students that have left and have gone to four-year institutions and are coming back to the community. We are very visible.

I get along with the rest of the faculty real well. I am one of the faculty leaders because I am in the union. I am in contact with most of the faculty all the time and in many cases have to represent them. I do that well because I have never been one that is frightened of any type of authority figures. That is my particular personality, so I kind of got picked up as a faculty leader. I don't know how it started. When I was going to school, we talked a lot about that in my field. A long time ago when they used to call industrial arts "manual arts," the type of people that they put into that were the ones that they didn't think could make it academically. Academic people (not all of them) sometimes tend to think they might be just a little bit above you because you are doing something like this. That does not exist around here. Number one, I would match my brain and wits with any of the academic people. I don't cower away from them, and I am not afraid to get involved with them. When we were first hired, we went to these workshops and these meetings, and we all got to know each other and to understand each other and what we were teaching and what we were trying to do. If you don't get involved in things around the campus, which is normally done by the academic people, they tend to start looking down on you.

Some of the teachers are good maybe in their field, but you know, they can't balance their checkbooks, they have trouble getting their shoes tied. Some of them are very bright, but they are living in a different world. I consider myself a regular guy and practical as hell. I tell my students that maybe I can never figure out a theory of relativity, but I can deal with what I have to deal with, a real world sense. I am real world, money talks. We are constantly talking money. People think that I am capitalistic; I tell them yes, that I am. When my student leaves here, I want him to know how it is going to really be out there, not how it should be. The social scientist can deal with how things should be, but my students have to know how it is. You know, you can't eat social change, and you don't put clothes on your wife's back and your kid's back sitting around pondering. I am talking about dealing with people who don't have jobs and who are looking for them. That is what they come here for.

I have had so many jobs in my lifetime and this is probably the best one that I have had, without a doubt. But I might start my own business. Life is exciting: If you get tired of it, go do something else. If I need to, I have the money to do it. You see, vocational teachers are never trapped. I tell my students that. That is the one thing about having a trade. They can snatch a white-collar job out from underneath you real quick, but if you have a salable trade, there is somewhere that you can always go to work. I guess my job means security. It is important to me because I have a message to get across. I think I am highly talented in my field and I want to pass it along. This is the best way I know. I think I bring some reality to this institution that is lost, maybe, in the other classes. And so I think that I have a real function. Teaching this class is much like teaching a biology class; we are not working on frogs, we are working on motors. I tell my students about my background. I tell them I am as talented as a doctor. He is working on people, and I am working on something mechanical. And in many cases, it is just as highly complex.

Profile: Scott Muller

Scott Muller teaches in an air-conditioning service and repair program at a community college in New York state.

I spend most of my time teaching. Right now my teaching assignment consists of three courses. One is a theory course that meets once a week for two hours. That course is very tough on the students and tough on me because they are always wondering just how far we are going to go, what's expected of them. So each time we meet, there is a lot of communication about when is the next test going to be, what is it going to cover, that kind of thing.

We are stuck with these two-hour sessions; they are marathons. You can just see the blood drain from their face after about an hour and a half. Every Friday I take the first hour of the two-hour session and make sure I address a topic that is emotionally, motivationally, and on a gut level pertinent to my students. It doesn't have to be technical. It is a pattern I have developed over the last year. It started when I saw that I had two students troubleshooting a piece of equipment in the lab, and they knew just enough to feel that they knew a lot more. And they think they knew enough to figure anything out. With that preconception, they very often block the real problem in the system. They can't really accept that they haven't come to a solution yet. They keep backtracking or insisting they were right. I wanted them to realize when they're troubleshooting a system, they are taking nothing but their pure intelligence into it. It scares some of them that they can't bring anything with them, and to me the next step is to show them that it's a pure esthetic educational experience because you are working with nothing but your perception. It is almost like sculpting. You just have this pile of clay and you are forming it, only you are forming in your mind.

What I wanted to do was to get the ones who were having trouble with their troubleshooting attitude to recognize that they don't have to carry those burdens with them. They can be an "ignorant" unknowing student and that is really a good mode to be in; that is a very pleasant experience. They don't have to always know. It is funny, because there were about four or five of the tougher guys that resisted. They keep showing up, and it is like they are there to dispel and disprove. They do not like this soft science approach, but they got dragged into it almost against their will: "Yeah, but I am not like that," that kind of approach.

I try to get them thinking about who they are and where they are going or where they are possibly not going. We were talking about economics. Economics to me is just some huge microorganism that is growing. It is like biology. I said, "What are your chances? You are in a very high growth field right now. You have a very good chance of at least getting entry-level employment—second fastest growing technological field in the country, next to computer science." Through a few linkages that I made, their jaws dropped a little bit when they realized that of all the people a shrinking economy can hurt, it is the entry-level graduate. He is the one that is locked out. So suddenly they go from a high-growth field to a no-entry field.

The larger context that I brought was that technical education is not enough, skills are not enough. You have to have not only a general education, but you have to have some sense of self that transcends whatever you are doing. You have to have an idea of not just what your mind is but who you are. Technical students have an orientation toward discrete answers, and that is a false orientation. Technologies are not any more discrete than humanities. They can be made discrete through discrete study, but when it comes right down to the application of technology to life, there is no right or wrong. There are always grey areas. I thought they had to get that. It is very esthetic, working out problems.

The heat-transfer lab meets for three three-hour sessions a week, and it is one of the pure delights of teaching. You get the hands-on, the best instructional mode by far. There is no substitute. You have got to have the direct experience. The students have projects in which they are immersed. We have to teach them how to use a meter, how to use wrenches even. It is amazing how many people cannot use wrenches. You just take it for granted if you have been doing it for twenty years. They build the simplest of systems that, when they plug it in, tosses heat out here and picks it up here. They take basic theory measurements, such as temperature, pressure, and mass-flow rates. Then they start to tackle controls. For instance, a refrigerator eventually needs to be defrosted. There is a whole series of controls required to do that, and different piping. So after they build the system, we have them sophisticate it with various assignments, and then after they have their simple little systems built, we have them work on the commercial systems we have purchased. That is all real equipment. We have data simulators. They cost about $7,000 apiece. It is a solid-state simulator of a system with meters built-in, so that you take electrical readings and do troubleshooting.

I can remember being in school and still thinking, "I am doing this because it is practical, because I want to feed myself." I can relate to that behavior. A lot of my mature students, "retreads" as I call them, that are coming back for additional education, have that as their goal: a salable skill. You have to respect that; they make the best students as far as absorbing. They always do the homework.

As far as some of the kids right out of high school, I don't have a disciplinary problem, but I can tell when I have attitudes kind of floating around the back of the room. For instance, you assign material prior to a test, and it is a good chunk of material. You can see where it represents three or four hours of study, easily. They moan a little bit; it is almost an involuntary response when they get the assignment. The mature student looks forward to crunching out the grade, that sense of progress; he doesn't moan so much. The one that moans so much is the one that feels that this is uncontrollable. He has got to study again. I can verbalize to them that there are other reasons for taking this test, other than to victimize them. They should look at it as a learning experience, and it is a way to validate their abilities. In the back of my head, I know how they feel. I know that they are not working in the same context as a more motivated student, so they feel victimized. They are constantly struggling with that question, "Is this worth it?" They have not made that decision. They are there, but they really haven't on a gut level said, "I am here because I want to be." They have yet to really give in to that and force themselves to make that decision. I mean if everyone sat down for about ten minutes and said, "At the end of ten minutes, I have got to decide whether or not I am committed to what I am doing," you can imagine the shuffle at the end of ten minutes, because I think an awful lot of people would have to change. But most people don't confront themselves like that, and students are no exception, so they just kind of dribble along in the process.

The orientation that these students have is a result of people telling them that they are not strong in math and science. Their parents probably aren't employed in technical fields. Most of them are blue-collar workers. These kids aren't necessarily low-I.Q. Many of them have never been convinced by their school system or their parents they should or could achieve academic excellence. One of the nice things about what I teach is it doesn't really rely on anything else. I teach them how to use a meter. I teach them Ohm's law. I show them enough algebra to manipulate a few equations. We are really starting from ground zero, so I feel I get a pretty true picture of raw, animal intelligence in the kid. By the time they are troubleshooting a system, they are holding three or four elements in their mind, doing some minor manipulations, and some pretty demanding memory work; they have got to remember where they have been and where they are going. I don't see any difference in their intelligence—with very few exceptions—any difference between them and the engineering students.

I have a student, he is my only minority student in the class. I have been aware since the first day that I have had him in my class that he lacks self-confidence. Very, very quiet kid, very nice kid, but just not at all convinced that he is ever going to grasp this material. Unfortunately, I think he is one of these people that somehow has been hoodwinked into thinking that after fifteen weeks you will know it all, and he doesn't realize that the process is very important, getting there is as educational as knowing it at the end. I've tried to point out how successful he is. He has a high B average because he is willing to do the work and he is willing to accept the fact that it needs to be done in a certain systematic way. He doesn't assume anything about it. He just takes it at face value each day and looks at it. But at the same time, I'm trying to relax him enough to make him recognize his own progress. Hopefully, everyone gets to that point by themselves, but I like to accelerate that process by saying, "Listen, you are doing fine. Look at what you have done." Try to build up his self-confidence so perhaps he can achieve more. But in one sense it is frustrating because I haven't been successful. He still thinks he doesn't know a thing, and it may be two or three years before he realizes how much he has learned.

One of the frustrating parts of teaching a vocational student or someone without self-confidence in technologies is that many of them have a defeatist attitude. You have to spend a year or two overcoming that. I am still in the stage where I am recognizing it. I am able to recognize the person that is working off the negative instead of the positive, and what is holding him back. I am trying to justify the fact that these kids could do more than society expects them to. They have been tracked, they have been conditioned by their families. I think they are much more capable. However, I get some kids that are just academically almost out of the system. They can just barely stay in the classroom, and usually the problem is memory. They just can't retain more than one or two elements at a time. They can't refer back to what they don't have. When you have got a system with fifty elements and you can't keep two of them in your head at a time—from the day I recognize that, then I say, Can I get this guy a job at a parts counter? How do I orient him to a job where he is not going to be a failure?

I talk to my students a lot. A kid will express a defeatist attitude. I'll say, "Where did you pick that up anyway—your father tell you that? A teacher tell you that? Someone told you you can't do this? I haven't told you—who's telling you? Are you telling you?" I'll try to reduce it to that level. I get a constant education as to the orientation of my students by talking with them.

Most of them are very reluctant to talk about communication with their fathers. These guys don't want to talk about their dads in any way, it seems. They will talk about their mothers saying "You should be stable, you should get a job," that kind of thing, but they don't want to talk about their fathers. I think the fathers' careers are a very touchy subject. They are very willing to talk about school and the injustices of grade school, junior high school and high school and the social problems, the social cliques, that they were excluded from. They were all aware of social exclusion.

I would not say any of them are destined to be drudges. It will depend a lot on their perception of their jobs. A lot of them will work for small to medium-size business where your boss, your foreman will get every inch out of you that he can. Every calorie in your body, he will ask you to give. It will be up to the graduates to say, "This is all I have got to give, and this is the quality of work I am going to do, and this is the pace at which I am going to do it."

I think it takes a lot of ability and a lot of adjustment, personal adjustment, to be a good technician. Technicians are not respected as they would be, say, in Europe, as a tradesman or a craftsman. Here they are underpaid and there is no job security. [In Europe] there is no equation between a maintenance person or a service person and a custodian, and a lot of people in this country see them as almost equivalent roles. You are in a building at night—you must be emptying the wastebaskets. A good car mechanic in Europe is a very well respected individual. Because most of them are well trained and they have more training and factory experience than a lot of them get here.

I still maintain a good technician has to be thinking about six hours a day and doing things manipulatively two hours a day. The first thing I tell my students when they are approaching an area that is complicated: I say, "Remember, for every ten minutes, you should be thinking an hour." If you don't feel comfortable sitting in front of a customer thinking, doing drawings, and really working through the problem, then get in a truck, make an excuse, get out of there. That is another problem: when you are paying someone fifteen dollars an hour, the last thing you want to see them do is sit down and think, but that is the most productive mode they can be in. They want to see them working like crazy—tote that barge, haul that bale.

I try to make sure my students don't feel limitations especially because they seem to have been relegated to the lower academic rungs by public view or academic view. Vocational programs tend to be a first and last stop in a lot of people's minds. So if anything, I try to convince them that this doesn't have to be their last stop, that this learning can be the beginning of continually turning themselves on to it. I want to make sure that they don't perceive this as their only shot at it.

They have lousy English skills, terrible. Now English skills are something you learn, you develop; they become reflections. It is like having a mirror constantly build your mind up. They have not ever developed that skill and, as a result, they are almost atrophied in that area. Most of their families have told them, or shown them indirectly, that they are not going to be doctors and lawyers, that they are going to be part of the working class. Their perception of the working class, the blue-collar workers, may or may not be pleasant. Some of them view it as being very unpleasant, but they see themselves relegated to it.

The classroom experience is fine, there is no problem there. I don't mind the preparation. I get good feedback from the students, I get a sense of progress and all that; but I am always looking for something a little more stimulating on a professional level. I have decided maybe I will write something. I feel that my approach is not a common one. Sometimes it is nice to be different. Sometimes just teaching is lonely in itself, regardless of how you do it. There are levels of lonely, and I think everyone goes through little mini-cycles of burnout. Around Thanksgiving, everyone is going through a mini-burnout cycle, and when you feel stress, you feel that you are at the end of your wits. Then you start to lose your enthusiasm with the students. You start to lose your curiosity about teaching techniques. You are not going into the class looking forward to being with people; you are going into class looking forward to getting through to the next lecture. When it reduces itself to that

level, then that can be lonely. I feel sometimes professionally lonely.
I feel that I may have a sense of quality that either I am too naive
to give up right now or that no one else shares.

Profile: Leonard Braddock

*Leonard Braddock is in his fifties and teaches
in a technological program in a community college in
a mid-sized city in New York state. Before teaching at
the community college, he had taught math at a state
university and had been in industry.*

We have a technology program that I coordinate for the
school. It is a unique program. It got started because of interests and
influence of the local power company where they used to employ
some 150 people in the testing field. I was not here the first year that
the program was in progress. The following year we took in twenty-
four freshman, and of that twenty-four, we graduated sixteen. We
are looking to graduate between thirty-five and forty this spring.
The program has been very popular principally because of the
prospects of jobs in the industry. We were graduating people and
their average starting salary is in the order of $17,000.

The first year that I was here, I taught all the testing courses,
and I had one student who was graduating from the program that
year working in a part-time capacity helping me. This year we hired
another gentleman, and he now shares the lecturing responsibilities
with me. We are looking to put on another one next year. We just
find that we can't get the job done the way that we would like it,
can't coordinate it as well as we would like to, by using part-time
staff. It is very difficult to maintain an interface with them.

When I taught at the university, I never had more than two
preparations. That's not the case in the community college. And I
really believe that you don't get as much out of the faculty because,
in truth, they are overworked. I find that eighteen hours is an awful
lot of contact when you are trying to develop the courses, expand
the program, and do the teaching as well. I really believe to do a
good, thorough, conscientious job, especially in rapidly changing
areas such as materials technology, that is too much of a load. I

don't find that I've got the energy that I would like to spend on developing curriculum. I find it a real hardship in trying to do all that I want to do with an expanding program.

We take attendance, a state requirement, so initially that is what happens in the classroom. I don't like to take attendance. It is something that bugs me. The first year that I was here there were only nine people in the class. After a couple of weeks, I got to know them all very well and now we have classes where there are as many as thirty people in them. There are people here with financial assistance programs, requirements in the state of New York. People who are on these kinds of programs, you have to take attendance. The G.I. Bill—they require attendance, so we do it. It is a school requirement, and I go through that motion.

I try to be very formal in some parts of the lecture because I find from my past experience here that if you just try to be a regular joe, they kind of seem to take advantage of that situation; so you have got to maintain the proper instructor-student interface. I've tried it other ways and it doesn't work. The students are pretty young; they are fresh out of high school, and they were not good students in high school. They are the kinds of students that have been underachievers, and so you don't crack as many jokes as you would like to.

The school has an open-admission program. We have tightened up the requirements in the testing program by saying that you must have two and one-half years of high school mathematics to get into the program; you must have two laboratory sciences to get into the program, one of which should be either chemistry or physics. Testing is nothing more than applied physics, and people coming here with no physics background or chemistry background we find just can't handle it at the level that we think it should be taught. Once the program got popular, it was easy to crank up the requirements, and the hope always was of getting a slightly better quality student. I'm not sure that that has happened. It seems to me in the three years that I have been here, the age of the student has gotten younger.

I concretely observe that the students are here because there are no jobs available in the area. They don't want to go into the service; they figure they might just as well go to school as do nothing. I see very, very few students with a genuine interest in the program. That improves between the first and the second year. As you might suspect, the attrition is pretty heavy between the first and second year. They just don't come back. We take in sixty freshmen; we look to graduate thirty-five to forty. It is troublesome. I would like to teach much of the program on a little higher level. I think that the first two years of college credit really deserves that. This is not a vocational school; they are taking courses here that potentially could transfer to other state schools and get a four-year degree.

The service that I am trying to perform for them is one of getting them ready to go out and work in industry, and I know what's there in that industry, because I spent a lot of time in it. And I know what a good technician or a good specialist should be able to handle. And we are not even keeping pace with the technology; it is changing faster than I can almost read about it. In industry you train people to turn out an instrument, twist a bunch of knobs, and look for certain specific things, and they get good at doing that; they really don't understand what it is they are doing. In a program such as we are trying to run here, we want them to be able to do that when they get out into industry, but we want them to understand the basic laws of physics that apply, and that is the difference.

You can't talk about anything in physics without a very heavy orientation in mathematics; it is impossible. I am trying to get these students aware of where equations come from rather than learning equations just for the sake of learning them, so we go through a lot of derivations. That is difficult sometimes to do at their level. We are beefing up the math requirement in the program so that they can understand a little bit better the origin of some of these expressions that are very necessary for them to work with. We try to build on very basic physics principles and develop from that point of view. For example, I ask very often early in my classes in radiography and in ultrasonics, "Explain what we mean by frequency." The students coming here don't have a feel for what frequency is all about. Here if somebody doesn't know what a logarithm is, you take the class time to tell them, but at the technical college, you didn't have the time for that. If you were teaching in a math program there, and you had four hundred sophomores taking sophomore mathematics, you had no choice but to keep pace with the outline. Everybody had the same homework assignments, everybody took common midterm examinations, common finals; your troops had to be up with everybody else. But in this program if the students can't handle it, we go back and we pick it up again. I am adjusting to it; I like it. It is very rewarding at the end of the year to have your students get a good job, then go out in industry and hear back from their employers that they are really doing well. And I think that is worth something.

I am writing this textbook. I bought the only available textbook that one could think about using. It is a book written in Germany. And it is not a textbook: It is a good reference book. There is no structured sequence in it that allows you to teach from it so that the students get the proper background. The only other thing available was this home-study type of training material that comes out of the industry. And they just aren't in-depth enough for college credit. So it's been a real challenge and a lot of work.

I have written at night. I work probably twelve hours a day. It is the only time that I get to write. I work on it weekends. I wrote some of it some last summer between consulting. My consulting activities pick up more heavily in the summertime. It has been a very unique experience for me. I got a whole batch of physics books, and I began to study the portions of those books that I thought I would need and began to develop some notes in building my own thinking. And what I tried to do was give the students a little background to simple harmonic motion as a place to start: What do we mean by a transducer when it vibrates? Then I sat down and tried to put together what I thought would be good background for them. And I did it with models which don't require the use of calculus.

I write drafts of it, sometimes I write it and I rewrite it, and I put figures in and then I change the figures, and when I get that finished I am never satisfied with it, and I give it to my wife and she types it. I am not satisfied with it then; but I have to have something, and if I waited until I got satisfied with it, I would never give the students anything. Right now, I am writing it and using it faster really than I can get it written. I came to realize that I can't get this thing done as fast as I need it. I have written probably five chapters out of, what I would guess, maybe twelve.

About my consulting work: I made sure that it was there before I came here and they had recognized that as a part of my being here. I think it is important for people who work in technologies to maintain a currency with a technology, and there is no way to do that if you sit in an office in a school. You know, it's one thing to read about new developments and it is another thing to be a part of them. It is like a second job, except that it doesn't involve that much of my time. I work probably typically a couple of days a month down there and, I would say, a couple of days at home.

I am available for consultation with students in my office hours. I have a group of students who are having a lot of difficulty. Maybe this is a wrong impression. I just get the notion that among sorts of students that we get at the community college, they are the kind of individuals who if they can read it and maybe struggle a little bit with it [say], "OK, we will give it a shot," but if they try to read it and it seems on the surface to be overwhelming to them, I think they just give up. I hold little classes for extra help, and they can come if they want to. I have a higher regard for students with somewhat less ability who've got an attitude of willingness to work than I have for people that I know damn well have got a good background and could do the work but have a poor attitude and don't care.

Rather than think about levels of intelligence, I try to think in terms of a student as being a good student, a poor student, a better student, because this is not necessarily a characteristic of their innate intelligence, it's more what their attitude might be. I don't think people should be separated on the basis of intelligence. I think they should be separated, if there is going to be any, on the basis of attitude, and willingness to work, and performance. They are either good students or they are poor students, and that is not really a function so much of their abilities as it is their attitude. Anybody who is accepted into the program, if they want to, can do the work.

People have to want to be there. They have to want to learn. If they want to learn, they will do some thinking in that process. That is the way that I judge people in classes; I look at what I think is their attitude about how much they want to learn. If they show me that they really want to learn, I will work very hard for them; I get students who come to work, come to class drunk, and that kind of thing. You just can't have that kind of individual out working on a safety system in a nuclear power plant. I get a little discouraged sometimes. I have been teaching a course in materials; we use a book that they use at the sophomore level in the materials department of a nearby four-year school. The students tried to read it and got discouraged and, as a consequence, they just gave up reading it entirely. And I tried to make a very comprehensive final exam; I tried to have it touch on the highlights of everything. And they didn't do well with it. I tried hard, and I just don't think that it was all that effective. I think a simpler book might have been more to their advantage than to try to work with this one.

My son the other day said, "You know, you think about a community college in terms of a learning experience as compared to a thinking experience." If you dwell on that, you get the notion that in better four-year schools, people are trying to teach them to think. Whereas I think historically, in this state at least, in community colleges the emphasis has been strictly on learning; you learn this so that you can go out and work at this and make a living. And not enough emphasis on thinking, you know. There is a subtle difference between the two, and I think about hopefully incorporating some of both in this program, even though it is a terminal two-year program after which people are supposed to go to work in industry. I want them to learn how to think.

One of the things that I like about teaching is the opportunity to learn; and I guess I am a person, whether in teaching or whatever I have done, I have always had an intensity to want to learn things. I think I am more intellectually inclined than I am pragmatically inclined. On the other hand, the things that I enjoy doing as a hobby are very pragmatic kinds of things. I have never really thought about me in terms of being an intellectual. I really get very excited about learning things and studying. So much sometimes to the point where I get preoccupied with it and I let other things that I also enjoy kind of slide.

I enjoy it, but it is intense, and I need to take periods of time to go to my hunting camp and look at a rock. The kinds of thinking that I like to do, the intensity with which I like to pursue the subject that I am interested in, are beyond the scope of what they consider our role to be at the community college. I like to be able to help people learn to think. The methodology of approaching problems, the analyses that you use, how you get started are more important than the mechanics of being able to solve the equations. I would like my students to be able to think, at whatever level they are able to handle it. I don't see that side of me being satisfied in a lot of depth at the school, which is perhaps why I am pushing myself in the direction of writing the book. Maybe I need that book to satisfy that aspect of my personality.

I am told that I am going to be offered a job at a company which is going to be at a salary that I'm not going to be able to turn down. I'm going to turn it down because it isn't stimulating enough. You know, in industry I think more people spend more time worrying about, "Let's see where is my next step, where am I going next," rather than the day-to-day job. They seem preoccupied with, they are always looking for, praise and satisfaction. I'll find my own satisfaction from the things that I do, and I don't need praise and promotions and that sort of thing to make me happy. The next step for me is to finish writing this book, which I find a lot of satisfaction in.

ᗯᗯ 11 ᗯᗯ

Minority Faculty:
Working for Equity

Profiles and excerpts from interviews of faculty who are members
of minorities in this country are interspersed throughout the book.
The following profiles of two black faculty and one of Mexican-
American descent are presented together, however, to illuminate the
complexities that faculty who are members of a minority face when
they work in a predominantly nonminority institution.

The individual personalities of the faculty who appear in
this chapter are different. Their subject matter—secretarial studies,
physics, and history—is wide ranging. Two teach in California and
one across the country in New York state. Yet their profiles reveal
similar experiences and touch on many of the same themes. Their
experience of their work in community colleges is significantly
affected by the fact that they are members of a minority and that
their relative numbers are few in their colleges. (See Kanter, 1977,
for a full discussion of the effect of relative numbers of women and
minorities on their work experience in a corporate setting.)

The minority faculty contend with all the issues their nonminority colleagues do, and many more. They must also face issues
of racism in their everyday work. Once they secured their positions
in their colleges, the profiles indicate, they had to work harder, and

do their jobs more thoroughly and more conscientiously, lest they find themselves subject to criticism not normally directed toward their nonminority colleagues. The interviews revealed a readiness on the part of minority faculty not to interpret every slight or awkwardness that they experienced in the college as an indication of racism. Their nonminority colleagues, on the other hand, often seem unable to see them first as colleagues and second as of a different color.

The following profiles reveal that a significant amount of conscious energy of minority community college faculty who work in predominantly nonminority settings is consumed with dealing with inequities. That time and energy is costly to the minority faculty themselves and also represents a serious loss to the students and the college as a whole. The experience of inequities revealed by these minority faculty gives food for thought to those who would consider the complexities of the struggle of community college faculty to provide equitable educational opportunity for their students.

Profile: Josephine Saunders

Josephine Saunders, in her thirties, teaches business and secretarial courses at a community college in New York.

I came here in '76 and was the first full-time black instructor that they had had here. There was a lot of adjusting to me when I first came, and to a certain extent, that is still going on. My first couple of years here were difficult. I guess that's the only word that I can describe it with. The first year that I was here, I had to let students and faculty know that I had proper credentials, and that there was nowhere on my diploma that said that I was only supposed to teach black folk.

I was the first black person that they had had any real contact with, so they didn't really know how to deal with that. There were instances of my having to justify everything that I did. One instructor could walk into a classroom and say, "This is it," it would be accepted. I had to walk into the classroom and say, "This is it," and I would have to justify why I said it. I think it was just they were not used to dealing with a black person. For them it was a new experience.

Some of the students have gotten to know me really well. The students who want to work take my courses because I do have high criteria for my students. They know now that I can teach, and I know the subject matter. But every now and then, for new students who come in, it sometimes gets to be a problem. "Why don't you correct the way Miss So-and-So does it?" or "Why don't you give your test the way Miss So-and-So does?"

The second year that I came here, there was lots of talk about cutbacks and some teachers having to leave. One instructor came to my office and said, "You don't have to worry about leaving because you are never, ever going to get fired," and I said "Why?" and he said, "Well, you are the only black person here." And I said, "What does that have to do with it?" and he said, "Well, you know, that's why you are here." In essence what he was telling me was that I was the school's token at that time.

I would have expected that things would have been a lot better as I grew into the job. The first year I ignored a lot of stuff because that was, I thought, just part of getting used to the job and the people. You are tested and students test you and colleagues test, but six and half years later, it's no longer a test, or it is a test of a different sort.

There are just certain things that people are not willing to accept about me, being black and the way that I am. One of the comments that was made to me was, "You never come to see any of us in our offices," and I say, "Why must I come to you?" Again, that's a concept some whites have. This whole busing thing, you know, about black students must be bused over there, but you know whites can't be bused; it's a one-way kind of thing. So I come in, and I do my work, and I leave, with a minimum amount of interaction.

It's frustrating for me, because the interaction with colleagues I think is important. At lunchtime I go in and find a table and sit down and eat. Usually alone, because the person that I talk with, when I have an on-campus hour, has an office hour and we are not allowed to leave our offices during office hours; we should be there for the students. So I usually go and grab something to eat and that takes about one-half hour. I don't mind eating alone; that's the way that it is. When I lived in New York and I worked at the high school, it was not uncommon for one of the guys to come and say, "Why don't we go out to lunch together?" and if he were married, we would go out and talk about his family or whatever. It was very difficult for me to understand that here you are not allowed to establish a real healthy relationship with someone of the opposite sex who is married; that's taboo. I remember asking once, "Can we go down and have a drink or something?" Oh no, that was the wrong thing to do.

I don't perceive myself as being powerful in this division. No, I don't. When I came here, I was told that they would be glad to have my input as far as the skills center was concerned, because they knew that I had experience with one from the ground up. So I offered my input at meetings and the suggestions were politely put aside, and then two months later someone came up with the same suggestion and it would pass. That happened a couple of times, and that was again, I thought, because I was new. But it continued to happen. I got to the point where I started to document stuff just for my own sanity. There have been opportunities where I planted seeds, and no problems, they passed. I guess knowing that they were mine gave me some satisfaction, but no one else knew it. I am a lot quieter at meetings now than I used to be. Now the way that I feel about them is that I go to the meetings if there is any voting to be done. I vote, and I listen to what is said, and that's pretty much it. As far as coming in with suggestions or ideas, I don't do that anymore.

It hasn't been all negative. I've met and worked with some really super students, and I think that the thing that has probably kept me here was that I still get excited about what goes on in the classroom. There are students who learn and, you know, you can almost see when the light comes on, so that still excites me. I guess when that stops I will quit because all the other hassles really are not worth it.

I enjoy lecturing and I enjoy talking in class. I think the fact that I have worked in the field also adds to my ability to make that stuff come alive in the classroom. I can tell them that what's in the book may not work and I can help them with the theory and the practical part of it. I get excited when students just take off and go with the typing, for example, because it is individualized—no one person has to be held back. I have one woman who finished the course last week, almost a month before the course ended. It was obvious that she just caught on, and she did the work and she was excited about doing it. When they ask questions which tell me that they have been reading and they have been thinking about what they have read, that excites me. To have a student start out with a D or F and then end up with a C or with a B, I can't help but think that the two of us did that; along with my help, the student was able to move from one point to another. And that keeps me here.

I would like to be able to do more of the things that I did in the clerical skills program, do more grant writing, and then still stay in teaching. The clerical skills program was an opportunity to help another group of people. I've got people in my family who had to quit school and didn't have a chance to get the high school diploma, so I guess I have a soft spot in my heart, so that it was easy for me to work with them. I know that once people leave high school for whatever reason—if they left because they had to go out and work or the women because they were pregnant—they don't usually come back. The women who came into the program said that they didn't really want to go back to their neighborhood high school because they were older and they would be stuck in a classroom with younger people. They didn't have the credentials to go on to a four-year school so the community college, being where it is, is a unique place to address those people. And we were right in the community and we had the equipment. They could come to us without having a high school diploma, if we could set the program up and set the times that were comfortable for them, because many of them had families, small children, so they couldn't make it all day, for example. So this program ran from nine to twelve, so that by one o'clock they were out of there and they could pick their kids up in the afternoon and be home when they got home from school.

Given the number of years I've been here, I probably should have, I don't know how to put it, I should have more say, for example, in scheduling. I'm not talking about times. I'm talking about my not being given all the correcting courses, for example. The shorthand and typing are just correcting courses, and maybe that's just the way that I felt: that if you spend time there for a while, you should get less of them and have some diversity. There are two of us who get the beginning level courses. It's difficult to have three typing courses in one semester, and a shorthand. That is all correcting, so you go nuts. You correct all the time and I think that could just be spread around evenly. There are people who have been here a couple of years longer than I who will say, "I don't want typing," and there are people who have not had typing for a couple of years. There are people who prefer not to teach certain courses and don't have to teach them.

The division chair with the registrar will make up a master schedule for the division. She will give me a schedule, and this time she said, "These schedules are already concrete so no changes." So I couldn't change it if I wanted to. Last year I had all eight o'clock classes and that was rough getting through that. I would have an eight o'clock, nine o'clock, and then have three hours break, and then another class in the afternoon. And on Friday, I came in for one class. That's the way the schedule happened to work out that particular semester. It bothered me a lot at first because I saw the inequities in that system that they had, and people would say things like, "I got to get my kids out to go to school, so I can't have an eight o'clock class," and I didn't have any kids so I really didn't have an excuse for an eight o'clock class. It would have been nice if I had maybe just two or three eight o'clock classes. I just didn't get a lot of sleep. I always wanted to get the papers back the next day because they couldn't go on until I gave them the feedback. Then I'd have to get up in the morning at six-thirty so that I could get out of here to get to an eight o'clock class. Sometimes I got there five after eight, so that they would be standing outside waiting for me. It was hard. But I got through that semester.

When I first came here, I think that, in some ways, I was a lot stronger than I am now. It is just the constant battle has made me weak, and that's why it becomes easy for me sometimes to say I'm not going to fight it. Not that I was very vocal, but I would sit in a meeting and if I heard things going on in the meeting that were wrong, I would say, "I think we are doing the students a disservice."

For example, at one point we were talking about raising the standards for typewriting. The standards that we had when I first came were really very low and they were not a challenge to the students at all. I went to a meeting, and some of the teachers said that this is the way it has always been, and I had no qualms about speaking up and saying, "I think we are wrong. I think we are just not challenging the students enough." It took a good while for that to get changed, but it did get changed. Now I hear things and I don't hear. It is a kind of a complacency, and I guess I don't like that, because that's not me, that's not how I was. It should be the other way around: the older you get, the stronger you should become.

It's difficult for me right now because I don't feel that I'm using the education that I do have and I know I'm not using all the skills that I know I've got. And in a sense I guess I'm feeling stuck right now. I'm not utilizing, I'm not doing the best that I can do. I work with people and I'm good with my students and I know that. The students who are willing to come in there and work, we move, and that's perceived as being hard. The students always say it is hard, and then they get through it and then they appreciate it afterwards, and then they come back and they tell you. I think maybe I am underutilized.

I think that they may not be perceiving it as a racial thing, but they often don't look beyond my color and that, in effect, impairs their vision. I see color when people make me see color. In a good number of instances, my colleagues have made me see color. In effect, I think they don't see beyond the fact that I am a black person. One person on the faculty is European and had not really had a lot of contact with blacks, so he came to my office just to find out and ask questions and I can appreciate that. I would prefer people asking questions because it is a sign that maybe they really don't know and would like to know, rather than making assumptions that could be wrong.

I'm angry because I have to fight and I thought that kind of fighting was behind me, and it's not. This is 1982 and I did a lot of that kind of fighting in '64, so how many years is that? You know, when I look at it, not much has changed. There has been the illusion that there's been change. I'm angry that I have to still fight the same kind of fight. Fighting for job, fighting against what is

obviously ignorance and prejudice—that was the same kind of fight
I was fighting in '64.

Profile: Robert Thatcher

*Robert Thatcher is in his forties and teaches
physics in a California community college.*

When I came here it was just teach, teach, teach. If I wanted
to do something else, I could do something else, but teaching would
be primary. I had an adjustment to being around just whites,
colleagues basically white. The only shocker probably was the
notions, the ideas, that students would have about you when you
walk in, in terms of your qualifications. A lot of students here had
never had a black instructor, had never been around black people.
Now all of a sudden you got a black instructor. It was an eye-
opening situation for them. The first year that I taught here I taught
a night class. When I walked in they asked me whether I was
subbing for the regular instructor and I said, "Yes," and so when
I came back the following week, they said, "You're still subbing."
"Yes, I'm still subbing." I think it was about the third meeting that
they finally discovered that I was the instructor.

It seems like employers ask a little more of blacks. Maybe not
"ask" but demand a little more. A little more pressure is put on
blacks. I think a little more pressure is even put on me here at this
college. Invariably, the first week of school, students tend to ask a
hell of a lot of questions, questions that are not even relevant to the
topic, and I think it's a situation of feeling you out, seeing whether
or not you know the material. I don't sense that same type of
attitude when they go into a white instructor's class. I think it's
assumed that he or she knows. But I think sometimes with a black
instructor, it's "Prove to me that you do know and then I'll listen."
If I differ with the book, it's difficult for them to accept the fact that
I'm saying the author is wrong, period. But I think once I get going,
it's really like someone just opens their eyes. I've seen some white
instructors that I know weren't prepared, and there's no overt
pressure by the students to do anything about it. I've also seen a
black instructor that was ill-prepared, and he got a lot of direct

pressure. I'm not apologizing for either instructor. I think you should be prepared, but let's treat both people the same way.

Another example: there was a problem that came up in our physics text. The problem was going around in the department. I ran across the same problem and solution in another text. So I made a copy directly from the text, verbatim, didn't leave out anything, and I brought it to the department. Several of the instructors said, "No, it can't be right." I said, "Well, show me what's wrong with it." Well, they don't know what's wrong with it but [they insist], "It's not right. It's just not right." I was kind of disturbed. They think they're rejecting my solution.

As another example, our general science textbook—I fought the book bitterly. I said it was a lousy book and a number of people just couldn't accept that, so I just kept up so much noise that at the second department meeting, on the agenda was a reaction to all new books. When I came, I had several pages of specific notes. When they got to me I started going through very specific points. Before the end of the semester, just about the whole department was acknowledging that it was a lousy book. I find that if I have a criticism, I have to be very specific and detail it out, do all my homework; and I think sometimes other people might not have to do all that. One of the problems that you really have to watch when those subtle things are there—you've got to kind of ask yourself, "Are those things because of me, a person, or because of me, a black person?" I try not to be in the dark on anything, but I also really just don't try to magnify anything. You know, sometimes it can be you, the individual, period. It's independent of race. Color might be a factor, but it might be a minor factor, or it might be a major factor. I can't go into the heads of other people and I try not to, you know.

There was one instructor who had a hell of a time calling me by my name. He called me every kind of name. When I'd see him, I'd just call him another name and he got the message.

I had a student that called me "coach." "Hell, I'm not a coach," I told him. "I'm an instructor. You can call me by my first name, you can call me Robert, you can call me Dr. Thatcher, but I'm not a coach." Whites sometimes will call blacks "coaches." They have a bunch of strange names they sometimes address blacks with. When you sense that type of thing happening, you just say, "Look, I want you to get off and get on here," and I think when you make that clear, people tend to respect you. The basic thing that I try to do, whether it's on a social level or a working level, is to tell people to deal with me as a person, not any of these stereotype trips. Deal with me as a person.

I try to be very academic in nature; when I go into the classroom, I tell students, "I'm not here trying to win friendship; I'm here trying to teach you science. If you hate me and know my science, I've accomplished my job. If you end up liking me and learning my science, that's even better. If you end up liking me and don't know science, I've failed." For some, it's tough for them to accept that. Now whether it's accepting that because I'm black or accepting that because it's a different teaching situation, I don't even get into that. I'm just saying what I expect. You come to my class to work. I don't want to hear any excuses. When you complain that I work you too hard, that my exams are too hard, I don't get pushed out of shape over that.

I came out of the university with a Ph.D., not in physics—it's in education. I didn't know and I still don't know exactly where teaching might take me. I've really enjoyed teaching. I still enjoy teaching. But I kind of figured at some point I might want to do something else, and I felt that with so much experience in education, that if I could get some type of training that will pull from my educational background, that would be nice. So I have looked at administration as a possible alternative.

I thought the university would be a good opportunity. There were no blacks that I'd ever heard of that came out of the university, so I had no models, no images. Most of the blacks that went to college went to the state college. The university was just a mystery place for me. This lady, a black lady, was working on her Ph.D. at the time, and she asked me, "Why don't you work on your Ph.D.?" Then there was another instructor in the humanities who was working on his Ph.D. And he said, "Man, you should start on your Ph.D. You've got enough time." So it was that type of thing that got me looking at the university. All of a sudden I did see someone that I rubbed shoulders with that was actually there.

Normally it takes you two years to do your course work, but I had to spend a year going back and picking up courses. I actually was on the verge of quitting the program. You can get encouragement from home, but a lot of times they really don't quite understand the pressures that you're under. You're trying to be a family person, you're trying to teach full-time, and you're trying to go to school full-time. There's only so much pressure that you can stand, and I was just basically exhausted. As I worked on the degree and I saw the job mobility around here, and I saw whites in administrative positions and they didn't have a degree, then that began to tell me that the degree is really not necessary. Because I've seen a white without a degree and a black with a degree, and the white got the job. It kind of told me that really the degree is not the key.

Sometimes when you push a lot and you don't back up and regroup, I think you reach a point where you start burning yourself out. I think you have to feel rewarded about what you do. Over the last couple of semesters, especially, I've had a very high dropout rate. I've really been bothered with that because in the past, I haven't had a high dropout rate. I can't understand that because I feel that I'm working much harder. I'm doing, I think, a much better job. I gave a take-home exam; I said, "Get help from any source." But damn it, when you tell students they can get help from anybody and they don't do that, it makes you stop and say maybe I oughta tell them, "Everybody gets an A if you just come to class." Maybe when you reach that point, maybe you ought to begin to think about something else, because you've lost the desire to do what you originally set out to do, and that's to provide a legacy in terms of something academically.

One of the reasons I press so in terms of demanding from my students is because I don't see them as being "terminal" students. I teach my courses as if they are planning to go on to a four-year school, and I try to adopt some of the same attributes, characteristics, that an instructor in college would adopt, expecting students to be able to present problems in a logical and organized manner on paper. Students being able to explain problems, being able to analyze—I think those are important principles. I tell students that they will learn more than science in my class. They'll learn how to take notes, how to utilize the notes, how to go look for resource information. If you're having problems, don't give up. If something is not right, you ask questions.

I've always felt that everybody should have a legacy. Everybody should leave some type of imprint, make some sort of a contribution. Teaching is something that I can do. I can help others by doing that. I look back at my own struggling time in college and I say, "I should be able to make it a lot easier for people who come from essentially the same background—that is, where they didn't really get started in school." I try to keep that in mind, trying to leave some type of imprint. When you talk about tearing down racism and discrimination, you can do it in a peaceful way. I've always felt that you could change attitudes by actually being out involved in something where people are not accustomed to seeing you there. I see myself leaving an imprint in terms of doing something for society, helping the races see that they can be together. In the process of teaching physics, I have a lot of students who talk to me. They've never had a chance to just sit down with a black person and say, "How do you feel? What's it like? Do you have problems? Do you have pain, do you have joy?"

I think 90 percent of the time, in order to be successful, you've got to know a lot about the system, and I think that's what probably has helped me. Even coming here I know that experienced instructors like new instructors to sit down and talk with them, come in and visit their classes. Again, you know, you hate to draw any conclusions, but I find myself initiating more, exchanging tests, talking to people about classroom situations. I had several instructors that came in, but it was about how to handle a black student, rather than handling a student in general. It had to be something related to a black problem, you know, if they were to come in.

So I think I've really bent over backwards. I do the initiating most of the time. So here again might be one of those subtle things. As an example, two other instructors, or three of us, have eight o'clock classes together. I would always come and wait or make sure that they were ready to go, and we'd all walk together. But they didn't do the same thing for me. You see, you're always reaching out, but there's no one reaching back for you.

Profile: Daniel Ramirez

Daniel Ramirez teaches history in a California
community college. He is in his forties.

I know that being of Mexican background helped me get this
job at the community college, though I think it was also who I
knew. You can talk about affirmative action, or the most qualified,
but the old buddy system is still there when all is said and done.

When I first came here, I thought it was just a stepping stone.
I'd been trained to do research. Nobody talked about preparing you
to teach at a junior college. But the job market started to decline.
I thought, well, if things are starting to go downhill, maybe with
the affirmative action program I'm probably still in better shape
than most people are. It didn't turn out that way. The first offer was
a couple of years after I started here. A private college contacted me.
In this case I was in the driver's seat. They had good students. It
looked like a college campus, the ideal. I don't think they leveled
with me totally on the fact that they were trying to get minorities.
They downplayed that part. But I suspected that I would be the first
to be fired if they had financial problems. So in the back of my mind
was that if I got this job, I was leaving the security of the junior
college, where the future looked fairly bright, for a small college
where the economic future didn't look all that bright. So I turned
it down. A couple of years later, a professor I'd admired at my grad
school wrote me a letter saying they were looking for a person at
the university he'd moved to. It was half-time in the history
department. They were looking for a person that had administrative
abilities to work with minorities. I got a little bit excited about it,
but not all that much. A series of letters were exchanged with a lot
of different people, and then they had some problems of their own.
I kept thinking I don't really want to be an administrator. And so
it fell through.

When I got the offers at the junior colleges, I wasn't all that
enthralled because I knew that they didn't really care what kind of
research you did; nor did most junior colleges do anything to
encourage your research. They were interested almost totally in the
teaching aspect. At the university, even though the emphasis was

not on teaching, I had some great teachers. The best teachers were the best researchers. Most people don't realize that. They think it's either-or. Once I got to the junior college, I decided maybe I can fall into that same category. I always go in prepared. The lecture is always well organized, and in all my years of teaching here, I've always given back papers that are received at the next class meeting. I expect a lot from the students. I have to teach by example. So I've been very conscientious. It's gotten to the point where I actually like teaching. At first I was kind of afraid of it, and I certainly was not enthusiastic about it, but as time has gone by, I like getting in front of thirty people now.

I always make extensive notations on the blue books. I've never in my life given an objective exam, true and false, or short-answer or whatever, because at a junior college you're trying to teach people things beyond subject matter: You're trying to teach them responsibility; you're trying to teach them to communicate in written form and also verbally. It's possible not to know your students and not know anything that they've done if you do true or false types of exams two or three times a semester. I like to see what people have done, what they're capable of doing. I like to see if my past evaluation of them was correct or not.

When I first came here, I gave seven F's the first semester I was here, and I had three or four people come up to me and say, "We don't give F's at this school. What do you think you're doing? This is a junior college; we don't give F's. Are you trying to hurt the students or what?" As time goes by I've become less uptight in terms of standards. Times have changed too. We often forget that students are different now than they were fifteen years ago. Even if I went back to the university, I think there would be a difference. They're not going to necessarily want to put in seventy hours a week of studying. Maybe they didn't want to fifteen years ago, but they did it. There's also a generation gap.

This is kind of a marketplace. I know that if I'm going to assign seven books a semester instead of three, that there will be a good number of students that'll say, "Hey, wait a minute, this other teacher is teaching the same class—he's only got three books." Now they're not going to ask, "Is he trying to acquaint me with new ideas?" or "What is the value of this book?" They don't want to go beyond the stage of "There's seven books versus three books," and if I assign those seven books I'm gonna have half the number of students. I think that's sad, you know, because that wasn't the case at the university, where most people actually appreciated the efforts of the instructor to deal with ideas. It's sad, but you have to deal with it. I can't afford to wind up with under twenty students. The administrators always talk about intellectual integrity, integrity in the course and all that. They never tell us, "It's a matter of bodies, keep them in." But I know they don't like to see declining enrollment, and most teachers are confused because they're getting both of these messages. Of course, integrity is important. At the same time, we've got to do something to maintain the student numbers.

I was the first one in history to get a Ph.D. And people would make jokes about Ph.D.'s that displayed a kind of envy or hostility. But they were very rare—two or three times a year. My colleagues have an ambivalent attitude about the Ph.D. Most of them started Ph.D. programs and for some reason, they had to drop out. They're here and they realize they're going to be here; they're not going to go back to graduate school and get that Ph.D. I appreciate something I couldn't ten years ago: As in most professions, after your mid-thirties you realize that whatever you're doing now is probably what you're going to be doing for the rest of your working life. I'm beginning to feel maybe a little bit that way. I'm beginning to feel that maybe I really ought to get that book out and published because nobody cares what you did ten years ago or even five years ago, they want to know what you're doing now. I don't think that simply teaching in the classroom and being conscientious is enough. I wouldn't be satisfied just being a history teacher.

I try to maintain an interest in research. But now it's downright difficult to go home and work on an article or whatever. It's not my most important priority. I'd rather go home and read a textbook so I can prepare a lecture. But I still think it's important to maintain an interest in research and even in publishing, if possible, though I think those are two different categories. I see myself as a historian. "Historian" is the right word. Not just a history teacher because I've published. I think that's the distinction between being a teacher of history and a historian, and I've always wanted to be a historian. Therefore I think that research at the very least is important. You have to get out and go to professional meetings, and go to seminars, and talk and get involved in intellectual discussions, and do things that are difficult in this environment now.

In the past few years the most important things that have happened to me were the two summer seminars I went to. In the first one I was the youngest member of the seminar. I was the only junior college member. Everybody else taught at a four-year school. The seminar lasted two months and I came back and incorporated a lot of that stuff into my classes. What I'm proposing to do on my sabbatical stems directly from that experience. It really recharges my battery, and I started to remember what universities were like again. I think I had almost forgotten.

I find that in all my years of teaching, I feel possibly more positive now than any time in the past. Instead of getting burned out or feeling that I made the wrong career choice, the more time goes by, the better I feel about this particular line of work. I see it as a profession, and it's permitted me to do a lot of things that I think are important. My priorities include being involved with ideas and being a student for the rest of my life. To be good at it, you have to continually read. Teaching has permitted me to learn more and more, to become more knowledgeable. It's also permitted a great deal of leisure. We have three months, and we have a big holiday for Christmas, for Easter, and the leisure I enjoy. I've taken advantage of the time for the most part to travel.

Even initially I had some pretty positive feelings because I had been to junior college, unlike a lot of teachers here who never went to junior college, didn't know anything about a junior college, and didn't know anybody that went to a junior college. Many of them, I think, felt that this was a step down. My wife initially felt something like this; she'd never been to junior college nor did she know anybody that attended one. But my attitude was always different than hers because I'd been through this kind of a system and I'd remembered that some of my better teachers were junior college instructors. So the feelings were not all negative. But I was ambitious. I wanted to go to a university.

When I took part in these two seminars that I've alluded to, with twenty-four individuals from different academic backgrounds, it became evident to me that the junior college, especially the one that I was at, had a lot to offer. Talking to some of my colleagues that went to colleges, you also learn that many of them are bogged down with committees, with publish or perish. That university setting doesn't look nearly as attractive as it did ten or fifteen years ago. On the other hand, the junior college looks pretty good to me. The security here is, I suppose, a very big thing.

Some of the colleagues that I socialize with may know about my work; but even within the history group, most people don't know that I've published anything. Some of my other colleagues have published and I'm aware of what they've done. I've gone out and bought their books and I've read them, but we hardly ever have occasion to talk about subject matter in that way. I read my colleagues' books because I think it's professional courtesy. It's something—if you're working with somebody—you should know what they're doing and become knowledgeable about it. A few years ago, there was a display of faculty publications that was quite nice. There were fifteen or twenty books there, but there's no tremendous emphasis in that regard. You're not encouraged to do it; it's not expected, it's not part of your job. A junior college like this one— and this one's better than most—I really think does not stimulate the faculty intellectually. There's very little encouragement. At the same time, I don't feel that it discourages it. The opportunities are available if one is willing to pursue them. I think the initiative has to come from individuals. I don't complain about it because I think it's the individual. If you really want to do it, I suppose you'll do it.

Half of the students are really interested in history. They want to know who the great historians were, who Edward Gibbon was, and what historians have said about Gibbon. The other half don't want to pursue it that far, but the more I research, the more I'm able to satisfy their curiosity. Historiography is simply more than history. I think they do, in fact, see me as a historian. They make a distinction between having a Ph.D. and not. I think they're all aware of that, who has Ph.D's and who doesn't; and sometimes for the wrong reasons, they think it's important that you have a Ph.D. Most students, all things considered, would rather take a class from somebody that was very knowledgeable about the field rather than somebody who has a passing interest in that field.

With students, to have a Ph.D. is really helpful to me to maintain credibility, which I find I have to do being Mexican. I think there are a lot of people that assume that anybody with a Latin last name or any black instructor got the job because of affirmative action. They don't really belong here; they got a break; and maybe they're not as competent as other people. So having a Ph.D. breaks down the kind of resistance that you might encounter. I know that there are a lot of students here that have never had a black teacher or a Mexican teacher, so there's a certain responsibility that goes along with it. Many of them will get a positive or negative attitude of Mexicans because of the way that I come across in the classroom possibly, seeing how a lot of these kids have never seen a Mexican. So I want to project a professional image, and I want them to know that I have a Ph.D.

Ten percent of our faculty is black or Mexican. There are a few Asians. I was made adviser to the Mexican American Club years ago when students were fairly militant, especially Chicano students. I was asked to give a speech and be candid. I went up and gave a speech and said, "You know, I'm here to teach students primarily, not necessarily Mexican students." So my orientation was significantly different. Yet the students there were very positive about my orientation. A couple of my colleagues that were there, on the other hand, felt that I was selling out. "How can you say something like that?" was the way they put it, and one of them is always spurring me on, saying, "You know, you need to make more of a commitment in terms of your race." In the seventies we were often asked, "What have you done for your race today?" He still maintains that orientation a little bit. I never really maintained it, in part because of my training. It was an academic training, a training in history. It's hard to mouth easy slogans if for ten years you've had this kind of academic training. At the same time, I see myself as adhering to the Chicano movement. I agree with most of the aims of the Chicano movement. At first I had difficulties because in the area I came from, "Chicano" was a bad word. "Mexican-American" was the right word. I've come to accept "Chicano."

At the beginning I was considered more conservative. Now, I think, by most of my students, I'm considered more radical. Nobody wants to hear about affirmative action or prejudice or discrimination or the fact that we don't have enough Mexicans or that the university only has 2 percent Chicano students. That kind of information is not that desirable today, especially by people that are not Chicano. I still give that kind of information. My ideas on race and on other things haven't changed significantly since I was in high school. Sometimes they're popular and sometimes they're not.

Being Mexican was, through most of my life, probably a detriment. At this level it is a positive thing, because that's what differentiates me from other teachers in the minds of many students: that I come from a Mexican background, also a lower-class background. I've learned that the background has been positive in terms of teaching, that I can get their interest, whereas I might not be able to if I mirrored their background. At the same time, I try not to overdo it, try to maintain a sense of balance, because I think that's being professional. I don't believe in using the classroom to get people to march for a lettuce strike or this or that. My colleague's position, which I can appreciate, is that school is not an ivory tower, that it's part of society. I mentioned that even in high school I was a loner. I didn't hang around with the groups; I did not take a position that was popular with other people, and so I don't feel badly.

I am aware of race. I didn't marry a Mexican. My kids are not totally Mexican. I'm aware of all of that. In my own personal life, many of the faculty members see me as a representative of Mexican-Americans and many of them erroneously believe (and I've stopped trying to convince them that I'm not all that typical) that what I think about Cesar Chavez, or whatever, is what all Mexicans think. The group of people that I come from is very diverse in terms of backgrounds, and certainly few Mexicans are in the same situation that I'm in right now. I also try to make students aware of their stereotypes: the Mexican is illiterate, a dropout from education, a low-rider, and speaks in a funny dialogue. And so I perform a positive service just by being here. People come up to me and say, "You're Italian, aren't you?" or "You're Portuguese." They assume

I'm not Mexican "because you're not at all like a low-rider," and after a while I think it occurs to many people that the majority of Mexican people are not low-riders, that indeed if I'm not typically Mexican, I'm not all that atypical either. I think people like me do play a positive role at this level simply by being here.

12

Community College Counselors: Issues of Morale and Professional Status

Neither faculty nor administrator, counselors do the work of both. The profiles that follow reveal the wide range of counselors' work. They do academic, career, transfer, and personal counseling and advising. Sometimes they do therapy. They teach, sit on college committees, do program development work, and troubleshoot for the administration. They maintain a liaison with high schools, business and industry, and four-year colleges and universities.

Despite, or perhaps because of, the wide range of counselors' work, faculty can treat counselors as though their work—in comparison to that of faculty—is secondary. Counselors, on the other hand, feel that faculty are often too rigidly tied to their disciplines and career fields. Without a discipline or field to protect, counselors see themselves as advocates for students. Counselors volunteer for a wide range of college work in order to ensure that their perspective is considered, but the faculty seem more to tolerate than value their contribution.

As community colleges grew, faculty were willing to have counselors take over jobs they once did, but at the same time some faculty came to resent the increasing fragmentation of their relationship with students. Because counselors do not contribute di-

229

rectly to the growth of the number of F.T.E. (full-time equivalent) students enrolled, which is the basis of much of the funding community colleges receive, the work they do is sometimes not affirmed as being as central to the college as that of the work of faculty. Caught between administration and faculty, counselors sometimes find themselves unrepresented in faculty contracts, and yet without the power and autonomy of administrators. When represented in a faculty contract, counselors can find their interests negotiated away in order to protect the interests of the teaching faculty.

The result of these ambiguities is that counselors can find themselves near the bottom of the professional totem pole in community colleges. In many cases, counselors are treated as the scapegoats for what goes wrong in a college. The consequence of their low position on the totem pole can be a sense of vulnerability among their college colleagues. In many ways, the counselors we interviewed were deeply involved in their own search for power and opportunity, and for some, the most affirmative vision they had of their work was as a stepping stone to something else. The profiles that follow reveal the loss to the college in experience, sensitivity, and good work that this limited affirmation can mean.

Profile: Julia Alvarez

Julia Alvarez is a counselor in her thirties working at a suburban community college in Massachusetts.

Working here at the counseling center has opened my eyes tremendously to myself, to the world, to others. It was the turning point in my life. As the most senior member of the counseling staff now, other than the director of counseling, I do have a lot of overall office coordination responsibilities. I am in charge of the orientation program for incoming students, involved in general overall program planning and [in] basically working with the director and substituting for him when the need arises. In addition, I have the normal counseling and teaching loads that all the counselors have. I teach two one-credit courses each semester. These are personal development courses lasting five weeks apiece. I also have a case load of individual student counselees, and also I do a lot of walk-in, quick-question kind of counseling. For instance, people will be walking constantly in with questions about their academic program here, about transferring, about testing, about financial matters. In addition, we have other kinds of group activities such as the admissions counseling sessions for prospective students. We have transfer workshops for people who consider transferring over to another institution, and we have career workshops. I am, in addition, a member of the curriculum committee, and I am a member of the subcommittee of the curriculum committee. I would say that my job has a lot of variety. There is nothing boring about it. It is a challenge to have to change gears constantly. I feel that it is preparing me or training me extremely well to deal with any kind of high-pressure job.

Out of the fifteen-week semester, I teach ten weeks. The difficulty is getting prep time. I have a love-hate relationship with teaching. I dread it, but I love it. It is something that is not necessarily required of counselors. We got into the teaching field voluntarily. No one came down and said we had to teach. As a matter of fact, we had to fight several battles in order for the academic sector to grant us the authority to teach. We fought for that from a philosophical basis of really feeling that this was a need and it was an effective counseling tool. Our courses are fully credited and recognized throughout the college.

We do a wide variety of counseling that ranges from advising to therapy to personal counseling. A lot of the counseling is support counseling. For instance, one area that I am especially interested in is their math anxiety. You get a lot of referrals on that topic. I am not exactly sure how I started being interested in math anxiety, except for the fact that I enjoyed math and I have had good experiences with it throughout high schools and colleges. I was amazed to see the number of people that would come into my office and go on and on about how terrible a subject math was, how they hated it, how they couldn't do it. They were trying to get out of trying to take math, and it just struck me it was such a pity that people went around feeling this way about math, which for me was such an enjoyable subject. I realized that the difference is not necessarily how well you do but your attitude toward math and started looking into why people develop a different attitude toward math. At that time a lot of literature and articles were starting to come out on the subject. So I started collecting things and talking to a math faculty member here at the college. I ran a couple of groups in the day and in the evening. We ran one group last summer for sixteen women and one man.

I always felt that I could achieve anything that I wanted to based on my personal qualifications and not related to the fact that I was a woman. But as I look around, I have to face the realities of the system. For instance, as I look at the structure of the college, the president is male and until recently all of the four deans were male. If you look at other colleges, they have women in the position of dean of students, which has always been the bottom of the totem pole. The next rung would be the directors, and all of the directors are men. I will be excluded from positions at a high level because whoever is doing the hiring is picturing a man in that role and does not see a woman in that role, or may have a man already picked out. They picture a man.

I think that being a counselor at this college is more detrimental to me than being a woman. Counselors are considered the workhorses. They are really the lowest-level professionals that the college has, the ones that can be given all the extra work and the blame for things that go wrong. Counselors in the past have always been associated with administration. We are held in high esteem by the administration because we solve problems. We answer questions. We make the administration's job a lot easier. The problems come with faculty more than anybody else because they see us as administrators. They have no idea of the confidentiality of the counseling relationship, the diversity of our jobs. A lot of them feel that we just sit in our offices all day and wait for students to walk in and that is all we do. When they see us on all these committees, they feel we are on these committees because we don't have anything better to do.

In the first couple of years, I felt on top of the world, being a counselor. That is not enough of a motivator for me anymore. I don't like being at the bottom of any totem pole. I don't necessarily have to be on the top anymore, but I don't feel comfortable being at the bottom. I don't think that it is the right place for me. Feels like you are always struggling to prove yourself, to prove what you are worth. For instance, I don't feel comfortable standing in the outer part of my office because people walk by and get the impression that I am not doing anything. If they walk in Friday afternoon and there are three or four of us sitting around a table, they will drop a comment about the counselors sitting around talking to each other. So we are constantly having to be careful of our image. If I am going to talk to some other counselor, I usually go into one of the offices. We are very easy targets because we are involved in so many areas of the college. We are here for such a large number of hours, we are so visible, so accountable.

It seems that the lower you are, the more indispensable you become. I can identify with this having been a secretary, where you were really low. The pay, the status, everything. You were chained to that desk. There is very little recognition, very little incentive provided at that level, and the counselor is only a little bit better than that in terms of the amount of flexibility in our positions. It is a very structured position in that it has the framework of the hours of nine to five and you have to be available for every moment of every day, pretty much. And I was looking at salary figures; it turns out that we work 30 percent more days a year, and our salary is not even at 100 percent of what the faculty's are. We are at 90 percent. Salary speaks also in terms of being at the bottom.

In some ways our perceptions are similar to faculty members. We identify with the faculty to a large extent. We see the students on a day-to-day basis, are aware of students' needs. But we don't have a discipline to protect. Faculty feel that they have to uphold the integrity of the discipline or ensure a certain kind of quality. We don't really have anything like that we need to protect. So we feel that we are able to be quite student-oriented. Many times it boils down to having information about students and advocating for students. So I find that the counselors have a very strong student voice on committees and more of a liberal orientation than most of the faculty.

Some days it seems that the whole job is useless, like you are spinning your wheels. Other days it seems like you are accomplishing a great deal. There are lots of times when I have a sense of personal satisfaction. Let's say someone that I have been counseling has had a good week, and they have reached goals that they have set and feel really good about it: I feel a real sense of satisfaction that something is happening in my counseling. In the teaching the same thing: When I hear students talking about how they enjoy the class and how much they have learned and I see them participating actively, I get a real sense of satisfaction. From an administrative point of view, I have had a lot of successes. I have implemented new programs that have been successful, proposed different things that have affected the whole college, and that has given me a sense of satisfaction.

I see this position as a temporary one in my life. I don't see myself in this position five years from now. Hopefully, I won't be at this position two years from now. This position is an entry-level position, a chance for me to develop as an individual. But it is a dead-end professionally. The next position would be director of counseling. I see myself moving into some area of management. I enjoy decision making. I enjoy working with budgets and planning programs and implementing programs. I enjoy high-level responsibility. I enjoy independence. I enjoy hard work. Lately it is a little more of a chore to come to work. I kind of think of the day, and I realize there are going to be good things and not so good things, and I am not that excited about coming to work. That is why I am starting to think that it is probably time for me to start thinking of new horizons.

I feel that in terms of the educational hierarchy, that the community colleges are considered the bottom. I resent that. I don't like to be associated with something on the bottom, but most of the people who think of community colleges at the bottom are people who don't realize the uniqueness of the community college as an institution that crosses all sections of society. We had a breakfast two days ago to which we invited people from the high schools in the area. The main goal was to sell them on the idea of the community college where all their students can come, both the higher-level students and the student who never thought of going to college. We had some students who have graduated there to share a little bit of what the college has meant to them. The stories that we heard were just incredible. For instance, one woman was on welfare and she reached the bottom and someone told her about the college. She came through our Special Services Program and went on and now she got a fellowship at an Ivy League college.

I feel that I am performing a useful function. . . . The community college is designed for those people who have not had a chance, who are in a certain social and economic status through no wrongdoing on their own. A lot of people that are on welfare or have not had access to higher education could go to college, could enter a profession, or at least have the freedom to choose. These people grew up thinking that they have very limited choices, limited options. So it is kind of a social justice institution where you are really bringing people from a position of low self-concept, low economic status, to a higher position in the freeing of their minds and the opening of their options.

I feel especially that this community college for the most part has a clear vision of its role or its mission of finding persons where they are and helping them along to achieve the goals they set for themselves, assist them in setting those goals. I feel very good about working in this particular community college. Most people at this college have that mission of serving and so that is one of the reasons that I enjoy working here. A lot of colleges, four-year colleges and universities, do not set out to do the same thing that the community college has set out to do, nor should they. I would have a hard time going to work for Harvard; I would have a very hard time relating to Harvard's mission.

There is a certain area that I didn't mention that exists, and it bothers me and haunts me continually because of my background and because of what I know about justice and injustice. I feel that the society is very influential on its members; the American society [is] influential toward conformity. And I find that in spite of myself, I have been influenced to conform. It is hard for me to be a true rebel in the system. So I have conformed a lot to the community colleges' stated philosophy. On the other hand, there are these feelings that bother me a lot, such as [that] the community colleges tend to perpetuate the system in which there is injustice. The community college doesn't really question the basic premises of the way that the society is set up. It is not a revolutionary force in the community at all, and it doesn't do that much to change the way things are basically. I don't know what could in this society. To tell you the truth, this is one of the most conservative societies in the world. It tends to swallow people up into its influence rather than to teach people how to critique and how to examine it. It is an issue that bothers me, but it bothered me more at the beginning than it does now. I realized that I conform more now.

It is easier to fit in. I question less. The most revolutionary that one gets in a system like this is pointing out when we are serving ourselves rather than serving the student, but we don't affect society; structures continue to be the same. I find myself defending positions that in the past I have never defended. Here I find myself saying things that in the past would never come out of my mouth, feeling certain ways, feeling very comfortable with my position, feeling very much an individual, a lot of individualistic feelings. In the past I used to care a lot more, and I was willing to sacrifice more of my own. When I felt that way, I was more a teenager or early twenties. As you grow older, you tend to become more conservative. So I can explain what has happened to me, but it bothers me that I have lost some of the vision of my past, the critical attitude toward my surroundings; and I feel it comes from almost feeling that you can't do much to change the system.

Profile: Richard Soletti

Richard Soletti in his early thirties, was a counselor in a suburban community college in Massachusetts until recently.

I think this is the best job in the college. It combines all of the parts of what is good about working in a college. Besides your general counseling duties, you have an administrative area, and my area was transfer. What I did was to just look at that area, really look at transfer here: who transfers, and how does it work, and really develop the idea of transfer. I had to do a lot of legwork: contacting colleges, building relationships, building up credibility for our college. Because transfer is really a relationship with another college and nothing to do with the quality of courses. In terms of actively meeting the four-year colleges and universities and inviting them here, we would have conferences between departments; they would meet our faculty and we would meet their faculty. We had "transfer days." These organizations, thirty colleges, come here twice a year.

Now my area is academic advisement. We work through data processing, assigning faculty members as advisers. By the collective bargaining agreement, every faculty member has to meet the student three times. We organize group meetings, select the rooms and handouts, notify the students when the meeting is, so that takes coordinating, getting letters out. It is a massive task.

We are involved at new-student orientation. It is orientation and assessment. New students come in to college, they are assessed, for English, writing, mathematical skills. Second, they are given an orientation by the counselors. The assessment information is given right back to the students at orientation, so not only do they learn about the college and how to select their courses but they receive information about themselves; that is built into the orientation system.

Another administrative thing that I do is that I am a member of the curriculum committee here. That is the committee that approves courses and programs offered by the college. And then we have staff meetings.

I have about twelve students that I see on a regular basis. Those are students that I would say are involved in long-term, psychotherapeutic kinds of counseling, transitional issues, or interpersonal issues rather than academic advising. Students can just come in and say that they would like to talk to a counselor. Our students would never dream of going for psychotherapy because they don't perceive that it is the kind of thing that they would need or want to have. They won't just come in and say, "I need counseling," and begin to talk about their problems. Not generally. It is usually indirectly developed. We set up regular appointments and maybe say to an individual, "We are going to work on a specific kind of problem or a specific issue that you want to deal with, and let us talk about it."

I am working on a project right now. We are developing a conference for reentering students, adult students. A one-day conference for adult students who want to come back to college. The format of the day will be a sampling. We will have a choice of fourteen different things, and people can choose a forty-five minute sample of two or three things. It will be cafeteria-style, like a college conference day. It is basically a recruitment effort. It is disguised as an altruistic function, but you know we are trying to get students in here. I am looking forward to it because it is my first big project in terms of working with other offices.

I am coordinating advisement with the assistant dean of faculty. Any time that advising is a major decision, I have to go back to the two deans to talk about it because what we're doing involves work load for people signing up students. It has all been worked out by formula. Any major decision that comes down, I will check with the director of counseling only because I have learned that sometimes I don't have the whole picture, so I can't just make a decision. I don't have any power. My power rests in having a director of counseling and a dean who believe in me. As long as I check with them and they know what I am doing, then my power becomes greater. I think I have learned that that is how you get things done here. Don't bypass the dean.

Academic advising is going pretty well. I am ready to give that up to somebody else. In other words, I am ready to take on the next level, whatever that might be. There is one more level. You go from counselor to director of counseling to dean of students. There are not that many opportunities in this institution or any institution. It is kind of tough. But this might explain why we have this informal hierarchy, a nonofficial way of moving up. You can say you were a coordinator of Transfer Affairs, a coordinator of Academic Advising, coordinator of Orientation, which means you were not just a counselor.

There is a mentoring system here, an informal one. I see myself and a couple of other counselors as being under the director of counseling's wing, and he takes care of us. He is the person that has taught me how to do what I am doing, and I just keep following him—that kind of mentor. He is just a little ahead and I am just trying to keep up.

I am starting to learn what this idea of counseling is all about. It takes a lifetime to get really good at it. There again is one of my sore points. The irony of it all is people look at counseling— you are just a counselor, you do this kind of stuff. How the profession is maligned! If people only really knew what it is about—to deal with another individual, and what it is to help someone make those kinds of decisions.

Administration versus counseling: I am torn. Because I like the counseling, I really like it. I really believe in it. What this human development stuff is all about, that is what counseling really means, and I am starting to grasp an understanding of it. I am torn. Which one do I really like better? I have to make up my mind, in terms of my future, if I want to get into private therapy, or if I want to get into administrative work, or if I want to get into teaching. I don't know.

I am the secretary to the union. That has taken a lot of my time. I really enjoy that part because there is a real battle to be fought, and the battle is recognition of professional staff, counselors, librarians. These people are not recognized as part of the faculty, not part of the bargaining, and we are not administrators. We are kind of in this limbo. And my battle is not only against the other members of the union but among ourselves—sometimes we don't even consider ourselves faculty.

Whenever you are dealing outside of the family of the counselors, you are at a new level. There is more to lose. Outside the office, it is faculty, administrators, and if I am on a campus-wide committee, there is a lot to lose. You represent the office. There is a lot of responsibility with that. I have known counselors who had horror shows in division meetings—people have turned on them and attacked them. The counselors came back bruised. Like academic advising: I have got to stand up there and talk to thirty-five math teachers. They are brutal. I think those division meetings are a good example of that kind of thing that could happen if you're embarrassed and they put you on the spot and they give you a hard time.

I really believe in what the community colleges can do—not sounding pretentious about it, but I think they have a definite role in higher education. Just the basic role of making what we have to offer accessible to many of the kinds of people that we are serving. To be part of that gives me a kind of a sense of meaning. Probably because of my own background. I am sure that has something to do with it. I mean the whole working-class-kid syndrome. I see me in a lot of students. There is no ivy on our walls. You just don't have that stereotypic student or family background type of people. Because we don't doesn't mean that the students are any less able or qualified, because we have students who are just as good, just as bright, and just as articulate as that other type of student. And I guess it is that—interactions with these types of people and seeing them move on and go on to bigger and better things—that kind of makes it enjoyable for me.

Why do you get into a profession? Counseling is obviously a helping profession, but I don't see myself as this noble saint who is saving all these people. I provide any assistance that I can in the form of information and guidance and teaching new skills, but I am not rescuing anybody. My own personal philosophy is that it is counterproductive to just rescue someone. You are not in the long run helping. In this business I look at myself more as a teacher, helping this person develop new skills to go on and become more self-sufficient. If they are helped, it is almost a by-product. I guess my sense of purpose is to see that person grow and develop, and that is the meaning I get out of it. I believe there are levels of helping. The initial reaction to help someone is to pick them up and that seems like helping: in other words, just to basically rescue the person. The real skill comes in when you can help the person develop to be a self-sufficient human being. To rescue is building a lot of dependence. I knew theoretically and in my academic training that these things happen, but not until I got really into it did I really get to see what counseling is.

I have already been approached as to whether I would consider a full-time teaching position, and I couldn't answer that. I teach part-time for the evening college. I have taught introductory psychology for the past couple of years, and a couple of different sections of psychology in business and industry. I am just wondering: If you teach a four-course load and all the other parts of teaching and you have your office hours, would I like to do that? I have my own office, I have a lot more flexibility, and I say, "Do I want to give that up?" I have always wanted to do everything, and I am afraid that I will miss something. Maybe I will do that someday. I am not sure when, but administratively your whole life [is] in the fast lane kind of thing; you can't really drop out; you have to keep working your way up. I am not sure that I want to get out of it yet because I think I enjoy that.

I have already found myself facing the administration dilemma more than the teaching dilemma. I have had good feelers on that. People are saying, "You ought to make your move now, it is going to be too late. Here is an assistant dean, you should apply for this; here is the director of this, you should apply for that," and I don't think I am ready and people say, "You are ready." I might be afraid, you know, uncomfortable—I like it here. That could mean anything, moving. I am not ready for all that change yet. I think I will know when I am ready. I know that I will outgrow this job. That doesn't mean that the job is not an important job, but I am looking for something else. I would like to move on and see myself be more influential, be more effective. I guess I think that all the projects that I am involved in—it is almost like a letdown when it is over. It is the process that is exciting, you know; it is the team work, the people, and seeing the fruits of your labor.

I feel good about the fact that I can give something back, some kind of contribution. You know I am basically a romantic. Education and awareness are really the things that are going to get you what you want to get. People are coming from a certain perspective and we are providing them with a totally new one, and that is a real strong sense of meaning, that I am a part of that process.

How I really put it all in perspective is that this is kind of like a stepping stone to whatever the next step might be. So maybe it goes back to saying that I don't want to just be a counselor. I think I want to use my experiences here to go on to the next level. I will have to find that level at some later date. It goes back to my other soap box, and that is that it is the nature of the profession that the rewards are not built-in. The next level is director of counseling. That is not a promotion; that is a job change. As a faculty member, you can be a really good teacher—an instructor, assistant, associate, and full: That is a nice ladder, professionally and emotionally. So what do you have in this kind of profession? You have burnt-out people. You have people that go, "Why am I banging my head against the wall?" I am doing it now, I enjoy it, but I say, "How long can you keep this pace up without any kind of rewards?" It is too bad. You lose a lot of good people. People say, "To hell with this, I am not doing this anymore." Look at all the people under thirty or around thirty. I mean we do not have any senior counselors at forty here.

Profile: Cheryl Collins

Cheryl Collins, in her thirties, works as a counselor and teacher in a California community college.

I didn't get hired at first as a counselor. I got hired as a teacher. I had three classes: a basic psychology class and two black psychology classes. Black psych had never been taught on this campus before, and I certainly had never taught it before and I'd never taken black psychology before, so we were all kind of starting at ground-zero. I can remember that first year actually having anxiety attacks. I tell people now that the only good thing about being a first-year teacher is that you never have to be a first-year teacher again.

I spent the first year doing the part-time teaching. I was hired as an instructor to teach classes three-fifths time, and then the position of counselor came open. So I got hired the next year as a counselor. Now I am the division chair. Counseling work is threefold: We do personal counseling, academic counseling, and educational counseling. It's real exciting to talk to students about majors, and to help them find a major or talk through a program, or set up a program. But I wouldn't want to do that for the whole time that I was in my office. I also run groups. They are called "counseling groups," not "therapy groups," but what they are are therapy groups, where students get together once a week for an hour and a half and talk about whatever personal problems or situations they may need some help in. I like to do that. I find those groups tend to be primarily women, which is not particularly uncommon not only in a school system but outside of the school system. The groups and the personal therapy get me away from the day-to-day "what does it take to transfer to the university" situation.

Then I teach. I usually teach one class a semester. It may be in the evening and it may be during the day. There have been very few semesters when I haven't taught something at least once a semester. I like the change about the job; I like the fact that I can see somebody in personal counseling; I like seeing groups; I like being in front of the classroom. Most recently I've taught psych of women. I've taught black psych, I've taught fundamental aspects of psych, I've taught social psychology of women. I lead a structured class; I demand a lot of work. I have a pretty strong reputation for what I do in a classroom.

At the beginning, because I was an inexperienced teacher and an inexperienced counselor and I was the youngest in the whole system, I took everything that I did really seriously. . . . I took on much more responsibility for students and felt like I was responsible for them. Trying to find that balance, I tell them, "I will talk to you about the kinds of classes that you need to take, but I won't set up the schedule." Some of them just want you to do that, you know, and I won't do that. I don't think that facilitates independence on their part. It makes them dependent on me, and I don't see that my responsibility is to make them dependent on me as a counselor. I think that it is my responsibility to make them not need me. My function is to become obsolete in a couple of semesters.

We had some black students who had some difficulty coming into the counseling center. The structure in the center—there's that big desk and it's not a real friendly place to be in. One black student came in and got into my office and had to bring a friend with her. I mean, the system just intimidated her. I ended up having to talk to the department chair at the time and his impression was, "Hey, this is a wonderful, beautiful, lovely center: I mean, why would somebody not come in here to see you?" What I needed to do and what I did do was go down and sit in the cafeteria for a while, and then once I made some initial contacts with the students, say, "Now go up and make an appointment to see me."

The other half of my job is time doing division chair business. Signing papers. It is a lot of paperwork. Requests for using a room in the counseling center. Minutes. We go over the minutes from the meetings, those have to be okayed. Those kinds of things. Then, of course, stuff comes in, requests from other division chairs and heads of counseling around the state. How

many counselors do you have? What is your load? They want to
know what are we doing and so there are requests for what's the staff
breakdown, what is the ethnic breakdown, what is the sex breakdown, salaries, that kind of information. We have what is called a
"college transfer day" that we do in the fall, and that's a big event
for us.

There is a division-chair meeting with the president every
other week. The president sits at one end of the table, and the dean
of instruction sits at the other end of the table, and the rest of us
sit and listen. It is a very structured meeting. It's very formal to me.
I'm the only female full-division chair. There is another woman
who goes there because she is a dean.

I still find myself being on guard for things in meetings. I
think that language changes when I come in. I think it is a
combination of not only being female but I think that there is the
issue of being young, being black. I mean, it's often very hard for
me to figure out which one of those things that they are responding
to, if any. I have to be aware of the issues around minority people
and around women. When I go into a meeting—whatever issue is
being discussed—I have to filter it through [the question], "What
does this mean to black students?" Whenever I go into a meeting,
I feel like I carry in that responsibility because in most meetings I
am the only minority person, and maybe the only woman. It is
trying to filter through not only what it means to a campus at large,
but trying to represent also women and minority students, because
when I go back to another meeting that is with women or when I
am talking to other women or other black faculty, then they see me
as their representative. It is like I can't just go in and sit at a
meeting. If somebody is going to speak up about how does this
affect women, or is this fair to women, or fair to minority students,
I feel like I have to represent that. It does feel like pressure because
sometimes I'll go into those meetings and I'll try to think through
[the question], "Am I seeing everything?" There may not be
somebody else there to bounce that off, and sometimes I'll make a
mistake and I'll go back and say, "I didn't think of that."

Black issues are not the same as the women's issues. When
we are talking about women, we are talking about, in general, white
women. Sometimes they expect me to be able to speak to those kinds

of issues, and sometimes I can't do it. And sometimes I don't want to do it. Sometimes I just want to be there and be me and listen to what is going on and sit back and not be smart, you know, and just exist like some of the rest of the people around the table. But I can't. I don't feel like I can very easily do that.

I have to admit that counselors don't have—I don't know on other campuses—but counselors don't have a really strong reputation. We get a bad rep from any student who comes through and thinks that they haven't gotten good counseling. We don't bring in money into the system because we don't teach. The number of students that we see and counsel, we don't get paid for them in the same way that the rest of the campus does. I think that many teachers think that we don't do anything. I think it is hard to be a counselor. I don't think that we are seen in the same way, having the same status as a teacher does. Recently the campus voted for us to have extra hours. Nobody else's load got increased and our load got increased. The whole faculty approved that. We couldn't get them to see that if they get our load, that they're next; at least the potential is there. But we were vulnerable. And that to me was an indication that they didn't see us as faculty members. It was saying, "You're not the same as us." The counselors were really upset about that. People retreated and went to their offices and said, "Here is my schedule, I am not doing anything else but this."

We had an article written in the paper once by a student who said that she had been to the counseling center and had gotten wrong information. Things change so quickly in counseling that it is very difficult to keep up on those changes and sometimes we make mistakes. But I think that we pay a very, very heavy price for those mistakes in terms of status. And teasing—people who are fairly close to me, they come through and tease in a joking manner. But when there is that much joking around, you can't help but feel that there is stuff behind that. It's like, "You guys don't do anything over here all day. Every time I come through here you are just sitting," or something like that. Well, it's just, it's wearing. Counselors feel that they are not valued in the system for what they do do. They will listen to us. It feels like we are the watchdog on the campus. We are trying to look out for the students' interests as opposed to sometimes what is most expedient for the computer or whose turn it is to teach, as opposed to what the students need.

I think that we counselors do tend to be the scapegoats. There are places outside this college that I feel more appreciated than actually on campus. I don't like it. It feels unfair, feels like I have to work harder. It feels like it puts me back in a place of having to prove my competence. Angry, frustrated, but none of those feelings are heavy enough. It's like they are there, but the goodies that I get are good enough to outweigh those things. I'm not disillusioned or disenchanted. They are things to deal with but they are not things that wear me out or depress me or that I get gloomy about. They are like, you know, that's the pits, but it's like, well, now we have to go out and try to do something about it.

I think that one would have more influence the higher one gets in the system. That may not be true. The reality may be that once you get higher in the system, you have less. But I think in terms of decision making, in terms of how money might be disseminated, what programs might be left in the system, and some awareness of the minority issues and women's issues at that level, it might be best taken care of by somebody like me. The next step, if I were going to do it, I would think that I would want to do it within the next couple of years. I've talked to someone about getting into the university administrative credentialing program. So I'm trying to figure out what it would mean with my family and husband. He said, "Do it."

What I am right now is a counselor-teacher. I'm not too sure that this is the most satisfaction that I can get. I am going back to the black and female business. There are so few blacks or females at that level that a couple of us need to go up there and find out what those folks are doing. I don't know how many faculty members there are at this college, but there are a bunch and there are only two black females. And two black female full-time folks is not a lot. There is one female black administrator. I don't think that there's any question; that female black administrator gets information that comes across her desk that she makes sure that I and other black faculty members get. She notices things. I think that I have sensitized some of the other faculty members and some other women in my own staff to notice those things for themselves as well as for me. They'll sometimes now see things and then they'll check it off and send it to me, and I think that it is just because I am there physically that they remember to do that, and I have made my interest obvious to them.

One thing that I was thinking about after the last two interviews was that I was sounding more like a crusader in some fashion as far as the black issue was concerned and the women's issue was concerned, and that it felt like I was saying that I had evaluated every deed and every relationship somehow through those two perspectives. I feel that it is important to me to say that I think that some people don't like me just because I am me. You know, I don't evaluate everybody and decide that they are either a racist or a sexist or an ageist or something. Those things are very important to me, but I try not to be fanatical about them.

I guess I am having a hard time thinking I will be a counselor for forty years and didn't ever try anything else. One needs to challenge oneself and try other things, and I would not like to say that I was the same thing for forty years. If I were going to be a counselor for the next forty years, if that's going to be it, then I also want to do a lot of gardening or I want to be a good cook or I want to be in class, I want something else. It feels like I want a constant challenge. I like to work the challenge to the point where I've gotten good at it before I move on. I don't just want to have stuff thrown at me all the time.

My daughter is so new I don't really know what it is going to mean to me in terms of my work. I like to work, you know; I think that's important for me to do that. I already know that she pulls some things from me that have never been pulled from me before. Some new stuff that I hadn't really thought about before, and I'm sure that there will be years and years of that. I feel I have to keep going because right now I'm at a very respectable level, being the division chair, a college instructor. In fifteen years I still want to be doing some other interesting things for her to model. I don't want to just stop here.

Part Three

Listening to
Faculty Recommendations

∽∾∽∽∾∽∽∾∽∽∾∽∽∾∽∽∾∽∽∾∽

In the ideal situation, administrators are in close contact with their faculty. In reality, the pressures of their daily schedules, the increasing demands from sources outside the college itself, and the internal bureaucracy developed to meet those demands often result in administrators' being consumed by their own work. They may lose touch with their faculty no matter how well intentioned they are. A rift develops between them and the faculty with whom they work.

Ideally, too, faculty talk with their departmental colleagues; they plan together, devise new programs, and share concerns in a spirit of collegiality that develops from shared goals and a willingness to work together. In fact, faculty work is often individualistic and insular, the energy demanded to develop new goals and plan new programs being an additional burden in an already overloaded schedule.

For both faculty and administrators, this insularity is a loss. Many shared experiences are not understood; a good deal of thoughtful exploration of concerns is never undertaken. Administrators come to see faculty as complainers rather than concerned educators. Faculty substitute quick greetings in the hall for meaningful collegial exchanges.

The first chapter in Part Three, Chapter Thirteen, focuses on a major area of faculty work that is at the heart of faculty sustenance, success, and work satisfaction and ultimately one of the keys to the success of a community college. Chapter Fourteen synthesizes what the faculty have said in previous chapters. Fourteen recommendations for faculty and administrative action are presented for consideration by all those who are concerned about improving teaching and the quality of education in community colleges.

~~~ 13 ~~~

How to Work with and Support the Faculty

~~~~~~~~~~~~~~~~~~~~~~

The False Dichotomy Between Research and Teaching

"I had always heard in school that the Ph.D. degree was the pinnacle of academia, regardless of what field you were in. I was going to be in chemistry, and I wanted to get the highest degree possible. . . . That coupled with what I perceived was my interest in research. . . . As my thoughts changed about research, the Ph.D. became less a prerequisite. As I matured, I was able to get away from the thought that to do anything in chemistry one had to have a Ph.D. I guess a little of the ego slipped away . . . I don't need a Ph.D. I need a master's degree to teach at a community college."

That was how Jesus Lopez (see Chapter Eight) spoke about his decision to give up his long-term goal to earn a Ph.D. in chemistry. Some fifty years earlier, Eells, an early student and advocate of the junior college, wrote: "It is very doubtful whether pure research of the university type should be strongly encouraged on the part of junior college instructors. Such work, if well done, is likely to consume time, thought, and nerve energy which is better expended on teaching and student contacts. Occasionally an outstanding man may be able to do both, but the major part of the

251

instructor's time and best intellectual energy should be given to the institution" (1931, p. 334).

Eells's and Lopez's statements, linked together by shared assumptions though separated by more than half a century, attest to the strength of the dichotomy between teaching and research in two-year colleges. In the mind of Eells and many early proponents of the junior college, the dichotomy was simple and unquestioned: Poor teaching that characterized some university classrooms at the time was explained and understood, to a considerable degree, by the fact that university instructors were engaged in research and their energies were diverted from teaching (Eells, 1931, p. 340). If junior college faculty were to concentrate on superior teaching, they should not be engaged in research.

Several factors combined to encourage that analysis. The notion of "research" narrowed and became separated from more traditional notions of scholarship as faculty in disciplines that were striving to achieve credibility in the developing university patterned their notion of research after the experimental and quantitative models in the physical sciences. To establish the "scientific" basis of a discipline was a key to acceptance, respect, and resources in the university. Furthermore, some of the most influential early proponents of the junior college were presidents of major developing universities. They hoped to enhance specialization in their institutions and in their research areas by separating the first two years of college from advanced studies, and reserving the role of research for the university (Breneman and Nelson, 1981, p. 6). Research itself became a specialized activity reserved for the few, and disassociated from the notion of continued learning and exploration in a faculty member's field. The result was the acceptance of what was essentially a false dichotomy between research and teaching.

Most significantly, that false dichotomy obfuscated the fact that at its core teaching at any level is intellectual work. Eells himself put it eloquently when he quoted Wilkins's description of teaching in Wilkins's 1927 inaugural address as president of Oberlin College: "True teaching is hard work. Relentless thoroughness in preparation, mastery of all that is new and should be known, long meditation, wherein the significant and trivial may reach their true proportions and the essential may stand out in focused clarity" (Eells, 1931, p. 389).

The attitude of mind reflected in Wilkins's description is necessary for any teacher at any level of education; however, the dichotomy between research and teaching established at the inception of the junior college—infusing the policies and practices of two-year colleges ever since—contradicts that notion of teaching. The dichotomy is so deeply entrenched in the community college that commentators who recognize, study, and describe its fallaciousness (see, for example, Cohen and Brawer, 1977, p. 53, p. 55) also are compelled to describe it as an almost immutable fact of community college life (Cohen and Brawer, 1977, p. 122).

Community college leaders must be concerned with the consequences of this false dichotomy. The interviews in this study with community college faculty in both academic and career curricula reveal that the consequences of separating research from teaching plague their teaching efforts, affect their aspirations and sense of themselves, undermine their intellectual energy, and conflict with a major source of satisfaction and renewal that should be available to all teachers as part of their work.

Some faculty in this study were conscious of the dichotomy and its destructiveness but felt that it was beyond their control. A New York state social science faculty member said, "You know, for years we talked about the community college . . . as a teaching and not a research institution. . . . The notion that there is a dichotomy between research and teaching . . . [is] the kind of fuzzy thinking that sets my teeth on edge. Teaching requires constant contact with information. . . . It requires that you constantly go back to the well. . . . You have to see what's going on. . . . If you cannot do the research yourself, you have got to have access to the research. . . . There are times it's very discouraging, because you know what has to be done. You know intellectually that you cannot do what needs to be done if you have five classes. It simply cannot be done. . . . It isn't because I am inept. It's simply because the conditions mediate against it."

The conditions of community college teaching reflect an absence of shared assumptions about its intellectual nature. From Laurence Bauer's perspective (see Chapter Nine), his administrators, many of his colleagues, and the legislature that funds his college all seem to misconstrue the work of a teacher. He said that in order to do his work well, he must spend as much time in preparation and study as he does in the classroom. His colleagues react ambivalently to him: "I am sort of jokingly referred to in the department as the guy who reads all the time."

Bauer realizes that members of the legislature who fund the college are intent on increasing class size and class load. They basically misperceive the work of faculty when they "jokingly" talk about the fact that they only work fifteen hours a week. As Bauer sees his work, his time at home reading, writing, and responding to students' written work is essential. But the administration of his college, responding to other pressures, disagrees: "The dean has sent a message down that the faculty should spend six hours a day on campus. . . . I don't see the occupation as one that is confined to the number of hours spent on campus."

Bauer carries out a portion of his teaching load in a nearby state prison, where he teaches long-term prisoners. His vision of teaching in the community college cannot be criticized as that of the so-called ivory tower. He is participating fully in his college's sense of new educational commitments. Yet he maintains that no matter who his students are, at the center of his efforts as a teacher is the intellectual work that must be accounted for in the structure of his day. Bauer had switched from the ministry to being a community college faculty member, but he observed, "I did not become a professor. That's about as well as I can state it." Bauer's comments are indicative of an enervating circle of misconception, response, and reaction that can occur in any institution.

Administrators and faculty must become more aware of the destructiveness of dichotomous thinking. As Epstein has suggested, thinking in dichotomous terms like "teaching versus research" reinforces "the notion of the we and the not-we; the deserving and the nondeserving; the competent and the incompetent" (Epstein, 1984, pp. 443–444). The dichotomy of teaching and research imposed upon and finally accepted by many community college faculty is both false and value-laden. Those who do research are higher on the educational totem pole than those who do not. As a result, the dichotomy with which community college faculty live every day takes a heavy toll on their self-respect. For Janet Ingersoll (see Chapter Seven), these issues played a major role in her decision to leave community college teaching. She realized that the low status of community college faculty was related to the fact that they were not asked to do research. She saw accurately that the heavy teaching load and the stipulations for faculty on how to spend their time on campus were reflections of the imposed dichotomy between research and teaching. Even the relatively high California salaries for community college faculty, which she described as "combat pay," were not enough to compensate for the loss of inner satisfaction—a loss that stemmed from the dichotomy between research and teaching in the community college.

For faculty who remain in the community college, the sense of their position on the totem pole sometimes becomes internalized. One veteran English professor, a former head of his humanities division in a respected California community college, said this about himself: "My sense of things with community college teaching at least initially was: I knew I was good, but I didn't think I was really good, and I felt that the community college was the appropriate place to be. . . . That was kind of my naive thinking at the beginning. I mean, since then I realize that there are a lot of people teaching in community colleges who are as bright and well schooled as those in many universities. Still, I think the norm is a kind of second level of achievement."

Lois Goodman, a psychology professor, has a Ph.D. in clinical psychology from one of the most highly respected universities in the country. She teaches in a community college in a relatively affluent metropolitan area in California. She spoke about how she and her colleagues have reacted to the separation of research and teaching:

> There's no peer pressure. I think that's what keeps tenured faculty going in good universities. There's tremendous pressure to publish, to maintain a reputation. . . . [Here] there is no support for that activity from the administration. . . . I'm not doing any research, so I'm not current in anything. After a while you begin to feel it. I think I'm really well

behind the times as far as new advances in my field, and it hurts. I don't think anybody notices. . . . I'm not putting myself down. . . . All things considered, this is a good place for me to be. The world hasn't lost much by my not being a researcher somewhere in a psychology department. . . .

I think all these things work together to produce the final product: it's a burned-out individual in some ways, or at least a person who has separated himself from the college to do other things with his life. . . . What I see happening more often than not is people finding other lives for themselves. They put in their time here and go off and do something else, invest in real estate or something. . . . They have classes early in the morning and then they disappear.

Thus for some faculty, separating research from teaching leads to decreasing self-respect and an effort to find both additional money and satisfaction in work away from the community college campus. That syndrome then prompts community college administrators to mandate or negotiate into the contract the amount of hours a faculty member must spend, not only on campus, but in his or her office. In response to such mandates, one Massachusetts faculty member said that he felt he had to "sneak" to the library and "hoard" his time away from the office. Thus, there is a circular path of faculty action and administrative response that becomes enervating for both faculty and administration as they fail to deal with the underlying issue of the separation of research from teaching in the community college.

The Ambiguity of the Doctorate in the Community College

Interviews in the study demonstrated a growing interest in the doctorate among some segments of community college faculty. To some degree the interest is a response to an increasing sense of job insecurity as a result of threats of reductions in force among faculties. Despite the fact that some faculty think a doctorate would earn them more security, having a doctorate places a faculty member in an ambiguous position in the community college. Misperceptions and distortions of what a program of study leading to a Ph.D. is actually like, a pervasive acceptance of the dichotomy of teaching and research among some faculty, and the imperative to reach out to a "nontraditional" population of students—all these have combined to produce an ambivalence at best and an antipathy at worst toward faculty who hold the doctorate.

In the late sixties and early seventies, when the number of doctorates being produced started to outrun the positions available in four-year colleges and universities, some community college administrations actively discouraged and screened out applicants who held doctorates. One community college president of that time said, "As a general rule, the community college is simply not the place for the person who is most excited about investigating new theories. The Ph.D. route is by no means per se a good preparation for the person who is going to spend his working days with freshmen and sophomores" (O'Connell, 1968, p. 15). The literature is replete with the notion that because community colleges are teaching institutions, they are not appropriate places for too many people with doctorates. One commentator recognized that it might be folly on the part of community college administrators to consider that all Ph.D.'s were incapable of two-year college teaching. He suggested, however, that although Ph.D.'s may be highly motivated and intellectually gifted individuals, to be qualified to teach in a community college they should be "retooled." Promising Ph.D. candidates should take part in "reeducation" programs in order to prepare themselves to teach in community colleges (O'Banion, 1972, p. 100). Such recommendations reflect the ambiguous meaning of the doctorate in the community college context. The doctorate, in effect, seems to simultaneously offer the possibility of greater status and of scorn.

One sure way for a community college faculty member to incur disfavor is to try to externalize the internal meaning that the doctorate may have for him or her. In the university where the majority of faculty members may hold the doctorate, there is a sense of understatement and confident modesty in not claiming the title "doctor." In the community college, where having the doctorate can set some faculty members apart from many of their colleagues, claiming the title can be perceived not only as immodest but also threatening to those who do not have the degree. Lawrence Bauer (see Chapter Nine) spoke of earning his doctorate as achieving one of the most important goals of his life. He appreciated the support his college gave him in earning his degree and the recognition his president afforded him when Bauer gave him a copy of his dissertation. He was not prepared for his department chairman's denial of Bauer's request that his office nameplate indicate "Dr." Bauer on it. He came to realize that his department chairman, who did not have a doctorate, did not "like the idea of having someone under him having a doctorate." Across the country in California, Daniel Ramirez (see Chapter Eleven) spoke of his experience as the first one in the history department to have a Ph.D. He explained that although it happened rarely, "people would make jokes about Ph.D.'s which displayed a kind of envy or hostility." As Ramirez explained, many of his colleagues had an ambivalent attitude about the Ph.D. and about doctoral programs, which some of them had in fact undertaken but which for a range of reasons they had dropped or suspended for the time being.

Kevin Riley, a humanities teacher in New York state, said, "When I got my Ph.D., I wanted to make it as big a thing as I could. In my own mind it was a big event. I worked eight years for it. I was proud of it. I didn't sense any great change in the faculty, though. I think that people (maybe I'm wrong about that) a lot of people wished they had it and wished that they'd worked for it." When he talked about what the degree meant to him, he said, "I wanted to feel that I could go as far as I could in the field. I would always have felt a little bit of a lack. And second, I wanted a ticket out of here." Rather than developing a way to affirm those teachers in community colleges who have earned a Ph.D., the colleges seem to sustain an ambivalence toward them which some faculty who hold the doctorate then internalize. The result is undermining to all concerned.

A number of times faculty in the study spoke of beginning a Ph.D. degree only to drop it. Their reasons for dropping varied. For some, family and economic obligations created a tension with completing the degree. As one veteran California division head said, "I think it was in the back of my head that I would go back and work on the Ph.D., but you see, when you start earning and you buy a new car. . . . It gets very luring. So you say the comfortable thing for yourself; you say, 'I wasn't really cut out to be a scholar.' "

While family and economic obligations sometimes were the reason for men to drop out of their degree programs, at least two of the women participants in the study spoke of how their doctoral studies were complicated by the fact that senior male professors in their department had not chosen to be their mentors. Not having a mentor and not realizing the importance of one in her doctoral program, one math teacher in a California community college decided that she just wasn't serious about math and dropped out of her program. Years later she said, "I have a little bit of anger toward the faculty. They had their favorites, and they [the favorites] were almost all men."

While the personal reasons for men and women who dropped their Ph.D. programs varied, two elements tied them together. First, the dichotomy between teaching and research established in the community college allowed them the option of substituting an externally defined sense of not needing a Ph.D. to teach in a community college for their internal sense of having wanted one. Second, the faculty in the study who had dropped out of their doctoral programs communicated a sense of omission in their lives and wistfulness about the degree. As one biology teacher in a Massachusetts community college said about the Ph.D., "It represents as far as one has to go. . . . I mean until you get it, you are not there. . . . I would like to go back and finish up."

Janet Ingersoll recognized the pattern when, after five years of part-time teaching in a California community college, she had to choose between pursuing her Ph.D. and taking a full-time community college teaching position. She chose to go for her Ph.D. She said, " . . . I think . . . that I would have always wondered whether I would have been able to go and finish a Ph.D. and get a different kind of teaching job and that is something I would have never been able to answer if I had stayed."

Some faculty who feel a pressure to get advanced degrees are turning toward doctorates from schools that will offer a large amount of credit for previous work at other schools and equivalency credit for extensive professional experience. One faculty member told us of having dropped his doctoral program at a university years ago, after having completed all his course work for the degree. He described the school that later granted his degree as "one of those new, uh, institutions where they accepted all the credits required to take the qualifying exam (at his first university) and then simply write a dissertation, which is what I did. I said the hell with it; I'm simply not going back to be readmitted and start from scratch."

Other faculty are turning to the doctorate in education. In a sense they are following the advice of commentators who recognize that teaching cannot be divorced from research and urge that community college faculty do research, especially in areas of pedagogy, student characteristics, and institutional effectiveness (Palinchak, 1973, pp. 244–247). Doctoral work in education for community college faculty can provide the opportunity to study the complex interactions among subject matter, students, social and organizational issues, and pedagogy. Even when such programs are first-rate, however, community college faculty who earn doctorates in education find themselves having to deal with a bias against degrees in education. As one faculty member described his situation, "Enough people know about the program to know that even though it is a Ph.D., it is in the school of education, you know, and they think it's not a first-rate intellectual achievement." The degrees from the alternative institutions and schools of education, whatever their intrinsic merit, carry with them an ambiguity that affects how community college faculty see themselves and their colleagues, and can contribute to that enervating sense, as Steven Zwerling (1976) put it, of being "second best."

Research, Writing, and Publishing

A significant number of faculty in the study did not accept the dichotomy between teaching and research; they wrote and published their work. Doing so elicited responses from their institutions ranging from acknowledgment to benign neglect to active interference. Lois Goodman, a psychology teacher in California, described the situation of some of her colleagues who pursue writing and publishing: "There are members of the faculty who write books and scholarly publications, but they are in the minority. It's certainly not from some outer pressure that they write. In fact, we've had faculty who were running off on the mimeograph here something for a book they were writing, and they've been told not to do it because it was school property. Somehow the administrators don't see that at all being related to competency in the teacher."

The faculty in the study who did write and publish talked of their writing as extremely satisfying personally and unrewarding institutionally. A teacher in a small-town, New York state community college said, "I have written a few articles and I love it. I love writing and I just wish that I did it all the time. . . . I don't need my writing for professional development here. People don't say, 'Hey, I read your article in last month's *Historical Review*. It was great.' People at this institution are generally not receptive to that type of thing."

Daniel Ramirez (see Chapter Eleven), who teaches in a large, well-established community college in a well-to-do, metropolitan area of California, expressed similar themes. He holds a Ph.D. in history from a highly respected California university. He told of finishing his Ph.D. at a time when the job market in four-year colleges and universities was shrinking rapidly. He described how he was reluctant to join the faculty of a community college because it would not encourage him to do research, even though he knew that at his university some of his most outstanding teachers were also the best researchers. He dedicated himself to trying to merge good teaching and continued research in the community college. He, in fact, has published one book and is working on a second, but few of his faculty colleagues in his history department either know of or have read his work. He reads his colleagues' works, because as he said, "If you are working with somebody, you should know what they are doing and become knowledgeable about it." He appreciated his college's display, a number of years ago, of faculty publications, but he recognized that the college did not really emphasize publication as part of faculty work. He said, "You're not encouraged to do it. It's not part of your job." While he recognized that the college did little to encourage faculty writing, he is also willing to see the issue as a matter of individual initiative and responsibility.

Speaking of his own present research activities, Ramirez said, "I try to maintain an interest in research. But now it is downright difficult to go home and work on an article or whatever. It's not my most important priority." Like the community college students London describes (1978) who take personal responsibility for their level of academic achievement, Ramirez is prepared to take personal responsibility for his loss of interest in writing, despite his awareness that the structure and policies of his college do not support writing and research in any case.

Anti-Intellectualism in the Community College

Ambivalence toward those who write and publish is indicative of one of the most costly consequences of the dichotomy between teaching and research in the community college: the intimations of anti-intellectualism that exist within the colleges. Martin Brenner (see Chapter Seven) said, "It's almost kind of a byword in the community colleges that we haven't been trapped into, you know, the publish-or-perish kind of approach to education. . . . There was a period of time, it seems to me, when there was kind of an anti-intellectual attitude (and that may have been in the four-year schools too) applied by the teachers themselves a little bit." Samuel Berger (see Chapter Nine) finally left community college teaching after some thirty years. He said that one of the primary reasons he left was the heavy teaching load and concomitant expectation that he would not spend his time doing research and writing. He said that by doing research and writing, he could even be seen as "allowing suspicion, that is to say, 'What is this guy up to? He is writing, you know. What for? He doesn't have to. Something strange about it.' "

Berger had spent a distinguished professional career in community colleges, had gone to one as a student himself in the late thirties, and had a tremendous loyalty to the community college movement. He carried Brenner's concern for anti-intellectualism even further. He prefaced his remarks by saying he had seen plenty of evidence of anti-intellectualism in the university, but that knowing that anti-intellectualism existed in the university did not comfort or compensate him for its existence in the community college. He said, "The whole approach is that we are here to teach and [that] teaching is unrelated to the life of the mind. Apparently, there is a cloud that descends and says, 'You don't have to do research.' "

Berger told of a fateful department meeting in which he and his colleagues were supposed to be discussing a total revamping of the social science curriculum in the college. He realized at that meeting that his colleagues were really not interested in thinking their way through the issues involved in the curriculum revision and that they seemed quite willing to take the "easiest way out, the customary way, and that was diffused through the entire system." He said he realized that day that there was something "profoundly wrong here." What was wrong is that some in the community college had taken on an easy skepticism about intellectual work; in its divorce of research from teaching and its attempt to reach the "nontraditional" student, the community college had separated action, teaching, and intellect. To Berger, there was no dichotomy between action and thought. He said to us, "The intellectual life is related to changing the world, making a more just, a freer society. . . . Part of what I can do about it happens to be an intellectual job." Berger finally decided that he could best carry out his vision of his work if he left the community college.

In California, Janet Ingersoll (see Chapter Seven) came to a conclusion similar to Berger's much earlier in her teaching career. The issue of intellectual seriousness was important to her decision to leave the community college. She talked about how the state had started to use the community college as part of the parole and mental health system. She enthusiastically supported the notion that mental health patients and ex-prisoners deserved effective community and rehabilitative programs. Their placement in the community college, however, meant not only that she had to work with students who were often out of place in the classroom but also that, in effect, the people in power in the state government did not think there was a lot going on intellectually at the community colleges. To her it indicated that state officials saw the community college as a "place that will babysit people who cannot get along elsewhere in the world." She saw the policy of using the community college as a repository for parolees and residents of halfway houses as perhaps a well-intended but still a very "discouraging" gesture toward those who teach in community colleges.

When Ingersoll finally made the decision to go to graduate school full-time and give up her community college full-time teaching opportunity, she said, "One of my colleagues at the community college who is a very eccentric but delightful man . . . had a fit when he found out I hadn't applied for the job. He went around telling people that I had delusions of grandeur, that I didn't know what I was doing, that I was far better off at the community college than anywhere else, and what in the world had gotten into me." But what had gotten into her is something that commentators on community colleges have been saying for quite a while. In 1960 Medsker found that 62 percent of the junior college faculty he surveyed agreed with the following statement: "The instructor usually has less opportunity to advance his own intellectual development in the junior college than in the four-year college or university" (1960, p. 189). In 1967 Garrison found from his interviews of junior college teachers that "Junior college teaching is going to be an experience in increasing professional frustration—especially insofar as personal and intellectual growth is concerned" (1967, p. 37). In a later part of his study Garrison points out that "Continuing professional refreshment is the basic question of job satisfaction on a long-term basis. For a teacher, as presumably for any other professional, such satisfaction is just as important as salary, if not more so. Among other things, 'job satisfaction' means regular opportunities for dialogue with colleagues; for additional specialized study; for continued growth and intellectual stimulation" (1967, p. 45).

In 1977 Cohen and Brawer found that the conventional assumptions about the inherent competitiveness between teaching and research did not stand up to investigation. They found that "The instructors who are oriented to research are an involved group. . . . They have an extremely high orientation toward their students and their teaching—'research orientation' and 'curriculum and instruction' showed one of the highest correlates of any pair of constructs. There is no support for the contention that an instructor's orientation toward research interferes with his teaching. On the contrary, the two may be mutually supportive" (1977, p. 55). In 1982 Cohen and Brawer summarized community college faculty response to the question, "What would make the workplace more gratifying?" in the following terms: "Faculty members would prefer spending more time on research or professional writing, their own graduate education, interacting with students outside their class, planning instruction, and conferring with colleagues" (1982, p. 85).

The evidence that has accumulated is convincing. The separation between teaching and research is a false but thriving dichotomy in the community college. Teaching is intellectual work, but community colleges stand in danger of becoming a part of, rather than an antidote to, the larger societal ambivalence that Richard Hofstadter describes as anti-intellectual (1963).

Because the basic nature of the work of teachers is intellectual, satisfaction with the work of teaching in community colleges is basically intertwined with the opportunity for continued learning, research, and writing. And here the history of the community college movement works against such satisfaction. Perhaps, as Cohen and Brawer have said, the community college "faculty will not become a community of scholars banded together in the pursuit of truth, discovering new knowledge, persevering and passing on the heritage of their culture. The pattern of two-year college development will not allow it" (1977, p. 122).

Despite the entrenched patterns and assumptions about teaching and research, writing, and advanced degrees, however, there is an enormous amount of intellectual energy among the faculty in community colleges, waiting perhaps not for a revolution in the structure of the colleges, but for some reasonable changes in the environment which could support rather than conflict with that energy. There is everything to be gained and very little to be lost when a community college administrator actively supports someone like Leonard Braddock (see Chapter Ten) who is researching and writing a textbook for his course on "materials testing." At the time of his interview, he had a job offer to return to industry. The company making the offer had hoped to put the salary at such a high level that Braddock could not refuse. Braddock said that what was meaningful to him about teaching was the opportunity to learn. He compared the intrinsic satisfaction of constant learning that he received from his work as a teacher to the external motivation and constant concern for moving up the corporate ladder that he perceived among his former colleagues in industry. He said unambivalently, "I'll find my own satisfaction from the things that I do, and I don't need praise and promotions and that sort of thing to make me happy. The next step for me is to finish writing this book, which I find a lot of satisfaction in."

The final chapter will explore some modest steps that community college boards of trustees, administrators, and faculty could take to work with, rather than against, the many community college faculty like Leonard Braddock who know that teaching is intellectual work and who want to act on that knowledge.

~ 14 ~

Recommendations to Strengthen Teaching and Enhance Educational Effectiveness

The Current State of Affairs

Despite all the differences in finance, governance, and organization of community colleges in Massachusetts, New York, and California, the faculty we interviewed in a broad range of colleges shared stories with strikingly similar themes. Almost to a person, they expressed a sense of loyalty and commitment to the idea of the community college. But the message they sent was clear: They faced serious problems which undermined their work and their colleges' effectiveness.

Near the end of interviewing in California, one faculty member said, "I don't know; I think something traumatic is going to happen in the next couple of years. . . . There's this expectancy of the boom going to fall on all of us. It's kind of an unpleasant feeling . . . hovering over the scene." Some hundred miles away, a veteran faculty member said, "I think a community college teacher, in the fullest sense of what that means, is a twenty-four hour commitment. I see colleagues, like those two guys I introduced you to in the hallway . . . that are tired of it. They're putting their time in . . . but they were both—ten years ago—enthusiastic, committed,

267

interested, innovative." A faculty member interviewed early in the study said, "The community college is becoming a petrified system. . . . It does terrible things to a teacher to be battling against an unresponsive system." And yet despite the serious concerns about the community college, faculty member after faculty member spoke of a love for teaching, much as Scott Muller did when he said, "I just kind of in my heart always felt that teaching, and teaching something useful, is one of the highest things you can do in your life."

False dichotomies permeated the everyday work of community college faculty and severely undermined their heartfelt commitment to their work. Faculty in both career and academic programs, for example, spoke of the gulf that seemed to be deepening between them. The growing division between career and academic faculty affected their collegial relations, their sense of worth, and the education their students were receiving. Many faculty on both sides of the divide recognized the irony that even as career programs became stronger in the community college and the role of the academic faculty diminished, those academic faculty still held the key to real opportunity and power for vocational students. Faculty on both sides of the divide recognized that vocational students would be doomed to dead-end jobs if they could not read, write, and think critically about their work. Many faculty spoke out clearly in favor of a concept of education in which the dichotomy between education and training, between head and hand, is overcome. They know from their everyday work what the Study Group on the Conditions of Excellence in American Higher Education concluded: "Increased access to higher education will mean little to millions of new students if the degrees they seek are weakened as credentials, whether by reduced standards or by overspecialization. . . . Access will mean little to the nation at large if its academic institutions offer fragmented, vocational curricula" (1984, p. 14).

Despite the increase of women on community college faculties, another injurious division is that between men and women faculty. The women faculty in the study, though working in three different states, spoke almost as one: They all said that women aspiring for administrative positions in the community college find themselves having to contend with unspoken assumptions about the norm of male leadership. When women are appointed to administrative positions, the positions are often "genderized" positions, like dean of students. Once in positions of leadership, women often find themselves alone among male administrative colleagues. They find themselves having to represent "women's interests" rather than thinking through issues and contributing as individuals. Likewise in faculty positions, women confront sexist attitudes about their salary and status and must contend with double standards, both in work and social situations in the college. They find that they must constantly cater to or figure out a way to go around traditional male assumptions about who has good ideas and how best to get things done.

Members of minorities on community college faculties do not have the advantage of increasing numbers that women faculty do. In those community colleges where they are a "Few Among the Many" (Seidman, Sullivan and Schatzkamer, 1983), minority faculty often play a difficult role as middleperson between minority students and a sometimes insensitive institution. Minority faculty spoke of "those subtle things" that happen in their relationships with their nonminority colleagues. Minority faculty recalled taking the initiative with their colleagues on a wide range of college issues, but being called upon by their majority colleagues only when the issue at hand was perceived as a "minority" concern. Minority members of predominantly nonminority faculties said that they felt they were more likely to be criticized than their nonminority colleagues if they made a mistake or did something questionable in their teaching. They spoke of the extra demands placed upon them because they were black, Hispanic, or Asian; and to a person, they expressed their willingness to do their work and their wish that doing the job were not such a constant fight. As one faculty member from Puerto Rico said, "I don't recognize a spot in this country that you don't have . . . racial considerations, and that really gets into your system, the racial situation going on and on everyday."

Whatever their gender or race, a significant number of the community college counselors in the study felt that they were at the bottom of the collegial totem pole. Neither faculty nor administrators in many colleges, counselors often do the work of both. In addition to advising, counseling, and in some cases providing therapy for students, they sit on committees, solve administrative problems, do liaison work with four-year colleges and universities, and teach. They are often scapegoated by the faculty for what goes wrong in the college. Because they do not have the autonomy of faculty, they are expected to be around all the time; and because they are around, administrators often call upon them to do what needs to be done. Yet they are frequently perceived by their faculty colleagues as not working very hard.

The totem pole effect on the morale of faculty is further complicated by the place of the community college in the hierarchy of United States higher education. Faculty must constantly contend with the nagging sense that teaching at a community college places them at the bottom of that hierarchy. Eugene Bowen (see Chapter Eight) said, "I think a lot of people say that the community college is wonderful, and it is a wonderful job that you are doing, on the surface. But then they say little things with subtle hints, and things come out that give you the deep-seated impression that they think your job is really not that great."

In the context of fragmented curricula, inequitable collegial relations, and low status in the hierarchy of higher education, community college faculty carry out their central teaching role. That role is complicated and made extremely difficult by a series of interrelated issues. Many faculty members in the study were caught in a serious conflict. They had high standards for college work, but they increasingly felt that it was becoming impossible to hold to them. Their students often came to them with undeveloped reading and writing skills. In addition, their students frequently had to work in jobs that were unrelated to their studies in the college and that competed with study time. If the faculty initially held to their high expectations for academic excellence, they thought many of their students would fail. If the faculty were swayed by their interest in the individual student's success, they often had to lower their sense of what it was reasonable to expect.

One of the consequences of this conflict of expectations is that students who have problems with reading and writing are being asked to read and write less rather than more. Students who come to the community college intent on preparing themselves for a job for which the college offers training tend to skirt as much as they can their alienation from reading and writing and as a result may be consigning themselves to dead-end jobs. English faculty are increasingly almost alone in bearing the burden of teaching writing to community college students. Faculty outside of English departments seem to be retreating from the issue, and an epidemic of machine-scored, so-called objective testing seems to be spreading through community colleges. In the more than twenty community colleges in the study, asking students to write is becoming less and less part of the teaching method of the faculty and less and less part of the process of educating the students.

Community college administrators, in search of innovations which will enable them to solve critical problems, are increasingly looking toward microcomputers and programmed instruction as a way out. Yet faculty who understand the complexities of learning to write know that the key to the process is the relationship between teacher, student, and subject matter and that this is a relationship for which a word processor cannot substitute. An unrecognized danger of the reliance on microcomputers to teach writing is that the process will tend to deepen the false dichotomy between subjectivity and objectivity which already plagues much of writing instruction and contributes to students' passivity (Finlay and Faith, 1979). Through a relationship with a sensitive and aware teacher, students can be encouraged to see writing as a process of discovering and ordering what they know from their experience (the "subjective") and relating it to what they are reading and studying ("objective" experience). In this way, relevance is not something faddish imposed on the material; it derives from connecting the students' experiences to what they are studying. That process of connecting is the task of a teacher of writing and it can be done only in a relationship with the student, for which no software has yet been devised as a substitute.

The issue of the expectations faculty have for their students' reading and writing cuts across all curricula in community colleges. Reading and writing are so intrinsic a part of learning, thinking, and personal power and opportunity, that those processes must be reestablished at the center of all curricula in the community college. Edward Thompson (see Chapter Ten), who teaches small machine repair, said, "The stigma that a mechanic can't read or write bothers me, and so I really make that thrust that you have got to be able to read. Our books get highly technical. Some you never get to."

Faculty receive a double message as they work to maintain the quality of their programs: It is essential that they keep both academic standards and also the number of students enrolled high. Faculty begin to feel vulnerable if they insist on a level and amount of reading that puts them out of line with their colleagues and leads students to withdraw from their classes. Dropouts plague their efforts. Recent commentators on attrition in community colleges tend to be very cautious about assessing the meaning of high dropout rates. Some even suggest that dropouts could be viewed as successes (Breneman and Nelson, 1981, p. 55). But to many faculty in the study, the student who dropped out was a serious loss. The dropout ruptured the essential relationship between teacher and student. The dropout undermined the morale of both faculty and remaining students. As one California English teacher said, "I have been bothered by the dropout, the kid who just simply disappears. It is an institutional problem. . . . I don't know how many countless faces are just lost in the mist. One kid sits in the back of the room for a month and then you don't see him anymore and you wonder, 'What did I do for him?'"

Administrators, aware of the reality of the dropout rate, sometimes enroll students in courses to a capacity that assumes that a significant number will drop. In so doing, they help contribute to the realization of that expectation. In order to maintain numbers, faculty are urged to join college recruiting programs, and colleges begin to lean over backwards to develop programs that will meet the so-called needs of students. One faculty member in a New York state community college described a proposal from his colleagues for a credentialing program for chef's assistants which would accept the fact that the students in it could not read or write effectively. Colleges may be leaning over so far backwards that they are forgetting that their students' learning and their dignity are correlated to the level of expectations their colleges have for them.

The interconnecting issues of standards and expectations, numbers and dropouts are complex. They belie simple solutions. Yet to approach the problem clearheadedly, funding agencies, governing boards, administrators, and faculty must keep at the center of their consideration what Cohen and Brawer have said quite simply: "The college that teaches best uplifts its community most. People must learn in college, or what is it for? More learning equals a better college; less learning a poorer college; no learning, no college" (1982, p. 357).

To work out these difficult issues at the heart of teaching and learning in community colleges, the faculty need space, time, and the flexibility to shift their energies. In 1967 Garrison wrote that "with the unvarying insistence of a metronome's tick, faculty pinpointed their most pressing professional problem with one word: time" (p. 30). Some twenty years later, the interviews in this study have indicated that the problem of faculty time and how it is spent continue to plague the work of faculty. Many faculty in this study described frenetically paced days in which they had little free time to think, plan, read, or reflect on what they were doing.

Teaching loads are not likely to be reduced for community college faculty in order to give them more time. This would require a significant shifting of funding among segments of higher education that would be heartily resisted. (See Astin, 1982, p. 164, and Cohen and Brawer, 1982, p. 353, for comments on the likelihood of equalizing higher education funding.) Although a reduced faculty teaching load in community colleges would be desirable, the real battle may well be to resist increasing that load.

If time is to be made available to community college faculty, it will come from reconceptualizing their role and relationship with students. This process may take even more courage than the fight to resist increased teaching loads. At the center of the reconceptualization must be a reconsideration of student-centeredness in community colleges. The interviews in this study indicate that this ethos has been carried to the point of diminishing returns for both faculty and students. Faculty are expected to reach out and care for the total student. Faculty are asked to individualize their teaching as much as necessary to ensure that students will be successful. Finally, faculty are expected to be totally accessible when they are on campus.

While faculty should not become calloused and impervious to the lives of their students, the student-centered ethos has clearly been overdone in the community college, with injurious consequences for both faculty and students. Faculty are treated as "fair game" when they are on campus. Faculty find themselves struggling to draw a line between on the one hand, concerns of teaching and learning to which they can legitimately and effectively respond and on the other, students' problems, for which they can take no effective responsibility. In a similar way, students in this environment can lose sight of what their responsibilities are and what is reasonable to expect of their faculty. While U.S. colleges and universities no longer act *in loco parentis* in social matters, there is considerable evidence in the interviews in this study that in community colleges the student-centered ethos encourages both faculty and students to maintain that relationship to some degree in their academic lives.

If this one issue were reconsidered and reconceptualized, valuable faculty time could be regained. Students would gain a different sense of their responsibility for their own learning. Teachers and students could more easily focus their relationship on the issues of teaching and learning. One veteran faculty member spoke of how he would like to relate to his students and be perceived by them: "I don't want to be a father. . . . I would by far prefer to be seen as a competent professional. I'm not sure that I am a good father. I am a good teacher."

A reconsideration of the issue of student-centeredness in community colleges would be a radical step. Part of the energy for the ethos is a response to the stereotypic image of university professors who are concerned only with their subject matter and research and care little for the welfare of their students. Yet the evidence is accumulating that such an image is distorted (Cohen and Brawer, 1977, p. 55). The dichotomy between being interested in subject matter as opposed to students is a false one at every level of education. Teachers interested in research and scholarship are not necessarily less interested in teaching. By reconceptualizing the relationship between community college faculty and students, a significant step could be taken, not only toward freeing time for faculty to concentrate with their students on issues of teaching and learning but also toward overcoming the false dichotomy that is established in community colleges between teaching and research.

For every hour spent in the classroom, dedicated community college teachers spend hours reading, gaining more experience in their fields, planning, and preparing. The precedents, policies, and practices established in community colleges, however, rest on assumptions that are fundamental misconceptions of the nature of faculty work. By separating teaching from research, by actively discouraging faculty from scholarship and writing in their fields, and by encouraging faculty to put all their available energy into student contact, the community college as an institution has eroded the essential intellectual core of faculty work. The irony is that the institution that has dedicated itself to good teaching has undermined the source of energy for good teaching. By separating research from teaching the community college has blocked central sources of sustenance and renewal from faculty.

Despite the pressure in community colleges against research and writing, individual faculty struggle to maintain their scholarship and writing in an atmosphere that is at best ambivalent toward those activities and at worst somewhat hostile. There is considerable intellectual energy and commitment present among today's community college faculty. With little or no extra cost, administrators could affirm and support faculty research, writing, and professional enrichment activities. At present such efforts often go unrecognized, unheralded, and are sometimes viewed as suspect. Community college administrators must take seriously the warning contained in the report of the Study Group on the Conditions of Excellence in American Higher Education: "We believe that keeping current in one's field is vital to good teaching and that any attempt to denigrate the importance of scholarship will be harmful to the quality of undergraduate education" (1984, p. 50). That message is different from the one community college advocates were stressing fifty years ago (see Eells, 1931, p. 334), but it is one that recognizes that access and excellence must be integrated for the sake of equitable educational opportunity.

In the mid-1980s, community college faculties are aging. Hiring has been drastically reduced, especially of full-time faculty. There is reason to believe that in the next twenty-five years, community colleges will join four-year colleges and universities in feeling the need to hire large numbers of faculty. Some students of

the field predict that American colleges and universities will need
to hire about 500,000 faculty members in the next twenty-five years,
thereby replacing the entire professoriat (Evangelauf, 1984, p. 1).
By recognizing and affirming the research and writing current
faculty members are carrying out, administrators would establish
important precedents for the next generation of community college
teachers.

At the core of many of the interviews with community
college faculty in this study were issues of power and opportunity.
(See Kanter, 1977, for a full discussion of the import of those issues
for the quality of work.) Yet few faculty spoke of unions or faculty
governance as keys to power and opportunity. What became more
and more clear in the interviews was that for faculty, as for their
students, learning was the source of power and opportunity. It was
clear from the interviews that if the intellectual center of teachers'
work were to be recognized, priorities in the community college as
a whole would be restructured and faculty and students alike would
be empowered as a result. Intellectual work cuts across rank,
curricula, gender, race, social class, and place on the community
college totem pole. Intellectual work was seen by the faculty as the
source of renewal and continued energy for doing their work. If the
community college can become a place in which societal ambivalence toward intellectual work is left at the front door, then both
students and faculty will experience a sense of opportunity that can
give new meaning to community college education and to the work
of community college faculty.

Recommendations for Action

Taking the first steps toward achieving these goals is no easy
matter. Every step taken in one direction may well create unantic-
ipated consequences from another. Yet governing boards, administrators, and faculties must be prepared to take matters into hand.
The words of the faculty presented in the previous chapters suggest
the following first steps:

Recommendation 1. Call a moratorium on new vocational
programs until joint committees of vocational and liberal arts
faculty are established to recommend ways in which the dichotomy

between vocational programs and academic programs can be bridged. The mandate of such committees would be to recommend how each vocational program in the college could be offered within a historical, social, and occupational context. The goal of the committees would be to recommend curricula and programs that would merge training and education and offer a more complete education to students enrolled in vocational programs.

Recommendation 2. Administrators must take the initiative on reviewing issues of equity among community college faculty. Passivity on these issues—waiting for grievances to be raised— establishes a climate in which complaint is the primary path to getting anything changed. Taking the initiative in formal reviews, holding workshops that alert administrators and faculty colleagues to equity issues, and establishing ongoing avenues of recourse without fear of recrimination are only examples of what a far-sighted administrator might envision. The report of the Study Group on the Conditions of Excellence in American Higher Education noted: "Students are quick to spot hypocrisies and inconsistencies in institutional behavior. They know when stated values are subverted by an institution's failure to apply the same standards of conduct to everyone" (1984, p. 52). In order to provide equitable educational opportunity for their students, administrators must develop an equitable working environment for their faculty.

Recommendation 3. Despite a national climate that has become passive about the goals of affirmative action, community colleges must recommit themselves to the goal of building a diverse faculty. While hiring is now limited, in the near future a new generation of community college faculty will be needed and hired. If the imperative for a diverse faculty is allowed to lapse, the attitude of mind necessary to do effective affirmative action recruiting and hiring will not be in place when hiring does begin again. A reaction stimulating such an attitude will then occur, but the crest of hiring will have passed and the positions will no longer be available. Consciousness of inequity and of the intellectual and social costs of racism and sexism must be kept alive by farsighted college administrators who can anticipate cycles of opportunity.

Recommendation 4. Establish "writing across the curriculum" programs. Writing is as important to students in vocational programs as it is to students in academic programs. English faculty should be encouraged by administrations to become the leaders of such programs. Faculty in English can be supported to attend workshops and seminars on the teaching of writing that emphasize a process approach. English faculty can then work with each department in the college as they institute a writing requirement for which the faculty in that department take responsibility. (A program similar to this is currently in place at the University of Massachusetts at Amherst.)

Recommendation 5. Make writing part of every class in the college every day it meets. Faculty should view writing not only as a product to be assessed at the end of a section of the class, but also as a means of asking students to think through subjects under discussion, and to discover and organize what they know. Such process writing as focused free writing (Elbow, 1982) can be one key to the active involvement of students that the report of the Study Group on the Conditions of Excellence in American Higher Education (1984) stresses as central to student learning.

Students can gain confidence in their writing when the connections between their experience and the subject being studied are explored and become a basis for further learning. Students' response to and interaction with the subject matter can become the texts for class discussions, which can facilitate students' going even further with the subject matter. Student writing, when it is guided toward bridging the dichotomy between subjective and objective, will reveal that their writing skills are not as inadequate as conventional wisdom would hold.

Recommendation 6. Administrators and faculty should join in adopting a moratorium on the use of machine-scored tests. There appears to be a growing reliance on such tests, partially in response to what faculty perceive as a decline in the verbal skills of their students. The use of machine-scored, "objective" tests encourages rather than arrests any such decline, and it promotes passivity on the part of students.

Recommendation 7. Administrators must resist the lure of innovation represented by the microcomputer. Because learning is a result of the relationship of teacher, student, and subject matter, microcomputers should be used only in ways that can be clearly shown to enhance that relationship rather than substitute for it.

Recommendation 8. All involved in community colleges must cooperate to develop an institution-wide response to the trend toward lowered expectations for community college students. Twenty years ago in Garrison's study, faculty insisted that they were able to maintain collegiate standards (1967). That is no longer clearly the case. Faculty who try to maintain high expectations of their students find themselves feeling vulnerable to the pressures of maintaining high enrollment. Ultimately the numbers of students who attend community colleges will be adversely affected by expectations that lack dignity for both faculty and students.

Recommendation 9. In addition to an institution-wide response to the issue of expectations, colleges must develop similar responses to the issue of dropouts. In the recent past, community colleges have developed new programs and new missions in order to attract students to their campuses. But such efforts are seriously impaired by the dropout phenomenon. Recruitment, admission, registration, add/drop policies, and the quality of the intellectual interchange in classes are all interconnected with events in students' lives that lead to their dropping out. The college has little control over events in students' lives, but it does have control over its side of dropout equations. A coordinated approach, involving the legislature, boards of trustees, administrators, and faculty will be required to address each interdependent factor in the equation.

Recommendation 10. While not urging a calloused disregard for the context of students' lives, administrators must encourage faculty to concentrate their attention with regard to students on those issues of teaching and learning for which they can reasonably be expected to take responsibility. The notion of student-centeredness in community colleges must be revised so that faculty are not treated as "fair game" by students and so that students take more initiative and responsibility for their own learning.

Recommendation 11. Administrators in community colleges must develop procedures and policies based on the assumption that faculty know their work best and want to do their work with integrity. The Study Group on the Conditions of Excellence in American Higher Education has urged that state and local administrators not intrude in the daily operations of public colleges and universities. The report said, "It is a legitimate responsibility of states to audit institutional practices, to demand evidence of their effectiveness, and to correct abuses. It is quite another matter to operate the institution from a distance on the assumption that faculty and administrators are either incompetent or corrupt" (1984, pp. 67–68). There is an important parallel in this recommendation for the campus administrator's assumptions about faculty. Faculty know the requirements of doing their work with integrity, and they should play the primary role in setting the conditions of their work day.

Recommendation 12. Administrators must hold the line on faculty teaching load. Classroom teaching is the tip of the iceberg in faculty work. Continued learning, preparation, planning, and responding to student work are all central to the work of teachers. While it may be unrealistic to suggest at this time that teaching loads of community college faculty be reduced, it is essential that governing boards and administrators begin a campaign to educate funding agencies about the full range of activities involved in community college faculty work. The suggestion that faculty teaching loads can be increased with little cost to the learning that goes on in community colleges is illusory.

Recommendation 13. Affirm faculty who have doctorates. The aversion to the Ph.D. in community colleges is based on false notions of the separation of teaching and research. While holding a doctorate does not automatically or necessarily make a person a good teacher, the attributes required for earning a doctorate are correlated with those required for good teaching. What is most important in teaching is a love of subject matter and of continued learning and an interest in sharing that love with students. It can be argued that it is especially important for faculty in community colleges to hold the doctorate. Faculty who somehow feel that they have not gone as far as they might have, whose pursuit of their own academic dream is somehow unrequited, can communicate their disillusionment to their students. Faculty who have gone as far as they can in their fields may be models for their students to do the same.

Recommendation 14. Recognize, affirm, and support the scholarship in which community college faculty are currently engaged. The split between teaching and research is a false dichotomy that serves to undermine the intellectual fabric of the community college. Concrete steps, like making college resources available for such efforts, listing publications, displaying faculty work in college libraries, and supporting faculty participation in professional associations and seminars, will indicate that such work is basically respected in the community college.

Recommendation 15. It was our privilege to interview over 100 community college faculty, staff, and students. Their words and stories are one path to understanding the core of community college education. Governing boards, administrators, staff, and students all have experiences which, in addition to those of the faculty, reflect the workings of community colleges. We recommend further research and a process of staff, faculty, and student development that will elicit their experience and the meaning they make of it. Their stories can then become texts that will further illuminate the workings of community colleges.

These recommendations are based on what seventy-six community college faculty had to say about their work. Listening to what the faculty has to say is important first, as the Study Group on the Conditions of Excellence in American Higher Education has noted, because "Faculty are at the core of the academic work force, and their status, morale, collegiality, and commitment to their work are critical to student learning. When we allow support for such a critical component of the enterprise to erode . . . we are compromising the future of higher learning in America" (1984, p. 11). Second, faculty face concretely in their everyday work the central dilemma of education in the United States: merging equitable educational opportunity and excellence. They know what they are talking about. It is in the words of community college faculty that legislators, governing boards, college administrators, and the faculty themselves will find a path to understanding and improving community college education.

References

Andersen, C. J. *1981–82 Fact Book*. Washington, D.C.: American Council on Education, 1981.

Astin, A. W. *Minorities in American Higher Education: Recent Trends, Current Prospects, and Recommendations*. San Francisco: Jossey-Bass, 1982.

Becker, H. S., and Geer, B. "Participant Observation and Interviewing: A Comparison." In G. J. McCall and J. L. Simmons (eds.), *Issues in Participant Observation*. Reading, Mass.: Addison-Wesley, 1969.

Breneman, D. W., and Nelson, S. C. *Financing Community Colleges: An Economic Perspective*. Washington, D.C.: Brookings Institution, 1981.

Chambers, M. M. "Analysis of State Funds for Higher Education." *Chronicle of Higher Education*, 1979, *19* (6), 6–9.

Chomsky, N. *Language and Mind*. San Diego, Calif.: Harcourt Brace Jovanovich, 1972.

Clark, B. R. *The Open Door College: A Case Study*. New York: McGraw-Hill, 1960.

Clark, B. R. "The 'Cooling Out' Function Revisited." In G. B. Vaughan (ed.), *Questioning the Community College Role*. New Directions for Community Colleges, no. 32. San Francisco: Jossey-Bass, 1980.

Cohen, A. M. *Dateline '79: Heretical Concepts for the Community College.* Beverly Hills, Calif.: Glencoe Press, 1969.

Cohen, A. M., and Brawer, F. B. *The Two-Year College Instructor Today.* New York: Praeger, 1977.

Cohen, A. M., and Brawer, F. B. *The American Community College.* San Francisco: Jossey-Bass, 1982.

Du Bois, W. E. B. *The Education of Black People: Ten Critiques 1906-1960.* (N. Aptheker, ed.) Amherst: University of Massachusetts Press, 1973.

Eells, W. C. *The Junior College.* Boston: Houghton Mifflin, 1931.

Elbow, P. *Writing with Power.* New York: Oxford University Press, 1982.

Epstein, C. F. "Ideal Images and Real Roles: The Perpetuation of Gender Inequality." *Dissent,* 1984, *3* (4), 444-447.

Evangelauf, J. "Founding Our Institutions Anew." *Chronicle of Higher Education.* 1984, *29* (11), 1.

Finlay, L. S., and Faith, V. "Illiteracy and Alienation in American Colleges: Is Paulo Freire's Pedagogy Relevant?" *Radical Teacher,* 1979, *16,* 28-37.

Garms, W. I. *Financing Community Colleges.* New York: Teachers College Press, 1977.

Garrison, R. H. *Junior College Faculty: Issues and Problems. A Preliminary National Appraisal.* Washington, D.C.: American Association of Junior Colleges, 1967.

Gilbert, F. (ed.). *1980 Community, Junior, and Technical College Directory.* Washington, D.C.: American Association of Community and Junior Colleges, 1980.

Gleazer, E. J., Jr. *The Community College: Values, Visions, and Vitality.* Washington, D.C.: American Association of Community and Junior Colleges, 1980.

Grant, W. V., and Eiden, L. S. *Digest of Education Statistics 1980.* Washington, D.C.: National Center for Education Statistics, U.S. Government Printing Office, 1980.

Hartz, L. *The Liberal Tradition in America.* San Diego, Calif.: Harcourt Brace Jovanovich, 1955.

Harvard University Committee on the Objectives of a General Education in a Free Society. *General Education in a Free Society.* Cambridge, Mass.: Harvard University Press, 1945.

Hofstadter, R. *Anti-Intellectualism in American Life.* New York: Knopf, 1963.

Hurn, C. J. "The Vocationalisation of American Education." *European Journal of Education,* 1983, *18,* 45–64.

Jencks, C., and Riesman, D. *The Academic Revolution.* Garden City, N.Y.: Doubleday, 1968.

Kanter, R. M. *Men and Women of the Corporation.* New York: Basic Books, 1977.

Karabel, J. "Community Colleges and Social Stratification." *Harvard Educational Review,* 1972, *42* (4), 521–562.

London, H. B. *The Culture of a Community College.* New York: Praeger, 1978.

McGrath, E. J. *Liberal Education in the Professions.* New York: Teachers College Institute of Higher Education, 1959.

Medsker, L. L. *The Junior College: Progress and Prospect.* New York: McGraw-Hill, 1960.

Meyer, T. J. "Two-Year Colleges Facing Serious Enrollment Decline." *Chronicle of Higher Education,* 1984, *29* (11), 3.

Moore, W., Jr. *Against the Odds: The High-Risk Student in the Community College.* San Francisco: Jossey-Bass, 1970.

Newman, F. *Report on Higher Education.* Washington, D.C.: U.S. Government Printing Office, 1971.

O'Banion, T. *Teachers for Tomorrow: Staff Development in the Community-Junior College.* Tucson: University of Arizona Press, 1972.

O'Connell, T. E. *Community Colleges: A President's View.* Urbana: University of Illinois Press, 1968.

Olivas, M. A. *The Dilemma of Access: Minorities in Two-Year Colleges.* Washington, D.C.: Howard University Press, 1979.

Palinchak, R. *The Evolution of the Community College.* Metuchen, N.J.: Scarecrow Press, 1973.

Pincus, F. L. "The False Promises of Community Colleges: Class Conflict and Vocational Education." *Harvard Educational Review,* 1980, *50* (3), 332–361.

Schuman, D. *Policy Analysis, Education, and Everyday Life.* Lexington, Mass.: Heath, 1982.

Schutz, A. *The Phenomenology of the Social World.* (G. Walsh and F. Lehnert, trans.) Evanston, Ill.: Northwestern University Press, 1967.

Seidman, E., Sullivan, P., and Schatzkamer, M. "The Few Among the Many." Paper presented at annual meeting of American Educational Research Association, Montreal, Apr., 1983. (ED 230 251)

Seidman, E., Sullivan, P., and Schatzkamer, M. *The Work of Community College Faculty: A Study Through In-Depth Interviews.* Final Report to the National Institute of Education, Washington, D.C., Sept., 1983. (ED 243 499)

Slutsky, B. "What is a College For?" In M. A. Marty (ed.), *Responding to New Missions.* New Directions for Community Colleges, no. 24. San Francisco: Jossey-Bass, 1978.

Sohn-Rethel, A. *Intellectual and Manual Labor: A Critique of Epistemology.* London: Macmillan, 1978.

Steiner, G. "The Distribution of Discourse." In *On Difficulty and Other Essays.* New York: Oxford University Press, 1978.

Study Group on the Conditions of Excellence in American Higher Education. *Involvement in Learning: Realizing the Potential of American Higher Education.* Final Report to the National Institute of Education, U.S. Department of Education. Washington, D.C.: U.S. Government Printing Office, 1984.

Trow, M. "Comment on Participant Observation and Interviewing: A Comparison." In G. J. McCall and J. L. Simmons (eds.), *Issues in Participant Observation.* Reading, Mass.: Addison-Wesley, 1969.

Vygotsky, L. *Thought and Language.* Cambridge, Mass.: MIT Press, 1962.

Watkins, B. "Notes on Community Colleges." *Chronicle of Higher Education,* 1983, *26* (7), 3.

Whitehead, A. *The Aims of Education.* New York: Macmillan, 1929.

Wolfe, L. "Enrollment in Two-Year Colleges Starting to Slip." *New York Times,* Feb. 26, 1985, p. 1.

Wolk, R. A. *The Higher Education Design Book 1980–81.* Washington, D.C.: Editorial Projects in Education, 1980.

Zwerling, S. L. *Second Best: The Crisis of the Community College.* New York: McGraw-Hill, 1976.

Index

287